Lecture Notes in Computer Science 7528

Commenced Publication in 1973
Founding and Former Series Editors:
Gerhard Goos, Juris Hartmanis, and Jan van Leeuwen

Minhua Ma   Manuel Fradinho Oliveira
Jannicke Baalsrud Hauge   Heiko Duin
Klaus-Dieter Thoben (Eds.)

Serious Games Development and Applications

Third International Conference, SGDA 2012
Bremen, Germany, September 26-29, 2012
Proceedings

 Springer

Volume Editors

Minhua Ma
Digital Design Studio
Glasgow School of Art
The Hub Building, Pacific Quay
Glasgow G51 1EA, UK
E-mail: m.ma@gsa.ac.uk

Manuel Fradinho Oliveira
Sintef Technology and Society
Industrial Management
P.O. Box 4760 Sluppen
7465 Trondheim, Norway
E-mail: manuel.oliveira@sintef.no

Jannicke Baalsrud Hauge
Heiko Duin
Klaus-Dieter Thoben
University of Bremen
Bremen Institute for Production and Logistics
High School Ring 20
28359 Bremen, Germany
E-mail: {baa, du, tho}@biba.uni-bremen.de

ISSN 0302-9743   e-ISSN 1611-3349
ISBN 978-3-642-33686-7   e-ISBN 978-3-642-33687-4
DOI 10.1007/978-3-642-33687-4
Springer Heidelberg Dordrecht London New York

Library of Congress Control Number: 2012947436

CR Subject Classification (1998): K.8.0, I.2.1, K.3.1, H.4.1, H.5.3, K.4.3, I.3

LNCS Sublibrary: SL 6 – Image Processing, Computer Vision, Pattern Recognition,
and Graphics

Typesetting: Camera-ready by author, data conversion by Scientific Publishing Services, Chennai, India

Printed on acid-free paper

Springer is part of Springer Science+Business Media (www.springer.com)

Preface

The Third International Conference on Serious Games Development and Applications (SGDA 2012) was organized as a satellite conference to IFIP-ICEC 2012 in Bremen. SGDA 2012 built on the successes of the First International Workshop on Serious Games Development and Application, held in Derby in 2010, and the Second International Conference on Serious Games Development and Applications, held in Lisbon in 2011. The aim of SGDA is to collect and disseminate knowledge on serious games technologies, design, and development; to provide practitioners and interdisciplinary communities with a peer-reviewed forum to discuss the state of the art in serious games research, their ideas and theories, and innovative applications of serious games; to explain cultural, social, and scientific phenomena by means of serious games; to concentrate on the interaction between theory and application; to share best practice and lessons learnt; to develop new methodologies in various application domains using games technologies; and to explore perspectives of future developments and innovative applications relevant to serious games and related areas.

The re-emergence of serious games as a branch of video games has introduced the concept of games designed for a serious purpose other than pure entertainment. To date, the major applications of serious games include engineering, education, health care, military applications, city planning, production, crisis response, and training. Serious games have primarily been used as tools that give players a novel way to interact with games in order to promote physical activities, to learn skills and knowledge, to support social-emotional development, to facilitate behavior transformation, to treat different types of psychological and physical disorders, etc. Many recent studies have identified the benefits of using video games for a variety of serious purposes. However, most serious games are still mostly focusing on the learning objective, and not so much on developing engaging and motivating user interfaces. In the world of entertainment games, there has been much more focus on the user experience. Therefore the organizational committee decided to co-locate SGDA with the 11th International Conference on Entertainment Computing conference, in order to foster the dialogue between the entertainment and serious games communities and support a bi-directional knowledge transfer.

The conference is supported by the GALA Network of Excellence for Serious Games; the TARGET (Transformative, Adaptive, Responsive and enGaging EnvironmenT) Project, which is a large-scale integrating project funded by the European Community under the FP7 (ICT-2007.4.3) and Digital Libraries & Technology-Enhanced Learning 2009–2011 (Grant Agreement N° 231717); BIBA-Bremen Institute for Production & Logistics; the University of Bremen; Glasgow School of Art; INESC-ID; the Technical University of Lisbon; and the

University of Derby. The University of Bremen hosted the third annual conference (SGDA 2012) on 26–29 September 2012.

A total of 22 papers on different aspects of serious games design and use were presented at SGDA 2012. We hope that participants benefited from the discussions and presentations held at the conference.

July 2012   Minhua Ma
                                                          Jannicke Baalsrud Hauge
                                                         Manuel Fradinho Oliveira
                                                                  Heiko Duin

Organization

SGDA 2012 was hosted by Bremen Institute for Production & Logistics (BIBA), University of Bremen, in cooperation with the Digital Design Studio, Glasgow School of Art, UK; SINTEF Technology and Society, Norway; and the TARGET project, which is partially funded by the European Community under FP7.

Conference Chairs

Klaus-Dieter Thoben	University of Bremen, Germany
Alessandro de Gloria	UNIGE, Italy
Jannicke Baalsrud Hauge	Bremer Institut für Produktion und Logistik, Germany
Minhua Ma	Glasgow School of Art, UK

Program Chairs

Minhua Ma	Glasgow School of Art, UK
Jannicke Baalsrud Hauge	Bremen Institute for Production & Logistics, Germany
Manuel Fradinho Oliveira	SINTEF Technology and Society, Norway

Local Organizing Committee

Jannicke Baalsrud Hauge
Heiko Duin
Matthias Kalverkamp
Rosa Garcia-Sanchez
Marcus Seifert

Program Committee

Esteve Almirall, Spain
Bjorn Andersen, Norway
Francesco Belotti, Italy
Riccardo Berta, Italy
Rafael Bidarra, The Netherlands
Daniel Burgos, Spain
David Bustard, UK
Paul Chapman, UK
Thomas Connolly, UK

Ben Cowley, Finland
Heiko Duin, Germany
Sara de Freitas , UK
Marco Gilles, UK
Alessandro Gloria, Italy
Poul Hansen, Denmark
Jannicke Baalsrud Hauge, Germany
Gabriele Hoeborn, Germany
Lakhmi Jain, Australia

Matthias Kalverkamp, Germany
Michael Kickmeier, Austria
Ralf Klamma, Germany
Marco Luccini, France
Minhua Ma, UK
Tim Marsh, Australia
Igor Mayer, The Netherlands
Paul McKevitt, UK
Rob Nadolski, The Netherlands
Jeppe Herlev Nielsen, Sweden
Andreas Oikonomouv, UK
Manuel Fradinho Oliveira, Norway

João Pereira, Portugal
Sobah Petersen, Norway
Elaine Raybourne, USA
Johann Riedel, UK
Luis Paulo Santos, Portugal
Marcus Seifert, Germany
Riitta Smeds, Finland
Ioana Stanescu, Romania
Marco Taisch, Italy
Klaus-Dieter Thoben, Germany
Wim Westera, The Netherlands

Sponsoring Institutions

Bremen Institute for Production & Logistics (BIBA), University of Bremen,
    Germany
Digital Design Studio, Glasgow School of Art, UK
SINTEF Technology and Society, Norway
Technical University of Lisbon, Portugal
INESC-ID, Lisbon, Portugal

Table of Contents

Don't Panic: Enhancing Soft Skills
for Civil Protection Workers

Ines Di Loreto, Simone Mora, and Monica Divitini

Norwegian University of Science and Technology
{inesd,simonem,divitini}@idi.ntnu.no

Abstract. *Don't Panic* is a serious game created to enhance soft skills in the crisis management field. The game is conceived to (i) add the fun element to training about stressful situations linked to panic management and (ii) teach skills such as communication styles, team management and coordination, time management, stress management and coping strategies. In this paper we present the first paper-based version of the game and its evaluation. The paper discusses the game design motivations, the methodological reasons behind its conception, and presentsa pilot study. Results show that, even in its paper version, the game is a promising tool if linked with adequate and realistic procedures. This opens methodological questions about the role of computer based serious games.

Keywords: Serious Games, Crisis Management, Civil Protection, Board Games, Evaluation, Soft Skills.

1   Introduction

Protecting the population during large events, emergencies, and disasters (hereafter *Civil Protection*) is a highly complex effort that requires coordination of different competencies, often under time pressure and in challenging environmental conditions.

Training of workers in this field is very challenging and has to take into account the need to learn not only specific skills, e.g. how to operate specific tools and how to behave during different types of events, but also appropriate communication styles, stress management, coping strategies and so on (hereafter *soft skills*) [1]. Challenges are connected not only to the complexity of the work to be performed, but also to its sporadic and discontinuous nature. In addition, civil protection requires the training of highly qualified professionals as well as volunteers to be deployed on the field, with varying backgrounds and competencies. A number of approaches are combined for training, including traditional training through courses and training material, coaching, simulated emergencies to recreate realistic working experiences [2], and structured debriefings to learn by reflecting on specific work experiences [3]. Serious games have also been proposed for this domain. (See [5] for an overview.)

In our research we investigate the use of pervasive and mobile collaborative serious games for crisis management and civil protection. In this paper we present *Don't Panic*, a game that aims at training soft skills in the management of situations where diffusion of panic might put population at risk. The decision to focus of panic

M. Ma et al. (Eds.): SGDA 2012, LNCS 7528, pp. 1–12, 2012.

prevention and management has different reasons. Panic might have catastrophic results (as demonstrated by the Heysel Stadium disaster [15], the Love Parade[16] or the 9-11[14] events) and the problem is transversal to any event, planned or unplanned, that involves a large number of people within a limited geographical area. Handling large number of people requires advanced soft skills, since it requires cooperation and communication among specialized workers and volunteers. In addition, simulations (that are effective for training in e.g. application of specific rescue protocols) are not very effective in this case because they would require the involvement of a large number of persons.A serious game based approach not only can help to cope with these limitation but also help participants to see things differently (and act differently) from the way they are used to.

The paper is organized as following. Section 2 presents related work; Section 3 describes the game; Section 4 its evaluation; Section 5 and 6 present considerations on the study for further development of the game and implications for the design of its computer based counter-part.

2   Serious Games for Civil Protection: An Overview

Crises are characterized by the absence of obvious solutions, the scarcity of reliable information when it is needed, and the lack of adequate time to reflect on and debate alternative courses of action. While simulation can help the crisis management team to find the optimal response to the crisis, serious games can help them for example in the art of optimizing the limited time that they have to develop creative responses to the crisis. The flexible rule structure can allow the learners to explore the game space, test hypothesis, and fulfill goals in a variety of unique, sometimes, unanticipated ways. The great degree of flexibility and range of plausible paths to success helps learners to develop a flexible knowledge base that can be applied to a variety of real world situations [4].

Now, while presented this way serious games could seem the panacea for all problems, there are two serious limitations to take into account. The first one is that participants will not learn everything they need to know from the serious game. "Learners will not learn to use a scalpel by handling a virtual one using a joystick, nor learn perfect bedside manners by "talking" with NPCs. Yet, just as pilots learn some elements of flying in flight simulators, medical students can learn some aspects of being a practicing doctor from serious games."[4] That's why we believe the use of both, real life simulations and serious games can add value to crisis management training. The other limitation we can list it's more linked to the "state of the art" of serious games for crisis management. As far as we now there are no "best practices" or at least a list of elements which are needed to create a successful "soft skills" training environment. We base this latter statement on an analysis we conducted on already existing serious games for crisis management and which is fully described in [5]. The games we analyzed (see for example [6] [7] [8] [9]) offer an interesting complement to traditional training. Though for none of them we have been able to find long-term evaluation of their impact, initial results of usage show they are promising tools addressing some of the limitations of traditional training. The available games greatly vary in terms of required organizational commitment, audience, and scenarios. They therefore provide a good overview of the spectrum of possible uses of games for training in crisis management, ranging from tools that can easily be adopted by a team to systems that require the involvement of top management, for example because of their cost as in [10]. The analyzed examples also provide some interesting lessons learned about how games can be designed to address some of the limitations of current training activities. For example, the usage of software agents, like in [11], can support the dynamic generation of scenarios overcoming real life simulations where scenarios are more or less pre-defined. There is however some issues that seems to be generally neglected. In particular: (i) there is limited link with an actual territory (i.e., the game takes place in an abstracted environment); (ii) there is virtually no possibility to play with roles; (iii) the importance of the debriefing phase is underestimated, (iv) there is no support for coaching (e.g. peer to peer teaching) during the playing sessions. The last two aspects are particularly critical because they are directly connected with the capability of a tool to promote learning.

3   The Game

The first version of *Don't Panic* is a cooperative board game inspired by games such as Pandemic [12] and Monopoly [13]. Each player starts the game as member of a *panic control team* that must work together to calm down people, preventing the biggest panic event humanity has ever seen. During the game session different potential panicking events will take place in the city represented in the board. Each player assumes a unique role within the team, with special abilities that improve the team's chances if applied wisely. In order to play the game a player gets a limited number of actions to spend on her turn. In this way the player has to think wisely how to use the actions he can do. The players have a limited time to calm down the situation, before the panic will spread and they will lose the game.

Learning Objectives of the Game. *Don't Panic* has multiple aimslinked to soft skills teaching and learning. In fact the game wants to teach communication styles useful to manage crisis events but also foster team building. That is the main reason why the game is a collaborative one and not a competitive one.The game was conceived to push local vs. global reasoning, problem dissection and making plans dividing the board game into zones and adding unpredictable events during the game which can create contrasting reasoning and priorities.In order to achieve these goals the game uses two means: the rules and the content. First of all the game rules are studied to push the player to put into practice the "best practices" linked to soft skills for crisis management. Secondly the content of the game reflects real life information and events linked to crisis management. This kind of game can be used with different targets form the crisis management team, to the volunteers, to common people (in order to sensitize them to the crisis management problem). In order to address the different targets only the contents (from more to less detailed) and not the rules of the game have to be changed. In the rest of this section we will present in detail each element of the game design underlining its potential usefulness in the crisis management field and in particular in managing panicking events.

Game Dynamics. A *Don't Panic* player gets a limited number of actions (4) to spend on her turn:

- *Calm down people in a sector.* This action simulate going on the field and calm people talking with them.
- *Move people from a sector to another.* The main idea behind this action is to demonstrate that moving the problem from a sector to another does not resolve it.
- *Move through keypoints.* This is a game linked action to allow movements over the territory.
- *Create/remove a barrier.* (to be done with the help of another player). Containing people could or couldn't be a wise action depending on the board situation.
- *Create an information center.* The information centers will be detailed in a following section. To summarize they symbolize the relationship between the crisis management team and the population.

In addition, each player's *Role* grants special abilities that are unique to that player. The game ends immediately in defeat for all players if the entire map has a panic lever higher than 50 panicked people. Players collectively win the game when (i) the panic can no more spread because of the barriers; (ii) There is nobody in panic on the map.

Game Components. Table 1 details each component of the game together with its serious role.

Table 1. Game components description

Component	Description	Serious Role
Board	Representing a real or virtual city the board is divided in sectors and presents paths and key points. If all the paths in a sector are secured through barriers (i.e. blocked) the sector is secured (that is the panic will not augment in the sector at next wave). However, only a non-secured path can let people pass from one sector to another.	The board is the main link to the territory. The game is conceived so that a general path could be applied to any city or territory
Pawns	The pawns represent the players in the game. The pawn moves towards sectors following keypoints and the player can act only on the sectors communicating with the keypoint.	While the pawns have the role of facilitators in the understanding of the position of the members of the team on the board, the fact that the player can only act on communicating sectors wants to simulate what happens during crisis in real life.

Table 1. (*continued*)

Component	Description	Serious Role
Timer	The timer is used to calculate the next panic wave. When the timer rings each already panicked sector will incremented by 5 panicked people. In the non-panicked sectors nothing will happen.	Add the sense of time stress to the game to simulate the limited time for decision making. We voluntary choose a timer with ticking and ringing to add the urge of taking decisions.
Role cards	Each player assumes a specific role (e.g., coordinator, crowd manager, volunteer, passerby and the like) in the game that can do particular actions at low cost.	The roles were chosen after analysis of realones. The passerby role was added to simulate the involvement of common people. Roles are used to push the players to coordinate with each other in order to take advantage of their specific abilities.
Events Cards	Events cards are, together with the Timer, the source of panic. Each round the player has to draw 2 event cards and apply their effects.	While the panic wave after the timer is a predictable event, the events card add the unpredictable aspect in the game, as the cards are draw by chance.
Information cards	Information cards diffuse information which is useful to manage panic. Only one card per round can be played and only by the current player. As Don't panic is a collaborative game, players may openly discuss strategies during the game and share information.	Information cards are conceived to pass real information on how to manage crisis. The fact that players have to be on the same keypoint to exchange cards symbolizes the effort in sharing the information.
Information Centers	Information centers help in lowering panic. Once an information center has being constructed, the effects of the draw event cards on the adjacent zone are cut by half. However creating an information center is a highly costly action. In fact if a player decides to create an information center this one it's the only action he can do for this turn.	The information centers are conceived to underline the importance of information management during crisis. While the information cards are more linked to information sharing in between the members of the team, the information centers are there to underline the importance of the communication with population during crisis.

Table 1. (*continued*)

Component	Description	Serious Role
Displays With Panic Numbers	Each sector of the game is equipped with a display to indicate the panic level on the sector. Chain Reactions: Once the panic number reach quota 50 (that is 50 people panicked in the zone) the panic propagate to all near sectors in an epidemic way	The serious role of the panic is linked to the chain reaction effect. Being in contact with panicked people can push other people to enter in panic.

4   The Pilot Study

In order to test the game concept we conducted a pilot study with crisis and emergency workers to validate game dynamics and elements before the implementation.We created then a paper version of the game as a first mock up for a following computer based version of the game.

Fig. 1. A game session

Don't Panic was tested with 10 Civil Protection experts belonging to different organization. In between our participants we had maxi emergencies coordinators, dog handlers, and medical emergency experts. We had 3 participants in between 20-29, 3 in between 30-39, 1 in between 40-49 and 3 in between 50-59. 7/10 participants were male. Participants spent in average 11 years working in the actual position and 8 years in other positions (always in crisis and emergency management) which allow us to classify most of our participants as experts (we had only 2 participants with less than 5 years expertise). We did not choose our participants basing on their expertise on game (video or not) but from the survey we discovered that half of the participants played "whenever they can" while the other half "sometimes". It is worth to note that the participants playing video games ranked "sometimes" while were the older ones playing cards or board games ranked "whenever they can".

To reproduce classical board game dynamics each session was composed of a maximum of 5 participants (Figure 1). The involved players were asked to play the game, to answer to a survey and finally to participate in a semi structured interview. In addition, the sessions were video recordedto analyze conversational exchanges, addressing leadership issues, team building and conversational styles. In the study we investigated:

(a) The potential acceptance of a game for skill training in crisis management
(b) The easiness of use of the game for the target
(c) The effectiveness of the game for soft skills learning

The first two aspects were derived from surveys and interview, while the latter one mostly through video and conversational analysis.

Regarding potential acceptance of a game in crisis management, results show that the game was very well accepted (in both cases we were asked when we will do another game session). To understand the reasons why, we can cite a couple of survey questions. When asked which aspects were the strong points of the game participants noted 3 times collaboration, 3 communication, 3 team building, 2 strategy/creativity and 3 excitement/stress. It is worth to note that this was an open question and the terms were chosen by the participants. As these are exactly the game dynamics inserted in the game this can be considered as a good result for the (c) point. In addition during the semi-structured interviews participants were asked if the game could be useful in training volunteers (in a general way, independently from soft skills). All the participants answered positively to this question, talking about the perceived importance during the game of decision making and making action priorities. For example one of the participants answered: "Yes, becausethe gamepushes you to createan overall picture,notfocusingon the singlepoint of concern" and another participant answered "It (the game) mightbeuseful whenit makes me understandthat someeventsare more difficult to manage thanothers, forexample,I might notknow thata chemical explosioncan create more panic than other kind of explosions or that a simplefirecan cause a lot of damages (for example contamination or not)". On the other hand it was also underlined that the game should not be the first access point for new trainees to the crisis management problem as it teaches procedures in a very general way: "It candefinitely be useful tovolunteer, although I don't know how much tothe event, because a wrong procedure obviouslycan be dangerous (to the event management)."

Regarding easinessof the game, the survey asked if the game was easy or not to play and if the rules were easy or not to retain. The game was ranked 4,6 (in a scale 0-

10 with 0 being very easy and 10 being very difficult) for both, rule retention and actual play session. From the video analysis we can write-in that the easiness of play was in part negatively influenced by the panic displays which had to be updated by hand at each turn. An electronic version of the game will compensate for this problem. On the other hand, the amount of rules is difficult to retain for a one-shot session.

Regarding validation of the game dynamics for soft skills,the results show that the collaborative board game is potentially useful for soft skills building. More in detail, the participants were asked in different questions if they felt that the game pushed them to communicate, collaborate and if they felt to be part of a team during the play. For the first question 10/10 participants answered that the game pushed them to communicate much (higher rate on the scale). For the second question 9/10 participants answered that they felt to be collaborating a lot (higher rate on the scale) during the game and 1 participant answered that he felt he was collaborating "a little bit"(smaller rate over the average). On the other hand for the team building part we had 6/10 participants answering that they felt clearly part of a team (higher rate on the scale), while the 40% answered "a little bit". We thinkit's worth to note that they felt to be collaborating even if they weren't feeling as a part of a team. The video and conversation analysis shows the emergence of evident leaderships in particular in one of the groups. In our opinion this leadership presence influenced the *Being a part of a team* answers, while on the other hand their professionalism (the consuetude to collaborate in an active way with strangers) explain the difference between the two answers. As this experiment wasn't linked to a debriefing part (which was thought to be integrated in the electronic version) and as it was a one-shot experiment we cannot deepen this aspect. On the other hand these answers reinforce us in two beliefs: (i) the necessity of a debriefing phase after the game session, and (ii) the need for a long term experiment in order to assess team building. This necessity of a debriefing phase around the topic of player's behavior was underlined also during the interviews: "From this gameyourealize whoworksin a constructive ratherthan destructive mood, who puts the others off tointervene andto cooperate, ifthere issomeone whohasa bad character... maybein the final analysisyoumightsay "but someone has made proposals and you have not even evaluated because you have preferred to listen to your best friend than common sense, and to say to another person "you'vegiven uptoo quickly,you were discouragedandhavegiven upto pursueyourideas.." To summarize, the perceived value of the game for soft skills passes not only through the communication aspect, but also though the identification of good or bad leadership/followers practices during the game.

Also for the reflection part we had interesting results. A question in the survey asked if the game pushed the participants to make a link with their past experience. 6/10 participants answered positively to this question. It's interesting to note that 3/4 participants which did not make a link with their previous experience were the ones less used to maxi emergences. For the other ones, because of the generated complexity the game management was similar to the real emergences management pushing this way a link with their previous experience.

5   Considerations on the Pilot Study

This section presents some considerations on the presented pilot study with the paper prototype.

Validation of the Use of a Serious Game for Crisis Management: Summarizing the results from the experimentation, *Don't Panic* can be useful for soft skills teaching in crisis management. As we have seen from the pilot study description, we had a high acceptance rate of the game for volunteers' training, and its usefulness for leadership or communication management was established.Another interesting point is linked to reflective learning. With this game we had the opportunity to validate not only that the game triggers different levels of reasoning (coordination and priorities for example) but also that the game pushes towards a reflection on past events. In fact most of the participants used previous experiences in real settings in order to manage better the current game. On the other hand it was underlined that a low fidelity implementation of the applied procedures can be counterproductive for training purposes. For this reasons after analysis we are upgrading some game dynamics.

Validation of Game Dynamics: The co-located, board game version has shown interesting aspects linked to soft skills: a high level of conversational exchanges, collaboration between players, a push towards quick communication styles.So whatever augmented electronic version of this game needs to reproduce in some way the outlined dynamics. However, to avoid the problems underlined in the interviews we decided to modify some of the game dynamics and structure the game to have two levels of triggers. Near the mission to avoid panic spreading we added another kind of mission (e.g., find all the blessed people in the territory). This kind of double level can help in (i) push the local vs. global optimum reasoning; (ii) add stress to the management. In fact if the players choose to focalize on the panic the blessed people can die and the other way round.

6   Implications for Design

We started our work conceiving the paper version of the game as a first mock up for a following computer based version of the game. However, results show that the actual version of the game is useful for its purposes (soft skills teaching) as is. We believe that this experiment is an interesting example about how we – as computer scientists- are used to think about the medium before thinking about the aim. From our point of view it was evident that this kind of game had to be a computer based one. The results from our experiments pushed us to ask ourselves other kind of questions. In particular we started to ask ourselves *when* a computer based serious game version is really necessary. To put it in another way: what can really do a computer based serious game for crisis management that other media cannot do? In order to find an answer to this question we are developing aserious game based on most of the rules of *Don't Panic* but conceived to be played in a semi-distributed way, allowing at the same time centralized management from the coordinators' part and interaction with the territory from the active workers part. This new game is now divided in two "zones". The first zone is the *coordination center*. In this zone play the players with the coordinator role. The zone use the same board described above augmented in an electronic way. In this board the coordinators have a general view about what happens in the territory. However not all the information are visible for the coordinators as several of them are accessible only by the on the field players. The second zone is an *on the field* zone. Several players go on the territory to do mission and collect information – mostly through mobiles or tangible tools - and they have only a partial view of the territory. In this way we can try another approach to the link with the territory and simulate in a better way the communication in between workers that happens during crisis events.

While we said that the paper version works well for soft skills training there are different elements a computer based version can improve.

First of all we can talk about the *game dynamics*. As we have seen thecurrent difficulty to update panic displays in the paper version influence the game experience. This is a problem that can be easily managed in an electronic version of the game. A computer based version can also help in managing in a more intelligent and efficient-from the learning point of view - way the information displayed during the game, or add a long-tail effect to certain actions. While these are minor addition they can certainly help improve the game experience and the teaching aspect.

Another important *learning aspect* that can be improved with a computer based version is the use of traces for reflection. In fact we can reuse the game traces once the game is finished to help players reflect on both (i) their behavior during the just finished game session but also (ii) its link with their past experience. Obviously this opens questions about which kind of traces are best suited for which kind of reflection. Final addition,also the coaching element already existing in the game can be improved. During the game more expert players give suggestion on how to manage a panic event basing on their previous experienceusing some kind of coaching by storytelling. In order to make this process useful for workers we can think about a notation process to foster knowledge exchange.

A distributed version of the game implies also reflection upontechnological choices. First of all a computer-based version of the board game part could be "easily" developed using a tabletop. However if we consider that in between our targets there are also volunteers one of the main constraint became keeping costs low, so the tabletop solution has to be dropped. A second aspect we have to take into account while developing the game is its portability. What we want to avoid in this case is to develop an ad-hoc game for each city the game will be used but at the same time keep a strong link with the territory.

7   Conclusions and Future Works

The board game presented in this paper was conceived to be the first step of a computer based serious game. However, results of our experimentation shows that the game is useful for teaching soft skills for crisis management "as is". These results pushed us to reconsider the role of computer science in Serious Games and to ask ourselves what a computer based Serious Games can really do for crisis management that other media cannot do. It's our opinion that this question will move our research focus *from Serious Games* for crisis management *to Transmedia* for crisis management (i.e. the use of different media from radio, to video to games for crisis management) and help in the integration with other non-game based tools used by crisis experts for teaching/learning in order to choose the best medium to carry a message. In this way we can create a more holistic approach to the crisis management teaching and learning problem.

Within this approach, we also plan to work on the identification of building blocks to be used for the development of serious games that address different needs and target groups in crisis management and civil protection. The use of a building block approach can promote the development of "quick and dirty" games (that is low cost, low fidelity games) that can be played by a larger community, including volunteer associations and common citizens.

Acknowledgments. The work is co-funded by NFR-VERDIKT 176841/SIO FABULA (http://teseolab.org) and EU-ICT 7FP MIRROR project (http://www.mirror- project.eu). We acknowledge the help of Regola (http://www.regola.it/) in organizing the experimentation. We thank all the participants, in particular Gianni Della Valle, for sharing with us their knowledge of the domain. The first author holds a fellowship from ERCIM - the European Research Consortium for Informatics and Mathematics.

References

1. Sagun, A., Bouchlaghem, D., Anumba, J.C.: A Scenario-based Study on Information Flow and Collaboration Patterns in Disaster Management. Disasters 33(2), 214–238 (2008)
2. Roberts, B., Lajtha, C.: A New Approach to Crisis Management. Journal of Contingencies and Crisis Management 10(4), 181–191 (2002)
3. Boud, D., Keogh, R., Walker, D.: Reflection: turning experience into learning, Routledge (1985)
4. Incident commander, the game, http://www.incidentcommander.net/product.shtml
5. Di Loreto, I., Mora, S.: DivitioniCollaborative serious games for crisis management: an overview. In: Proceeding ofd 21st International IEEE WETICE Conference (to appear)
6. Mora, S., Boron, A., Divitini, M.: CroMAR: Mobile augmented reality for supporting reflection on crowd management. International Journal of Mobile Human Computer Interaction 4(2), 88–101 (2012)
7. Disaster Planning and Emergency Management, http://emergency-planning.blogspot.com/ (accessed February 2012)
8. Sagun, A., Bouchlaghem, D., Anumba, J.C.: A Scenario-based Study on Information Flow and Collaboration Patterns in Disaster Management. Disasters 33(2), 214–238 (2008)
9. Stolk, D., Alexandrian, D., Gros, B., Paggio, R.: Gaming and multimedia applications for environmental crisis management training. Computers in Human Behavior 17, 627–642 (2001)

10. Hazmat Hotzone, the game, `http://www.etc.cmu.edu/projects/hazmat_2005/about.php`
11. Benjamins, T., Rothkrantz, L.J.M.: Interactive Simulation in Crisis Management. In: Proceedings of ISCRAM 2007, Delft, The Netherlands (2007)
12. Pandemic board game,
    `http://www.zmangames.com/boardgames/pandemic.html`
13. Monopoly game, `http://www.hasbro.com/monopoly/en_US/`
14. Report on 9-11, `http://www.9-11commission.gov/report/911Report.pdf`
15. Heysel stadium disaster, `http://en.wikipedia.org/wiki/Heysel_Stadium_disaster`
16. Love Parade in Duisburg, `http://en.wikipedia.org/wiki/Love_Parade_stampede`

Health Games

Taxonomy Analysis and Multiplayer Design Suggestions

Alex Gekker

Department of Media and Culture Studies, Utrecht University, Utrecht, Netherlands
Games for Health Europe Foundation, Eindhoven, Netherlands
gekker.alex@gmail.com

Abstract. This paper presents an exploratory research of health games in EU, focusing on the role of multiplayer in the health-games experience, utilizing the health-game taxonomy suggested by Sawyer and Smith [1], combined with a preliminary survey of fity existing European health games in order to point out existing trends and suggest currently untapped venues of exploration. First, a theoretical review is presented, utilizing framework from the humanities and cultural studies in order to address what seen as a design issue with contemporary serious health games. Then, the results of a quantitative study of existing health games are presented, and analyzed through an existing taxonomy. Last, based on the lacunas found in the taxonomy, a thorough theoretical analysis is undertaken on their possible reasons, and suggestions on design methodologies are introduced through a comparison with existing commercial multiplayer games.

Keywords: serious games, health games, game taxonomy, multiplayer, procedural rhetoric, asynchronous multiplay.

1 Introduction

Serious games are becoming a recognized venue of creative attempts to improve the life of others, and health constitutes an important aspect of these attempts. From so-called exergaming and up to the use of games in medical rehabilitation, games are employed for preventative and rehabilitative medical needs, and for, both physical and mental wellbeing. This paper presents an exploratory research of health games production in EU, focusing on the role of multiplayer in the health-games experience. I utilize the health-game taxonomy suggested by Sawyer and Smith [1], combined with a preliminary survey of 50 existing European health games in order to point out existing trends and suggest currently untapped routes of exploration. The research was carried out during an internship within the recently-founded Games for Health Europe foundation, aimed at promoting health games, and thus was designed to better the understanding of this field in the European region and subsequently facilitate additional research projects.

M. Ma et al. (Eds.): SGDA 2012, LNCS 7528, pp. 13–30, 2012.

The paper is broken into three parts. It begins with a theoretical review, to situate this research as utilizing framework from the humanities and cultural studies, in order to address a design issue with contemporary serious health games. Then, the results of a quantitative study of several dozen existing health games are presented, and analyzed through the aforementioned taxonomy. Last, based on the lacunas found in the taxonomy, an examination is undertaken on their possible reasons, and suggestions on design methodologies are introduced through a comparison with existing commercial multiplayer games.

In the first part I present the notions of play and games as reflected in literature, noting how modern attempts to use computer games for non-entertainment purpose stem from theorization of play and learning. Following, I discuss some of the terms surrounding the idea of using games for non-entertainment means, such as "serious", "persuasive" and "training" games, and their implications for different design methodologies within serious games. Specifically, I utilize Ian Bogosts' [2, p. 258] notion of procedural rhetoric on the ability of games to present arguments and how it might be used for the learning experience in health games.

In the second part, I sample and analyze fifty recent health game, created in Europe. The games were selected via a process which included initial semi-structured interviews with participants active in the health game field and following, a snowball sampling of game data from the web. Those games are then sorted out according to the health games taxonomy suggested by Ben Sawyer and Peter Smith which differentiate health games according target audience and medical field. I analyze the result in the scope of Bogost's procedural rhetoric, while sketching a common denominator for each category in terms of game mechanics, player interactions and their relevance to the aim of the game. The taxonomy provides an initial view of the European health games sector, and allows a more in-depth analysis by focusing on those taxonomy categories which lack examples. I note that the lacking categories are those tied in with multi-user interaction, and suggest looking into the design methodologies of mainstream multiplayer games for solutions.

In the final part I outline possible directions into future development of health games, particularly focusing on the multiplayer aspect of serious gaming. I propose that procedural persuasion can be achieved in multiplayer game by utilizing the notion of collaborative creation and collective intelligence popular in web projects such as Wikipedia [3]. This can be done by establishing the game space itself as influenced by player's actions and showing the reciprocity of multiple actors vis-à-vis this environment. To illustrate those principles, I analyze two radically different recent commercial games Minecraft and Dark Souls, and conclude by suggesting how similar principles may be implemented in a health multiplayer game.

The main premise of this research is that health games are beneficial practice which allow innovative approaches to various fields within medicine and healthcare. This research nevertheless does not dwell on demonstrating those benefits or detailing particular games and their specific effect. Though validation is an important aspect of the evolving health game industry, this practice is best left to medical professionals. My work focuses on a critical design approaches for health games, and suggests possible venues of improvement for those developing multiplayer health games.

2   Theoretical Framework

The notion of games for teaching and instruction is rather old, even though it might seem otherwise these days. German educator and the inventor of the kindergarten Friedrich Fröbel [4] has suggested that playing constitutes an integral part of children's upbringing. It was his understanding that play is the freiarbeit – or "free work" – and it is the primary through which the young acquaint themselves with the world. However, it is in the early 20th century that the idea of play as cultural, rather than educational phenomenon has risen, in the works of Dutch historian Johan Huizinga [5] who has set play as defining characteristic of human culture, pointing out its prevalence in such fields a war, politics, law and art. Huizinga emphasizes the distinction between play and work, and argues that the non-compelling, consequences-free results are a primary aspect of play and what distinguishes it from work. He notices how problem solving in various societies is equated with competition and proposes that answers to those problems (or, knowledge, in his somewhat narrow definition) can be treated as particular games, and be solved by finding the "rules" of the game, "grammatical, poetical or ritualistic, as the case may be" [5, p. 132].

2.1   Defining Games and Serious Games

"Games", along with the interrelated "play" are arguably one of the most disputed terms in modern scholarly work, stemming from such varied fields as classic anthropology [6], cultural studies [7] and design [8]. Bringing into the bundle "games" as incorporated into game theory of mathematics, statistics and strategy studies [9] and we have quite an overbearing term. For a good example of the discussion, I suggest visiting the website of game designer and researcher Ellis Bartholomeus, who in her continuous work identifies 15 repeating elements in the writings of 25 distinct game and play theorists, ranging from challenge to rules, from Huizinga to McGonigal [10]. The extent of this paper and its aims nevertheless are not geared towards a discussion of the many (and occasionally mutually exclusive) understandings of games.

   In this work I define games as digital programs, running on personal computers and/or consoles (with or without specialized peripheral devices), and which incorporate some feedback system using a graphical user interface, which allows the user a structured engagement with a rules-based world. In this context, health games are games used for improving the health and wellbeing of individuals. This improvement can come either in a way of direct engagement of the individual with the game or by the use of the game to improve the skills of medical professionals, caretakers and the like. This positions health games within the serious game paradigm, which emerged in the recent decade and calls for using games and game-based techniques for the purposes outside entertainment.

   Health games are therefore intervened with serious games, a term which itself is rather contested. Co-founder of the Serious Game Initiative Ben Sawyer defines them exclusively in accordance to the process of their creation: games that are for "serious" (non-entertainment) purpose, positioning it as a descriptive rather than normative term [11]. Game designer and critic Ian Bogost [2], on the other hand, rejects the term as being politically biased, aimed at enforcing the hegemonic culture of the political and business establishment at turning games into another source of power (in the Foucaldian sense) exerted over the player. Others have argued that serious games are necessarily tied in with pedagogy [12], are application for corporate/ business-related learning techniques [13], impossible to achieve without incorporating the social (learning) system that the player is situated in [14] or dependent on the interpretation of the player, who might use an "entertainment game" for "serious purpose" [15]. Unlike Bogost, I do not think the political appropriation of the term to corporate and governmental cultures invalidates its use. I do however think that the term 'serious games' conveys many different things to many different people, and thus attempt to narrow done my distinct sampling criteria. In her research on serious game as discourse Valentina Rao [16] summarizes the issue:

"Current classifications of serious games take into consideration to their educational content, learning principle, target age group and platform... but seem to blend indiscriminately aims, content themes and distribution sector". (p. 9)

2.2   Procedural Rhetoric in Games

My frame of analysis focuses on the way digital games encapsulate learning for players, but in a way that underlies the games' unique medium characteristics, utilizing Ian Bogost's ideas on procedural rhetoric. In his book *Unit Operations* Bogost suggests that video games can be defined as complex systems of interlocking "units" of meaning, and the process through which the individual player interacts with those units. An analysis rooted in unit operations stands in opposition to a perspective of holistic system-operations, and focuses on "modes of meaning-making that privilege discreet, disconnected action over deterministic, progressive systems" [17, p. 3]. Following this, he adds the notion of procedural rhetoric [2] and suggests that video games can make arguments exactly through the process of "leaving blanks" intended for player to carry actions in conjunction with the game rules, but with distinct unit operations rather than with the game as a wholesome object.

Bogost coins the term "simulation gap" to address the emerging meaning in the space between a game's procedural rules and player's subjectivity. He further claims that this simulation gap can be understood as a rhetorical (read, persuasive or instructive) device, by creating a system of interlocking procedural enthymemes. Enthymeme is the rhetorical device of leaving proposition out of an argument to be filled by the listeners themselves ("John Doe cannot be trusted, as he is a politician", suggests that all politicians are not trustworthy). In a game based procedural enthymeme, a player is encouraged to fill the gaps by his action, conditioning him towards a certain viewpoint. In our case, inducing learning is tied to the ability of influencing thoughts and behaviors and thus health games must be persuasive about their goals. To view games as rhetorical system, therefore, requires us to analyze what is being left out of the game (what actions should be undertaken by the player) and how the procedural engagement with those blank space forms understanding about situations and processes.

For instance, when discussing the topic of exergaming (games intended for promoting active exercise), Bogost notes how the procedural rhetoric of the game Dance Dance Revolution (DDR) evokes the idea of the personal trainer, as the game suggests a movement to be carried out on a special control mat, and immediately gives the player both audio and video feedback on the performance of the move. Combining each move (unit operation) into the fluid process of semi-dancing, DDR taps the into the player's own goal of getting fit and encourages her to continue moving. The feedback of the game occurs not only as numeral evaluation of the points, gained by the correct execution of moves but also a feedback on how accurate the sequence was (thus a player may step on an adjacent space to the one required and still get some of the points and an encouraging message on the screen "almost got it!".

3   Methodology

For my procedural rhetoric analysis, a sample of health games was required. Fifty recent health game, created in Europe were selected via a process which included initial semi-structured interviews with six participants, who are active in the health game field, and following so a snowball sampling of game data from the web. Those games were sorted out according to the health games taxonomy suggested by Ben Sawyer and Peter Smith [1]. Next, I analyzed the results while sketching a common denominator for each category in terms of game mechanics, player interactions and their relevance to the aim of the game. I will describe each component in the following.

3.1   Geographical Frame

Only games developed by organization and companies coming from western and central European countries were selected. The reasons for that are twofold.

First, the research was carried out as part of an internship within the Games for Health Europe foundation (GFHEU), and thus it was centered on immediately accessible markets and organizations. Additionally, initial study showed considerable lacking of research into European health games, focusing strongly on the North-American sector. It was hypothesized that a research such as the one presented here might prove valuable in further comparison between the sectors in various regions

3.2   Time Frame

Only games developed within the last 5 years were chosen. An exception was made to games which have seen continue development in later years, either in the form of further titles, expansions or translations.

3.3 Sampling

I used sampling technique similar to the method used by Lagu et al. [18] in their research of weblogs written by health professionals. The team has identified 279 blogs written by health professionals, first by sampling blogs listed in relevant web directories and then by following reference links to other blogs while analyzing whether they fit the research criteria.

As heath games have even more arbitrary definitions then health blogs, I first approached six speakers (two of them keynotes) of the GFHEU conference, and held short semi-structured interviews with them. The interviewees were chosen on the basis of their talks and the need for varied backgrounds (medical, industry and academia). The goal of these preliminary interviews was to understand the speakers' vision of what constitutes a health game, as well as receiving specific examples of such games.

Following the interviews I added an online questionnaire which was sent to all the conference attendees and additional contacts. The answered questionnaires (n=44) together with the games collected from the interviews and literature review, has served as the basis for the snowball search.

Following the links on game websites, developer blogs and magazine reviews, games were selected and analyzed for compatibility with the research definition until a target of 50 games was reached. The sample target goal was set after various research indicated the average number of serious (not only health) games produced in recent years at approximately 80 games per year [15, 19, 20]. Thus, a sample size of 50 health games from the past five years was chosen as an effective representation of the field.

Additionally, projects that use existing (mainstream) video games were not included. The organization or individual sampled were required to develop their own tool, be it a health game or a middleware that allows the creation of such games (e.g. a game engine for modeling medical situations). The reason for that was the desire to witness how "serious" intentions are incorporated into the game starting with the design stage, utilizing the unique procedural rhetoric of the gaming medium, rather than appropriating an existing (unchanged) game as part of a broader treatment. Therefore, health games using existing games (or game engines) but modding them were included in the sampling, as they fit the ideas of procedural rhetoric.

3.4 Health Games Classification

After sampling games that met the research requirements, they were analyzed and organized into taxonomy for health games classification suggested by Sawyer and Smith [1]. The taxonomy (as it will be regarded henceforth) showcases the potential of games for influencing personal and public health (table 1). It is divided into four different *health game fields* (personal, professional practice, research/academia and public health) over five various *areas of application* (preventative, therapeutic, assessment, educational and informatics). Each of the twenty categories is not named, but rather presents a potential field or need to be addressed.

Table 1. Sawyer and Smith's health game taxonomy

Fields -> Areas of application	Personal	Professional Practice	Research / Academia	Public Health
Preventative	Exergaming Stress	Patient Communication	Data Collection	Public Health Messaging
Therapeutic	Rehabilitainment Disease Management	Pain Distraction Cyber Psychology Disease Management	Virtual Humans	First Responders
Assessment	Self-Ranking	Measurement	Inducement	Interface / Visualization
Educational	First Aid Medical Information	Skills / Training	Recruitment	Management Sims
informatics	PHR (Personal Health Records)	EMR(Electronic Health Records)	Visualization	Epidemiology

Sawyer and Smith's taxonomy, is not the only attempt to create a clear definition of the field. In their report on serious gaming industry, Michaud and his associates [19] separate the serious game industry into 4 distinct segments, defined by end customers, being Healthcare, Teaching and Training, Public Information and Business and Defense and Public Safety. Within the healthcare sector they divide it into private and public sector, with further listing of the following areas: In private (professional) sector there are games to persuade, to educate and therapeutic games. In public sector there are additional categories such as games to inform, brain training games and exergames (see table 2). Similarly, in her literature review on using games for health and physical education, Papastergiou [20] categorizes research done on health games. She suggests classifying studies in accordance with their aim: disease awareness, nutrition education, first aid education, acquisition of motor skills or improvement of fitness. Although the research focuses on classifying the research done using such games, rather than the games themselves, the classification still follows a framework similar to this of Michaud et al.

Table 2. Michaud et.al's classification of health games

Public	Private
games to educate	games to educate
games to inform	games to persuade
games to persuade	rehabilitation games
brain training games	
exergames	

The advantages found in the taxonomy over other classification methods for this research are that it focuses specifically on health games and is presented in the form of a two dimensional matrix, which allows a more organic view of the field. It is also well-matched to Bogost's ideas on procedural rhetoric. The games are arranged by coupling their "target audience" with the topics wished to be examined. The taxonomy promotes apprehensive understanding of procedural rhetoric by showing for example how the notion of "education", is in fact multi-dimensional, and receives different values by enacting the engagement of the "blank spaces" with player action, resulting in various kinds of arguments that arise from these games. A game designed to educate a doctor uses different procedural rhetoric than one to educate a public official on the consequences of vaccination.

4   Results

Overall, out of the 50 games reviewed, the top three categories account for more than half of the games in total (27 games out of 50 in the three categories combined). Those categories are preventative and therapeutic games for personal use and therapeutic games for professional practice. Preventative games for personal use include titles aimed at exergaming, brain training and other mostly-wellness related actives, a rising field within the commercially-aimed gaming industry and thus unsurprisingly popular. Therapeutic games account for games used by medical professionals to facilitate rehabilitation procedures.

Table 3. Number of games in each taxonomy category

Fields -> Areas of application	Personal	Professional Practice	Research / Academia	Public Health	total
Preventative	13	1	1	2	17
Therapeutic	7	7	3	3	20
Assessment	1	1	0	0	2
Educational	5	4	0	1	10
informatics	0	0	1	0	1
total	26	13	5	6	50

Out of all the application areas, the *therapeutic* proved to be the most popular (20 titles) with the *preventative* application area coming close with 17. Games for *personal use* are the dominant category, amounting by itself to 26 titles – more than half of the entire sample size. *Informatics* and *assessment* games are practically nonexistent with one and two titles, respectively.

However, the goal of this study was to point out tendencies rather than provide exact numerical account of the games on the market. Acknowledging that the sampling method may provide skewed numerical values, the overall inclination is present. I will discuss these findings in the next part.

5   Discussion

Looking back at the results we need to remember that those are games that attempt to go beyond the notion of entertainment and thus have a goal of influencing their respective players in a certain way. In other words, the procedural rhetoric of such games (the coupling of game mechanics and story) should stand on their own besides the content delivered in them. *Pony Panic* is a good example of game with a strong procedural rhetoric. The game announces itself as an exergame and played via two computers located within a 2-3 meters distance from each other. As players play a race game, they are prompted to suddenly change positions, and following, sprint towards each other in order to gain advantage in the virtual race by winning a short physical one. As the game lasts, its difficulty of the game is raised by increased virtual challenge as well as by physical exertion.

In the following part I will show that the most heavily populated categories of the taxonomy are those that have provide for both game designers and player a clear procedural rhetoric of coupling the game play with player actions.

5.1   The Solitary Health Gamer

The results of the sampling are not surprising, with the most abundant category being the most commercially viable. *Preventative* games for *personal use* exist as both physical (exergaming) and mental (psychological relaxation, brain training) variety. These finding correlate to those presented by Papastergiou [20] in her review of health game research, as the majority of research was focused on the use of (existing) exergames for improving the physical fitness of adolescents and young adults. Similarly, *therapeutic* games for both private and professional use address a clear need of creating a more engaging and rewarding therapy sessions. I will return to the lack of such games in the research and public health field later.

Analyzed according to Bogost's notion of procedural rhetoric, *preventative* as well as *therapeutic* games present the player with a simple simulation gap to fill, echoing the dynamics of similar non-game techniques: If you will carry out the action we describe, in a certain manner, you will be rewarded by (a) a feedback from the game towards your progress and (b) improvement in the way your body (or parts of it) function. As the premise (and therefore, the rhetorical argument) of such games focuses on gradual improvement over repeating series of actions, developers in this category have little problem designing such games, as this is the basic premise of most existing (non-health) games, and the challenge is applying non standard input or feedback systems related to the players' specific conditions. This can be addressed by using multidisciplinary design teams and involving the target audience in the design process, as was done by Lockyer et al. [21], who interviewed children, teachers and parents prior to designing a nutrition and exercise game for children. As long as the gameplay correlates with the learning goals of the game, and the target audience experiences it as such, designing similar games presents little procedural challenge.

As for training (*educational*) medical games, the (relatively) limited amount of titles found is surprising, especially when considering previous research regarding the popularity of such games in the US. Since the inception of the term "serious gaming" in the early 2000's, one of the primary conceptual frameworks with which such games were understood was that of a training method. In their book on serious games and the process towards manufacturing such games, David Michael and Sandy Chen [11] argue that the appearances of personal computers heralded their use for training and education. "Edutainment" software, featuring repetitive interfaces and tasks, had blossomed under the general umbrella term of "e-learning". While having many game-like attributes, this software had rather simplistic approach to learning, and had predominantly text-based, unimaginative and boring execution of merging training with interactivity based on existing game mechanics (what Bogost calls textual or graphical skins – the "dressing" of old games in new content). Serious game develop-er Kevin Corti notes that serious games differentiate themselves from edutainment and e-learning software by emphasizing game principles such as realistic environ-ments, clearly defined rules objectives and outcomes, adaptive to the player, require application of non-textual cognitive abilities and are truly enjoyable [13].

If analyzed from procedural rhetoric perspective, educational and training health games are approaches to learning, focused on providing the player a simulation gap which can be filled with knowledge later applicable in the physical world. In other words, the player is expected to experience certain gameplay demands and respond in a way that will teach him or her something. For example, in a game *Air Medic Sky 1*, the player performs the role of a doctor who must cope with incidents related to team communication and safety, utilizing decision making skills and advanced bio-feedback controller that affects his or her actions in the game. The game suggests to the player that those skills and the control of one's physiology (heartbeat as indicating calmness level) are viable in actual medical practice as well.

Similarly, education theorist James Gee argues that (even commercial) computer games can be approached as examples for creating better educational tools, as they promote a type of learning based on what he calls "situated cognition". Gamers gen-erate their knowledge about the game world from interacting with it, rather than fol-lowing the more traditional education paradigm of training-exam-application of knowledge. Mitgutsch and Weise [22] have shown that not only player have the abili-ty of using previous knowledge and support of fellow gamer communities –their gam-ing capital [23, 24] - to learn the rules of new games, but are also able to alter their knowledge recursively, and re-structure it in accordance with alternative game design. Overall, training and educational games provide a clear framework for both the game designer and the players in how they should be designed, built and played. This is what Bogost refers to as "procedural literacy" – the ability to "read and write proce-dural rhetoric—to craft and understand arguments mounted through unit operations represented in code" [2].

So far I have addressed the *preventative, therapeutic* and *educational* games, applied to *personal* and *professional* practice areas. Those categories host the largest amount of games from the sample and I have argued that this has to do with the ease of the designers to tie the premise of the game to its gameplay mechanics, and thus achieve efficient merging of the game and serious elements. In the next part of the discussion I will address those taxonomy categories that are sparsely populated.

5.2   The Procedurality of Multiplayer

When looking at the European health games analyzed through Sawyer & Smith's taxonomy, a clear picture arises. There are a lot of *preventative, therapeutic* and *educational* games aimed at *personal* and *professional practice* users, both commercial and non-commercial. Some *therapeutic* games are also present in the *research / academia* and *public health* categories, although in fewer numbers. Other categories show anecdotal examples at best.

I would like to argue that the lack of games in those categories stem from limited understanding on procedural rhetoric of the multi-player oriented serious games. To explain this statement I will need to address three distinct arguments:

1. The procedural rhetoric of games in those categories is tied to the multiplayer practice.
2. There is currently no good conceptualization of how such procedural rhetoric works (for serious multiplayer games).
3. Therefore, games in those categories are seldom being developed.

The blank categories in the taxonomy are those of *research / academia* and *public health* categories along with the assessment and informatics application areas. The common thread running through them all is their reliance on cooperation between the various stakeholders for successful operation. Modern research and academia is a complex process in which scientists and researcher engage with both human and technological components in order to advance certain assumptions or developments [25, 26]. Public health is similarly related to the relations between interested parties such as medical professionals, corporations and decision makers. Games related to assessment will similarly have to deal with the complex web of relations between the patient and his symptoms on the one hand, and the medical establishment on the other. Same goes for informatics, as the application of game mechanics to medical databases (both on personal and multiple scales) will require multiple parties[1].

The idea that effective learning is reliant on effective interaction with the environment is not new. Soviet psychologist Lev Vygotsky [27] introduced the notion of social constructivism, which situates the learner as participator in a dynamic process involving himself and other members of his society. The learner observes interactions within his cultural group, which allows him in time to *internalize* those practices into his own repertoire and later *appropriate* them for his own use, while perhaps giving them a unique meaning (such as the use of a pen develops over time from technical reproduction of a mentor's guidance to a distinct writing style and the ability to formulate one's own ideas on paper). Social constructivism views cognition "a complex social phenomenon... distributed – stretched over, not divided among – mind, body, activity and culturally organized settings (which include other

---

[1] I leave out the discussion on whether some of these fields (informatics in particular) should be attempted to be made into games. Unlike the training and educational games, those categories are less obvious in this context. Suffice to say that Sawyer and Smith predict such categories and present examples of medical solutions for each category.

actors)" [28, p. 1]. To effectively teach on situations involving the complexities of multiple participants, games should attempt to involve additional human players as participants.

Some of the research done on the effects on (non-serious) multiplayer games focuses specifically on the way social interaction between players promotes learning. Multiplayer games feature official or unofficial learning fields, where players share game-specific knowledge with newcomers and among themselves. This occurs while inside the game space but also on additional platforms that are created in parallel to the game (wikis, forums) and serve as places where games (as cultural objects) are deconstructed and reassembled into a form that benefits their players (tutorials, Q&A sections, quest walkthroughs etc.). Some scholars view those external platforms as the main drivers of player learning, viewing them as massively creative collaboration [29] or a unique form of paratextual transgressive play which challenges the dictum established by the game developers [24]. On the other hand, Constance Steinkuehler [30], a games and education scholar, rather emphasizes the unique way that the in-game interaction forms around immediate (situated) actions that the players must perform. For example she presents an account of how an "apprenticeship" is undergone in a massively multiplayer online role playing game (MMORPG) by an experienced player who recognizes newcomer's inadequacy in the game world and offered to guide her, offering to show her interface shortcuts but also guiding her on the ethics of the game world (in this case, not to clutter central recourse gathering area, and try to avoid going in the same direction as other players). Remarkably (and important for the case of health games) this information is "given 'just in time', always in the context of the goal-driven activity that its actually useful for – and made meaningful by – and always at a time when it can be immediately put to use" (p. 526). Drawing from such "apprenticeship" socialization for our discussion of multiplayer based learning, we should incorporate how the learning which occurs is both of the game mechanisms and of the implicit social codes and dynamics present in it.

So far the majority of attempts to create multiplayer serious games environments focused prominently on the MMROPG and its structure. Digital sociologists Ducheneaut and Moore [31] identify three main components which make MMORPGs into potential learning environments: players' self-organization, instrumental coordination (ways for a team of unfamiliar players to work with each other) and sociability (the "out-of-game" elements that develop, such as humor or the interest players show in each other's offline life). They suggest that "Going a step further the experience-points-based achievement systems in MMORPGs could easily be transformed into educational-credits-based achievement systems in which students accumulate credits for accomplishing educational tasks" [31, p. 99], a statement taken critically especially since it is not backed up by any concrete suggestions on how to do so. Similarly, instructional design scholars Childress and Browsell [32] describe how a distance learning class was enhanced by creating a common meeting space in *Second Life*, the massively multiplayer online virtual world. Leaving aside the question of whether *Second Life* constitutes a game, those (and similar) attempts concentrate on transferring the learning activity into the domain of the 'paratextual' [24] game activities, i.e. those that lie outside of the game space and in the broader game literacies of the player. Obviously, a class conversation via three dimensional avatars differs from similar conversation in physical space or via textual chat, but such discussion has nothing to do with the game's objective. In the same manner, designing a multi player health game should focus, from a procedural rhetoric point of view, on how the game promotes relevant notions (research cooperation, managing health records) in a unique way by being both **a game** and **multiplayer.**

This means that building a game just to replicate a class dynamics, or copying an online puzzle game mechanics which allows for some multiplayer but infusing it with health-related terminology will do no good. A player engaging in a multiplayer health game is required to understand **why** other players are present in the game, and **how** the interaction with them is relevant to the game goal(s). To conclude: the focus on MMORPG-like games for kindling cognitive learning processes is misplaced, since the procedural rhetoric of those games is focused on developing social interaction for the purposes of monster-slaying, not engaging in complex learning.

Theoretical framework might not be a major factor for commercial games, but for serious games it is a decisive consideration. Despite dismissive remarks about how "easily" MMORPGs environment could be transformed into learning environment by gaining "some kind of new ability for their in-game characters whenever they reach a new level" [31, p. 99] the reality is that few serious games have managed designing such mechanic. Instead those games often offer textual or graphical 'skins' – repurposing an existing game mechanic to include a message of sorts. I argue that one cannot build a multiplayer game without understanding how the multiplayer aspect in itself constitutes an argument in the overall game rhetoric towards the player. To construct multiplayer health games we must look elsewhere.

5.3   Building Multiplayer Health Games

Procedural persuasion can arguably be achieved in multiplayer game by utilizing the notion of collaborative creation and collective intelligence popular in web projects such as Wikipedia. This would be done by establishing the game space itself as influenced by player's actions and showing the reciprocity of multiple actors vis-à-vis this environment. To illustrate those principles, I will discuss two radically different commercial games *Minecraft* and *Dark Souls*, and conclude by suggesting how similar principles may be implemented in a health multiplayer game.

Minecraft is a curious phenomenon in the concurrent game production landscape. Low-budget and featuring low-resolution blockish graphics, the game became a major success, earning more than €23 million in its first year alone [33]. The core mechanic of the game is an open, randomly generated world, in which the player can manipulate basic building materials such as wood and ore to create tools of increasing complexity, gaining the ability to extract better materials and thus construct more elaborate structures. The player faces the environment which features generated enemies that attack on certain conditions. The game is complex and unintuitive, and an unskilled player may face problems surviving the first "day" in Minecraft's world.

This complexity has sprouted a vast paratextual network of player-to-player help, including the "usual suspects" such as a wiki and forums but also modes of multiplayer games (initially Minecraft was single player only) where gamers craft the gameworld together, "learning by doing" and assisting each other to develop better design skills to master the game. Digital law scholar Greg Lastowka [3] argues that Minecraft exemplifies the web 2.0 spirit, by allowing amateur creativity to blossom, uninhibited by draconian copyright and content control so popular in other sandbox and user-generated-content-reliant games. What is interesting however is that by creating an open system which provides limited guidance, developers encourage players to generate the game-specific knowledge by themselves. Minecraft is all about construction, design and manifestation of ideas. The training provided in the player communities correlates precisely with the game's goals, and is not exogenous to them, as in the case of many "educational" MMORPGs. From a procedural rhetoric perspective, this is a game about creation, constrained in a way to evoke discussion on ways to facilitate such creation, within the game space and in its immediate vicinity.

Dark Souls is, in a way, the exact opposite of Minecraft. It is a well-funded studio console sequel of the "dungeon crawler" action genre, in which your character is required to traverse hostile environment fighting off enemies and survive traps. Both games were released the same year but they look and feel as if separated by an abyss. And yet a similar thing unifies both – minimalist introduction and unforgiving learning curve from stage one. Dark Souls has been hailed as one of the hardest games to play, in terms of its reward/punishment mechanics and player progress. This dungeon crawler features a distinct crawl, rather than a leisurely walk in a park so common in modern games. Dark Souls features an interesting limited multiplayer game, embedded into the game mechanic. The game is single player in its core, but the presence of others is felt in two ways. First, occasionally apparitions of other players appear out of thin air, doing battle with enemies unseen to your character. You cannot interact with them in any way, and their sole purpose is moral support of sorts- reminding you that there are others out there fighting the same war as you do. The other mode is more interesting. Players can leave notes to each other in certain areas, warning what lies ahead. One can choose from a pre-set phrasing, never giving out about the nature of future danger besides a general "trap ahead". Additionally, one can choose to collect additional in-game resource, which will allow her to call other player for help, but also leave her open for "invasions" from hostile players, with irredeemable consequences for the player character in case of defeat.

Dark Souls features "asynchronous multiplay" [34] – a design technique that allows different players to interact while not playing at the same time. This mechanic is most known from current generation social Facebook games, but unlike them, here it carries meaning within the game world. The game encourages the players to constantly balance risks and rewards, and puts every other player in a dualistic rival-ally position. The game design makes sure that the player is reliant on the entire community (both in-game, in the form of notes and external paratextual sources) but as players progress in game, others begin to constitute a threat rather than opportunity. This prompts constant alertness, adaptability and creativity of the player, as well as a tension of what can and cannot be shared with the community and to what detail.

Let us envision what can be learned from those two examples towards a design of a health game correlating to one of the empty taxonomy categories.

A health game must be low cost, as it is likely funded by public or not-for-profit organizations. As the case of Minecraft has shown, this is not a problem as captivating gameplay can be created with minimal graphics. In fact, such game may be based on the Minecraft engine, substituting for example the building blocks of ore and wood into rudimentary representations of biological hierarchical systems. Furthermore, as the number of players (at least in the initial stages) will be low, such game would feature asynchronous multiplay, allowing for example, different classes of students from various time zones to share a common gamespace. Such game may feature a pervasive environment, which continues to function detached of the players' action, thus prompting a sense of urgency and necessary collaboration between the participants. Finally, as seen in Dark Souls, imposing limits on communication might actually stimulate learning, a notion which might come as counterintuitive to many educators[2]. Our game might deliberately limit player communication, thus encouraging them to continue deliberations and problem solving on other platforms (such as Facebook groups or designated forums), making them play along each other against the game.

6   Conclusions

This paper emerged from the work with Games for Health Europe, in an attempt to critically examine the status of health games. My aim was twofold: present an annotated snapshot of the relevant games present on the market and point out possible areas of improvement. My focus has been on the serious game initiative which advocates the use of games for non-entertainment purposes, and its co-founder Ben Sawyer's taxonomy of health games and their possible uses, which I used to organize the games sampled.

Following, Ian Bogost's notions of unit operations and procedural rhetoric were introduced as a method to analyze health games as systems of interlocking units, where meaning is generated by interaction between the player, the game rules and the "blank spaces" in the game to be filled by the player's actions. I have argued that an effective health game would be one that allows learning to occur through the game mechanics, and thus must be considered in the prism of what procedural rhetoric the in-game actions convey.

Finally, I claimed that the lack of games in certain taxonomy categories is related to the need to present relations between multiple human participants, in a way which is hard to imbue without a multiplayer game design. Yet, current procedural gameplay

---

[2] See for example the work of Manton and Maple [35] on creating an asynchronous virtual world to facilitate learning between schools. The world featured turn-based mechanic and mostly modes of conversation between participants during each turn, which in my opinion is counterproductive to the idea of a multiplayer on the one hand and asynchronous multiplay on the other.

conceptualization of serious games in general and health games in particular lacks the multiplayer aspect, and so such games are not being developed.

I propose combining design techniques from commercial games to create a procedural rhetoric argument about how creative collaboration is necessary to approach certain health topics. These include asynchronous multiplay, deliberately hindered communication and environment which invokes experimentation and construction.

In addition, it is my hope this paper will lead to a follow up research, since currently no other publications on health games specific to the region could be found. One possible direction is an institutional exploration of the European health game scene and mapping of the stakeholders which engage in the design and propagation of such games. Another venue is a comparative analysis of the European and US health games scenes, while noting America's apparent head start in serious games application versus the European focus on governmental grants and more publicly-funded development. Lastly, an attempt for user-tested game design based on those conclusions would serve to substantiate procedural rhetoric as design strategy for games.

References

1. Sawyer, B., Smith, P.: Serious games taxonomy. In: Serious Games Summit, GDC (2008)
2. Bogost, I.: Persuasive Games: The Expressive Power of Videogames. MIT Press, Cambridge (2007)
3. Lastowka, G.: Minecraft as Web 2.0: Amateur Creativity & Digital Games. SSRN eLibrary (2011)
4. Fröbel, F.: Die Menschenerziehung. Weinbrach (1826)
5. Huizinga, J.: Homo Ludens: A Study of the Play Element in Culture. Temple Smith, London (1970)
6. Geertz, C.: Deep Play: Notes on the Balinese Cockfight. Daedalus 101, 1–37 (1972)
7. Cassell, J., Jenkins, H. (eds.): From Barbie to Mortal Kombat: Gender and Computer Games. MIT Press, Cambridge (2000)
8. Salen, K., Zimmerman, E. (eds.): The Game Design Reader: A Rules of Play Anthology. MIT Press, Cambridge (2005)
9. Aumann, R.J.: Game Theory. In: Durlauf, S.N., Blume, L.E. (eds.) The New Palgrave Dictionary of Economics, pp. 529–558. Nature Publishing Group, Basingstoke (2008)
10. Bartholomeus, E.: Game elements, http://www.ellisinwonderland.nl/gmotiv/Gameelements2.html
11. Michael, D., Chen, S.: Serious Games: Games That Educate, Train, and Inform. Course Technology Inc., Boston (2005)
12. Zyda, M.: From visual simulation to virtual reality to games. Computer 38, 25–32 (2005)
13. Corti, K.: Games-based Learning; a serious business application. Informe de PixelLearning (2006)
14. Salen, K.: The ecology of games: connecting youth, games, and learning. MIT Press, Cambridge (2008)
15. Susi, T., Johannesson, M., Backlund, P.: Serious games–An overview. University of Skövde, Skövde (2007)

16. Rao, V.: How to Say Things with Actions I: a Theory of Discourse for Video Games for Change. In: Think Design Play: The Fifth International Conference of the Digital Research Association, Hilversum (2011)
17. Bogost, I.: Unit Operations: An Approach to Videogame Criticism. MIT Press, Cambridge (2006)
18. Lagu, T., Kaufman, E.J., Asch, D.A., Armstrong, K.: Content of Weblogs Written by Health Professionals. Journal of General Internal Medicine 23, 1642–1646 (2008)
19. Michaud, L., Alvarez, J., Alvarez, V., Djaouti, D.: IDATE - Serios Games, 2nd edn. IDATE Consulting, Montpellier (2010)
20. Papastergiou, M.: Exploring the potential of computer and video games for health and physical education: A literature review. Computers & Education 53, 603–622 (2009)
21. Lockyer, L., Wright, R., Curtis, S., Curtis, O., Hodgson, A.: Energy Balance: Design and formative evaluation of a health education multimedia game. In: EDMEDIA 2003, pp. 2721–2724 (2003)
22. Mitgutsch, K., Weise, M.: Subversive Game Design for Recursive Learning. In: Think Design Play: The Fifth International Conference of the Digital Research Association, Hilversum (2011)
23. Consalvo, M.: Zelda 64 and video game fans. Television & New Media 4, 321–334 (2003)
24. Consalvo, M.: Cheating: Gaining Advantage in Videogames. MIT Press, Cambridge (2007)
25. Latour, B.: Pandora's Hope: Essays on the Reality of Science Studies. Harvard University Press, Cambridge (1999)
26. Latour, B.: Reassembling the Social: An Introduction to Actor-Network-Theory. Oxford University Press, Oxford (2005)
27. Vygotsky, L.: Mind in society. Harvard University Press (1978)
28. Lave, J.: Cognition in practice: mind, mathematics, and culture in everyday life. Cambridge University Press, Cambridge (1988)
29. McGonigal, J.: Reality is Broken: Why Games Make Us Better and How They Can Change the World. Penguin Press, New York (2011)
30. Steinkuehler, C.A.: Learning in massively multiplayer online games. In: Proceedings of the 6th International Conference on Learning Sciences, pp. 521–528. International Society of the Learning Sciences (2004)
31. Ducheneaut, N., Moore, R.J.: More than just "XP": learning social skills in massively multiplayer online games. Interactive Technology and Smart Education 2, 89–100 (2005)
32. Childress, M.D., Braswell, R.: Using massively multiplayer online role - playing games for online learning. Distance Education 27, 187–196 (2006)
33. Orland, K.: Minecraft Draws Over $33 Millio. In: Revenue From 1.8M Paying Customers (2011), http://www.gamasutra.com/view/news/33961/Minecraft_Draws_Over_33_Million_In_Revenue_From_18M_Paying_Customers.php
34. Bogost, I.: Asynchronous multiplay: Futures for casual multiplayer experience. Other Players 6 (2004)
35. Manton, R., Maple, C.: A Networked Multiplayer Game to Facilitate Pupil to Pupil Contact Within the Context of a School Twinning Scheme. In: IADIS International Conference e-Society 2006, pp. 70–75. San Sebastian (2006)

Games Mentioned

Air Medic Sky 1 (2011) Vision Shift Studios / Utrecht Medical Center [PC computer] Utrecht

Medsim (2005) Medsim [PC computer, additional peripherials]. http://medsim.nl/

Campto(2008) Medpict / Ja.Games [PC computer, web]

Minecraft (2011) Mojang [PC computer, web]

Dark Souls (2011) From Software/ Namco [PlayStation 3, Xbox 360]

Second Life (2003) Linden Labs [PC computer, web]

Zombies, Run! (2011) Six to Start [iOS, Android] London.

A Serious Game for Training Balance Control over Different Types of Soil

Bob-Antoine J. Menelas and Martin J.D. Otis

[1] University of Quebec at Chicoutimi (UQAC), Department of Mathematics and Computer Science, Quebec, Canada
bamenela@uqac.ca
[2] University of Quebec at Chicoutimi (UQAC), Department of Applied Sciences, REPARTI Center, Quebec, Canada
Martin_Otis@uqac.ca

Abstract. It is known that the type of the soil can affect balance. Here we report a serious game designed for training users at maintaining balance over five types of soil (broken stone, stone dust, sand, concrete and wood). By using an augmented shoe and proposed navigation metaphor, in this game, the user is invited to browse a maze while standing balance over the physical grounds. During the exploration, exercises targeting assessment of balance control are suggested. To insure the effectiveness of this training program, four exercises based on the Berg Balance Scale and the Tinetti Balance Assessment Tool are incorporated in the game.

1 Introduction

Falls represent a major factor in the frail elderly. In developed countries, we observed that nearly half of falls among elderly caused minor injury while 5 to 25% sustained serious damages such as fracture of the proximal femur [9]. Beyond the physical injuries, in many cases, falls leave a psychological impact due to the fear of falling. As a consequence, even without an injury, a fall can cause a loss in confidence and a reduction of mobility. This can lead to a decline in health and function and contribute to future falls with more serious outcomes [5]. These observations have promoted the development of multiple programs dedicated to prevention of accidental falls. Given the multifactorial aspect of falls, these programs have to target several factors that can constitute a certain risk of fall [3]. In this way, several programs have coupled the practice of physical exercises to analysis of balance and gait. Others have been focused on control of vision, hearing and blood pressure. Our research project aims at taking all these factors and even several others into account. Here, we consider training balance control via exercise programs.

Balance control via exercises has been an active research topic in the last decade, multiples approaches have been proposed. However, to the best of our knowledge, no

M. Ma et al. (Eds.): SGDA 2012, LNCS 7528, pp. 31–42, 2012.
© Springer-Verlag Berlin Heidelberg 2012

research has yet integrated the type of soil in training programs targeting improvement of balance control. Given that the type of soil, that a person walks on, may affect his balance [17], our work aims at helping users at maintaining their balance over several types of soil by using a serious game.

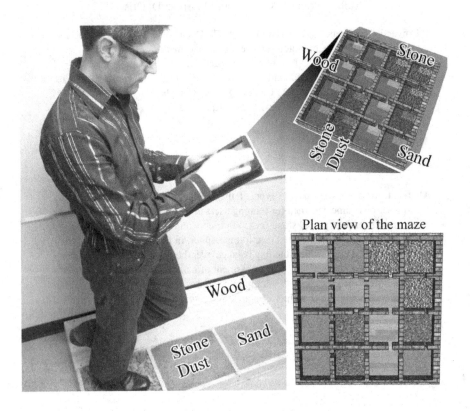

Fig. 1. A user is playing the game while standing on one leg

By playing this game, we want to bring the user to experiment balance control over several types of soil: broken stone, stone dust, sand, concrete and wood. To insure the ecological validity of the system, it combines elements of the real world, to an interactive virtual environment. The game is designed in order to be usable for the realization of home exercises. In the proposed game, the user is invited to browse a virtual maze having five types of ground (see Fig. 1). During the exploration, fitted with an augmented shoe, the user has to face several distracting stimuli designed in order to bring him at realizing movements similar to those that occur at the beginning of a spontaneous loss of balance. Delivered stimuli are based on exercises targeting balance assessment (Berg Balance Scale and the Tinetti Balance Assessment Tool). During this process, various measures relative to the user's posture and its heart rate are measured in order to check how the situation affects the user.

The paper is organized as follows: related work are presented at section II, the developed serious game is detailed in section III and the conclusion in section IV.

2   Related Work

Various studies have proved that balance control plays an important role in fall prevention. As a result, it has been incorporated into multiple programs aiming at fall prevention. Previous researches show that practice of exercises can reduce the risk of fractures. By helping to maintain bone mass, it allows to improve notably the stability posture. Madureira et al. have shown that balance training program is effective in reducing the risk of falling in elderly [16]. Traditionally exercise programs were delivered in a class situation or individually by professional physical therapist [18, 20].

To alleviate several constraints regarding such an approach (cost of transportation, schedule management, etc.) new methods that use some technological devices have emerged. Exploited approaches range from pure visual system (like the Nintendo Wii-Fit) to vibrotactile feedback embedded in a cell phone [8, 10, 14]. In [8], a 6-week home-based balance training program using Nintendo Wii Fit and balance board is presented. In the same way, Grosjean et al. have combined the Nintendo Wii Fit platform to traditional physical therapy interventions [10]. Also, Lee et al. have described a cell phone based vibrotactile feedback system dedicated to balance rehabilitation training [14]. Realized experiment shows that real-time feedback provided via a cell phone can be used to reduce body sway.

Looking at the literature, we observed that physical characteristics of the soil have not been considered for training of balance control. For person with gait disorder or losing autonomy, it appears that walking on different type of soil could be a challenge and may represent a risk of falling. Moreover, it has been demonstrated that the type of soil may affect the gait [17]. As result, it seems quite important to help users at maintaining their balance over different types of soil. Considering the promising results of cited studies, we have developed an interactive game for balance training over different types of soil.

The proposed game combines elements of the real world, to an interactive virtual maze. By exposing the user to various destabilizing events (perturbations) the game aims at helping users strengthen their lower limbs while learning facing perturbations that can occur in daily activities. Moreover, by using an interactive shoe, the dynamic of the users and his ability to maintaining postural stability after a perturbation are logged in real time. In the following, we describe the game.

3   Proposed Game

With this game, we want to design an environment that can help users at training their balance over several types of soil. Given that successful previous balance training programs have usually run over a long period [16], we designed the game in a way so that a user can experiment it over a long period. Among several other requirements, it has been designed to be fun, interactive, safe, ease to use and usable at home.

In this game, the player is invited to browse a virtual maze as fast as possible while standing balanced on a specific type of soil. To do so, fitted with an augmented shoe, to move in the maze and to perform exercices, the player remains physically at the same position and uses the metaphor presented in subsection 3.1.1.

3.1   System Overview

The game presented in this document requires a physical setup and an instrumented shoe. This section briefly summarizes these two components.

3.1.1   Interactive Shoe

Recently, we have developed an intelligent system that aims at prevent accidental falls related to conditions of the physical environment of the person (slippery ground, steep slope, etc.), or abnormalities of its gait. This system is centered on an augmented shoe (right part of Fig. 2). This device counts, on one side, a set of sensors that serves for characterizing the dynamics of walking, the posture of the user and the physical properties of the environment. For example, they measure the velocity and acceleration of the foot, bending of the sole and forces applied at five points under the foot (as seen in Fig. 3). All these sensors are exploited to compute the risk level associated to physical characteristics of the environment. On the other hand, this device brings together several actuators aiming to transmit vibrotactile signals to the user. These signals intend to attract the attention of the user towards situations deemed dangerous by the control system running on a *Android* device (tablet or smartphone). For more details regarding the interactive shoe, one can refer to models of instrumented shoes like [1], [7] and [21]. As part of this game, for each soil type, we used these sensors to measure the variation

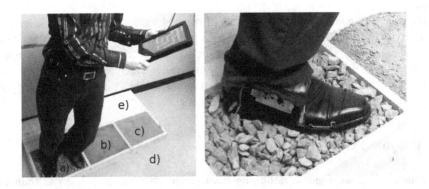

Fig. 2. Setup used for training of balance control (left side). Interactive shoe (right side)

of several parameters (acceleration, sole bending, applied force by the user, etc.) when maintaining or recovering balance.

Another sensor used in the system is a portable wireless device that helps to measure the electric activity of the heart. This heart rate monitor is designed for cardiovascular training - running, jogging, or any kind of strenuous exercise. Its main component is a heart rate monitor strapped over the chest with bluetooth capabilities. This device reads and transmits the heart rate to the *Android* device.

3.1.2   Physical Materials

Our work intends to fulfill the gap observed in the literature about balance training over different types of soil. To ensure the ecological validate of this work, even though we propose a serious game, we wanted to use physical soils. Moreover, in order to cover a wide range of soil, three granular (deformable) and two non-deformable materials were used as type of ground. The three granular materials are broken stone, sand and dust stone whereas concrete and wood were the non deformable. These materials have been selected because of their rheological characteristics and their relatively high rate of use in living environments. In the context of the game, they spread out in a tray as shown in Fig. 2.

3.2   Metaphor Used for the Displacement in the Game

In the proposed game, the user has to browse, as fast as possible, a virtual maze while standing balanced. Since the goal behind the game is to improve balance control over different types of soil; it seems appropriate to exploit body interactions for displacements in the maze. Moreover, it has been showed that such interactions may enhance the engagement of users in the games [2].

For this, interfaces such a *Microsoft Kinect*^{TM} could be considered. Indeed, a recent study used the *Microsoft Kinect*^{TM} to assess kinematic strategies of postural control [4]. However, such a system does not really fit our need since it can not be used to evaluate all aspect regarding the balance of the user of different types of soil. We therefore have prefer our device; it includes several sensors that can be used for evaluate the balance of the user.

The navigation metaphor used is based on the repartition of the forces applied to the sole of the shoe. To navigate the user just has to swing (see Fig. 4). As shown in Fig. 3, two types of sensor measure the forces reparation in sole: the FSR force sensors and the bending sole. Therefore two components let to compute the displacement of the avatar in the scene. The first uses the direction given by the vector forces computed by the (FSR) force sensors. The second component measures the angle of the sole bending to produce a proportional movement in linear direction (forward) (see Fig. 5). These components are determined as follow:

- The total force and moment applied on the sole by the user generate a wrench $\mathbf{h}_a \in \Re_{6 \times 1}$ which is computed by equation (1). The position A is the reference

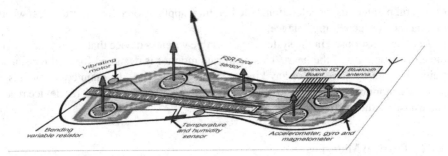

Fig. 3. Instrumented sole exploited for navigation in the game. Arrows in red are the force measurement at each sensor. The sum of these arrows is represented by the black arrow.

frame in the game, B is the reference frame of the shoe, $^A Q_B \in \Re_{3 \times 3}$ is the rotation matrix between reference frame A and its counterpart B. Also, m is the number of sensors inserted in the sole at the position $\mathbf{q}_i$. B is located at the center of pressure applied on the sole in a upright posture of the user. The vector $\mathbf{h}_r$ is a projection of the vector $\mathbf{h}_a$ on the plane described by the virtual ground which gives the direction of avatar's movement as seen in Fig. 6. The amplitude of the projected vector gives a proportional movement in the maze. In the current version, a Hooke constant $\mathbf{k}$ is used to compute a variation of displacement as described by the equation (2). The current position of the avatar is $\mathbf{s}_a^n$, at the discrete time n.

- The sole bending is evaluated with a bending variable resistor which gives only one angle θ as shown in Fig. 5. This angle is thus used to move forward. Since the bending is proportional to an angle θ, we compute a displacment in the maze $\mathbf{s}_y^n$ with the equation (4) using a proportional constant k_θ which reflects the sole curvature into a linear movement.

$$\mathbf{h}_a = \begin{bmatrix} \sum_{i=0}^{m-1} {}^A \mathbf{Q_B f}_{a_i} \\ \sum_{i=0}^{m-1} (\mathbf{q}_i \times ({}^A \mathbf{Q_B} f_{a_i})) \end{bmatrix} \tag{1}$$

$$\mathbf{s}_a^n = \mathbf{s}_a^{n-1} + \mathbf{h}_r / \mathbf{k}, \text{ with} \tag{2}$$

$$\mathbf{s}_a = \begin{bmatrix} s_x & s_y & s_z & s_\theta & s_\psi & s_\phi \end{bmatrix}^T \tag{3}$$

$$s_y^n = s_y^{n-1} + k_\theta \theta \tag{4}$$

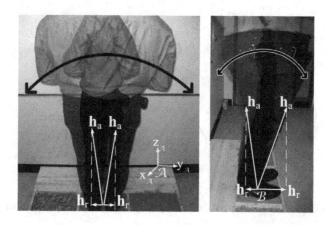

Fig. 4. Displacement with the navigation metaphor. Any swing of the user does generate a displacement in the maze.

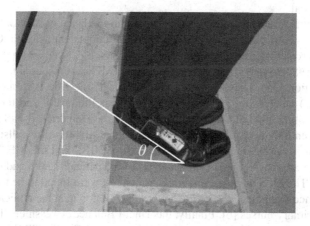

Fig. 5. Representation of the direction coming from the bending of the sole

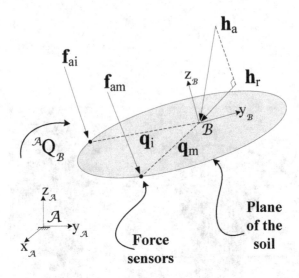

Fig. 6. Movement computation in the game used as navigation metaphor

3.3   Balance Control: Assement and Training

The goal of the game is to train people on maintaining balance on different types of soil. Because of that, assessment of the ability of the person to maintain balance plays an important role in the game. A special attention was paid to selection of exercises that can serve this goal.

Literature on assessment of the ability to maintain balance counts two main categories: 1) exercises or tasks based evaluation and 2) the patient's health. Our game is centered on exercises based evaluation.

Berg Balance Scale (BBS) and Morse Fall Scale (MFS) are two main tools used for fall risk prediction [24]. These tests are very different since the BBS analyzes some tasks (exercises) whereas the MFS approach analyzes the health and the gait of the patient. On the other hand, it was demonstrated that the Heindrich II Fall Risk Model (HFRM) is potentially useful in identifying patients at high risk for falls; some studies suggest that it can be more relevant than both the BBS and the MFS [13]. However, the HFRM approach concerns the analysis of the patient' health and do not cover exercises [11]. The MFS and the Functional Reach test were found to be time consuming and often inconvenient and were not better at prediction than the clinical judgments made by the primary nurses [6]. Finally, the Tinetti Balance Assessment Tool (TBAT) (described in [23]) was also compared with Functional Reach. TBAT seems to be the most suitable performance measure for evaluating balance in community-dwelling older people [15]. A comprehensive review of methods to assess the risk of a fall is presented in [12].

As seen through that brief analysis, Berg Balance Scale and the Tinetti assessment tool appear as most appropriate tests for exercises based evaluation. We have therefore integrated exercises proposed in these tests in our game. Proposed exercises are associated with some parts of the maze. During the browsing of the maze, while entering a section associated to an exercise, all motions (used to move the avatar) are disabled for the period of the exercise, a video presenting the exercise to realize is shown to the user. In the proposed game, selected exercises are:

- Standing unsupported with feet together;
- Turning in place;
- Placing alternate foot on step;
- Standing on one leg;

With the navigation metaphors (presented in section 3.2) and the sensors located in the sole of the interactive shoe (presented in section 3.1.1), it is possible to differentiate the four selected exercices and compute a score according to the success of the exercises.

3.4   Different Levels of Difficulty

The complexity of the game could be described by two components: the maze itself (number of paths, size of the maze and number of dead end) and proposed exercises. At the current version of the game, we do have only rectangular mazes: proposed route are only vertical or horizontal. Each little rectangle described by the route defines a particular zone and is therefore associated with a particular type of soil (sand, stone, dust stone, wood and concrete). As a result, in the current version of the game, the complexity is mainly determined by the complexity of the exercise to achieve on given type of soil. In general, MFS, TBAT and HFRM use three levels of risk (low, moderate and high). Since we use an additional level of risk in the game (type of soil), four levels of risk (low, moderate, high and very high) are implemented in the game.

At the current stage, the game counts three levels of difficulty. At the easiest level, user is invited to stand on both feet, there is no time constraint for the completion of the task and proposed mazes are the easiest. At the intermediate level, the task has to be completed in a certain amount of time while the mazes are a little more complicated. Although sometime the user has to stand on one foot, most of time he has to stand on both feet. At the hardest level, the time allocated for the completion of the task is reduced and at the meantime the mazes become highly interactive while presenting various obstacles to the user. At this level, when gifted with some bonuses, the user has the possibility to overcome certain constraints of the maze. For example, he may jump over a wall by placing alternate foot on step (the apparatus used for holding the soils as described in section 3.1.2). At this step, all the time the user has to stand on one foot. As a result, the use of both feet is seen as a mistake and generates a reduction of the score.

These three levels are designed in order to provide a progressive level of difficulty that will help the user familiarizing themselves to situation that can lead to accidental falls.

3.5 Score

To maintain the engagement of the player in the game, we consider all the factors described previously to evaluate a score. The score displayed in real-time is computed according to the execution of the exercise, the difficulty level and the time.

As suggested in the Berg Balance Scale, each exercise is rated on a scale of 0 to 4. The distribution of the forces measured in the sole determines the value accorded for the exercise. In fact, the computed value is inversely proportional to the standard deviation σ of the measured force $|\mathbf{h}_a|$ over the period of the exercise. Hence, when doing an exercise, the user has to stay in a fixed position in order to maximize his score: the more he swings the lower his score for the exercise will be. Each soil type has a difficulty level labelled D. The difficulty level associated for soil types are: concrete (or wood): 1, stone dust: 2, stone: 3 and sand: 4. To compute the final score, for each exercise, this difficulty level is multiplied by the score of the exercise. When the time of execution is considered in the game, the final value is inversely proportional to the time t with a scale factor α, as described by equation (5):

$$Score = \frac{D}{\sigma(\alpha t)} \tag{5}$$

This score aims at evaluating the level at which the user is able to maintain its balance on different types of soil.

3.6 Safety Issue

One of the main advantages of using a serious game for balance training resides in the fact that the game can be experimented at home. However, this raises a number of problems related to player's safety. For this, several design choices were made in order to guaranty the safety of the player.

Although the game was designed to train and practice balance control, players should be aware that some of the proposed exercises may represent a risk. For example, previously we mentioned that using deformable soils increase the risk of falling. More particularly, standing on one foot over the sand soil could be challenging for people with balance disorder. Furthermore, the current platform requires a location in a room free from obstructions that may hinder user's movements. Beyond these aspects, in order to prevent potential injuries, at the end of the analysis performed on the data logged from the ECG and those concerning the posture of the player, if a serious trouble is detected, the game is locked and invites the player to contact the costumer service because the game seems not to be appropriate to his profile.

4 Conclusion and Future Work

This paper described a serious game for training balance control over five types of soil (broken stone, stone dust, sand, concrete and wood). To provide an efficient training program, proposed exercises, used to assess the balance of the user, are selected from standard evaluation test. With the current version of the game, we are able to record various parameters that will inform us about the dynamic of balance control over different types of soil. Doing so, the game will let us identifying parameters which could lead the user to a loss of balance. This information will be useful for the design of a new generation of enactive shoe dedicated to preventing fall. Then, the shoe will use these parameters in daily activities (real situation) for warning users whenever a potentially dangerous situation occurs. Indeed haptic vibrotactile stimulus or auditory feedbacks can represent an alternative to visual feedbacks [19]. The warning signal can be generated via the actuators, located inside the shoe, which are able to synthesis different types of signal such as ecological icons. A longer term goal will be to replace the real soils by simulated one using a locomotion interface similar to [22]. Such an interface will promote better integration of the system in a clinic.

References

1. Bamberg, S.J.M., Benbasat, A.Y., Scarborough, D.M., Krebs, D.E., Paradiso, J.A.: Gait analysis using a shoe-integrated wireless sensor system. IEEE Transactions on Information Technology in Biomedicine 12(4), 413–423 (2008)

2. Burke, J.W., McNeill, M.D.J., Charles, D.K., Morrow, P.J., Crosbie, J.H., McDonough, S.M.: Optimising engagement for stroke rehabilitation using serious games. Visual Computer, 1–15 (2009)

3. Chang, J.T., Morton, S.C., Rubenstein, L.Z., Mojica, W.A., Maglione, M., Suttorp, M.J., Roth, E.A., Shekelle, P.G.: Interventions for the prevention of falls in older adults: systematic review and meta-analysis of randomised clinical trials. BMJ 328(7441), 680+ (2004), http://dx.doi.org/10.1136/bmj.328.7441.680, doi:10.1136/bmj.328.7441.680

4. Clark, R.A., Pua, Y.-H., Fortin, K., Ritchie, C., Webster, K.E., Denehy, L., Bryant, A.L.: Validity of the microsoft kinect for assessment of postural control. Gait and Posture (2012)

5. Cumming, R.G., Salkeld, G., Thomas, M., Szonyi, G.: Prospective study of the impact of fear of falling on activities of daily living, sf-36 scores, and nursing home admission. Journals of Gerontology - Series A Biological Sciences and Medical Sciences 55(5), M299–M305 (2000)

6. Eagle, D.J., Salama, S., Whitman, D., Evans, L.A., Ho, E., Olde, J.: Comparison of three instruments in predicting accidental falls in selected inpatients in a general teaching hospital. Journal of Gerontological Nursing 25(7), 40–45 (1999)

7. Edgar, S., Swyka, T., Fulk, G., Sazonov, E.: Wearable shoe-based device for rehabilitation of stroke patients. In: International Conference of the IEEE Engineering in Medicine and Biology Society, pp. 3772–3775 (2010)

8. Esculier, J.F., Vaudrin, J., Beriault, P., Gagnon, K., Tremblay, L.: Home-based balance training programme using wii fit with balance board for parkinson's disease: A pilot study. Journal of Rehabilitation Medicine 44(2), 144–150 (2012)

9. Ganz, D.A., Bao, Y., Shekelle, P.G., Rubenstein, L.Z.: Will my patient fall? Journal of the American Medical Association 297(1), 77–86 (2007)

10. Grosjean, A., Fabbri, E., Feldheim, E., Snoeck, T., Amand, M., Keuterickx, C., Balestra, C.: On the use of the wii fit in reducing falling risk factors and improving balance for the elderly. Kinesitherapie 10(107), 41–45 (2010)

11. Hendrich, A., Nyhuis, A., Kippenbrock, T., Soja, M.: Hospital falls: development of a predictive model for clinical practice. Applied Nursing Research 8(3), 129–139 (1995)

12. Howe, T., Rochester, L., Neil, F., Skelton, D., Ballinger, C.: Exercise for improving balance in older people. Cochrane Database of Systematic Reviews (Online) CD00 4963(11), 1–152 (2011)
13. Kim, E.A.N., Mordiffi, S.Z., Bee, W.H., Devi, K.e., Evans, D.: Evaluation of three fall-risk assessment tools in an acute care setting. Journal of Advanced Nursing 60(4), 427–435 (2007)
14. Lee, B.-C., Kim, J., Chen, S., Sienko, K.H.: Cell phone based balance trainer. Journal of Neuro Engineering and Rehabilitation, 10 (2012)
15. Lin, M.-R., Hwang, H.-F., Hu, M.-H., Wu, H.-D.I., Wang, Y.-W., Huang, F.-C.: Psychometric comparisons of the timed up and go, one-leg stand, functional reach, and tinetti balance measures in community-dwelling older people. Journal of the American Geriatrics Society 52(8), 1343–1348 (2004)
16. Madureira, M.M., Takayama, L., Gallinaro, A.L., Caparbo, V.F., Costa, R.A., Pereira, R.M.R.: Balance training program is highly effective in improving functional status and reducing the risk of falls in elderly women with osteoporosis: a randomized controlled trial. Osteoporosis International 18(4), 419–425 (2007)
17. Marigold, D.S., Patla, A.E.: Adapting locomotion to different surface compliances: Neuromuscular responses and changes in movement dynamics. Journal of Neurophysiology 94(3), 1733–1750 (2005)
18. Means, K.M., Rodell, D.E., O'Sullivan, P.S.: Balance, mobility, and falls among community-dwelling elderly persons: effects of a rehabilitation exercise program. American Journal of Physical Medicine and Rehabilitation 84(4), 238–250 (2005)
19. Ménélas, B., Picinalli, L., Katz, B.F.G., Bourdot, P.: Audio haptic feedbacks for an acquisition task in a multi-target context. In: 3DUI, pp. 51–54. IEEE (2010)
20. Nitz, J.C., Choy, N.L.: The efficacy of a specific balance-strategy training programme for preventing falls among older people: a pilot randomised controlled trial. Age Ageing 33(1), 52–58 (2004)
21. Noshadi, H., Ahmadian, S., Hagopian, H., Woodbridge, J., Dabiri, F., Amini, N., Sarrafzadeh, M., Terrafranca, N.: Hermes: Mobile balance and instability assessment system. In: Proceedings of the 3rd International Conference on Bio-inpsired Systems and Signal Processing, pp. 264–270 (2010)
22. Otis, M.J.D., Mokhtari, M., Du Tremblay, C., De Rainville, F.M., Laurendeau, D., Gosselin, C.M.: Hybrid control with multi-contact interactions for 6dof haptic foot platform on a cable-driven locomotion interface. In: IEEE Int. Symposium on Haptics Interfaces for Virtual Environment and Teleoperator Systems, pp. 161–168 (2008)
23. Tinetti, M.E.: Performance-orientated assessment of mobility problems in elderly patients. Journal of the American Geriatrics Society 34(2), 119–126 (1986)
24. Zhou, J., Fan, J.: Analysis of the effectiveness of morse fall scale and berg balance scale applied in the fall risk prediction for senile patients. Chinese Journal of Rehabilitation Medicine 27(2), 130–133 (2012)

Constructionist Learning in Anatomy Education

What Anatomy Students Can Learn through Serious Games Development

Minhua Ma[1], Kim Bale[1], and Paul Rea[2]

[1] Digital Design Studio, Glasgow School of Art, Glasgow, UK
{m.ma,k.bale}@gsa.ac.uk
[2] Laboratory of Human Anatomy, School of Life Sciences, University of Glasgow, Glasgow, UK
paul.rea@glasgow.ac.uk

Abstract. In this paper we describe the use of 3D games technology in human anatomy education based on our MSc in Medical Visualisation and Human Anatomy teaching practice, i.e. students design and develop serious games for anatomy education using the Unity 3D game engine. Students are engaged in this process not only as consumers of serious games, but as authors and creators. The benefits of this constructionist learning approach are discussed. Five domains of learning are identified, in terms of what anatomy students, tutors, and final users (players) can learn through serious games and their development process. We also justify the 3D engine selected for serious game development and discuss main obstacles and challenges to the use of this constructionist approach to teach non-computing students. Finally, we recommend that the serious game construction approach can be adopted in other academic disciplines in higher education.

Keywords: Serious games, game engines, game development, medical education, human anatomy, anatomy education, constructionist learning.

1 Introduction

Over the past ten years we have seen games technology become a commodity making it widely available and within reach of both professionals and enthusiastic individuals. Careful design makes games inherently fun and thereby entertaining for people of all ages, in particular, today's *games generation*. Given the high level of engagement that people exhibit whilst playing games it seems logical that combining the unique characteristics that make these games so engaging with conventional methodologies in education could provide a powerful means of encouraging students more effectively in learning activities. This concept forms the underlying principle of the idea of serious games coined by Sawyer and Rejeski [25]. In recent years serious games and game-based learning have received increased attention from researchers, educators, and psychologists [12], [15]. However, the majority of

M. Ma et al. (Eds.): SGDA 2012, LNCS 7528, pp. 43–58, 2012.

previous endeavour is about playing games for learning rather than making games for learning [13].

This paper discusses how 3D games technology can be used for human anatomy education and presents our experience of teaching students to develop interactive anatomy applications using a 3D game engine. The goal is to offer this as a case study for those wishing to create 3D educational content within an academic context and to incorporate computer technologies into their anatomy curriculum. It also shows what anatomy students can learn through serious game construction based on our practice on our MSc Medical Visualisation and Human Anatomy programme, which teaches students a combination of computer science, structure and function of the human body, anatomical and medical terminology, and cadaveric dissection techniques. Consequently, graduates from this course will be able to communicate 3D medical visualisation processes to a specialist audience and develop health-related products in a multidisciplinary team. The students that participated in this study are all from biomedical sciences background. They are engaged in this game-making process not only as consumers of serious games, but also as authors and creators.

This paper is organised into six sections. Firstly, traditional human anatomy education is reviewed and main challenges are discussed. The role of computer technology in education and training of future doctors, dentists, biomedical scientists, Allied Health Professionals, computer scientists and related professions is discussed. We then review previous serious games for anatomy education and higher education in general in section 3. Section 4 briefly describes the course design and the context of this study. The reason to select Unity 3D as the development tool for non-computing students is justified in section 5, and results are presented in section 6. Finally, we conclude the study and recommend that this constructionist approach can be adopted in other academic disciplines in higher education.

2   Human Anatomy Education

The use of computer technology, in particular computer graphics, has a long history within Medicine. However, its use within the teaching of medicine has somewhat curiously been overlooked. In a report entitled "Tomorrow's Doctors" [11] the General Medical Council highlighted the advancement of technology and its role in the education and training of future doctors, biomedical scientists, allied health professionals and related professions as a strategically important area for development. With technology developing at such a fast pace and forming key areas for strategic development in these areas it is clear that a unique opportunity for enhancing medical education is emerging.

Understanding the function and spatial context of human anatomy forms a fundamental building block in a medical student's education. At present anatomy is largely taught using a combination of three methods; book based learning, learning from physical models and cadaveric dissection. It is generally accepted that to gain a thorough and accurate understanding of anatomy a student should gain as much exposure to "real" anatomy as possible. However, due to the practical and cost issues in utilising cadavers for medical training, cadaveric dissection is often used sparingly and reserved for medical students rather than those training for related occupations. Consequently, the majority of anatomical education is based around learning from diagrams, images and physical models. This poses a number of problems. Firstly, it can often be difficult to appreciate the spatial relationships and physical sizes of the various components of the body from a photograph or image. Secondarily, the physical models of anatomical structures often lack the level of detail required to fully understand the various components. Finally, diagrams often form an abstract representation of the anatomical components, which if used on their own, can mislead students.

Over recent years, anatomy within medical education has seen a significant reduction in content delivered and time allocated to this subject [22], [33]. Also, with the loss of staff in anatomy that are skilled in teaching the subject, there has been an increasing need for new approaches to be developed in aiding anatomical teaching and training both for the educator and the student [3], [33].

The recent advances in gaming technologies puts forward interesting opportunities to expand upon these approaches to learning by bringing the lessons learnt from playing and developing games into the classroom. By combining computer models of anatomical structures with custom software we can present students with new ways of interacting with anatomy that could not be achieved during cadaveric dissections or in static images and diagrams.

3   Games for Anatomy Education

Serious games have been used for education in various formats (non-digital games, digital games, gamification, live action role play games based on pervasive technologies, etc.) and ways (commercial off-the-shelf games and bespoke custom-made games), and based on different philosophies of education (instructionist and constructionist philosophies) [13].

The majority of educational games on the market are instructionist games, which integrate game scenarios with the content to be learned. Constructionist educators take a differing viewpoint. Rather than asking students to play instructional games and learn from it, they provide students with opportunities to construct their own games. Learning can happen more effectively when people are active in making things.

The constructionist approach has been tested in non-digital game format by Carter [6], who worked with school children to design *Dungeons and Dragons* board games as a student-initiated, teacher-guided independent study. The games integrated different skills and subject areas across the curricula, including mathematics, social studies, written communication, artistic and creative development, social and emotional development. This approach has also been tested in digital game format [28] with computer science undergraduate students.

With the right authoring tools (more discussion on this in section 5), the game making process does not require expensive technologies and programming skills to create rich and interesting game worlds and characters. Our attempt to expand this approach to non-computing disciplines provides evidence of this.

3.1 Serious Games for Higher Education

There is a large amount of evidence available to suggest that the use of serious games for learning can make positive impacts on learning outcomes at all levels of education, ranging from primary [6], secondary [19], higher education [7], [14], and for children with special educational needs [35]. Educationalists often argue that the sophisticated computer skills and development costs required for producing these games prohibit their use in higher education. These obstacles can be overcome by adopting Commercial-off-the-Shelf (COTS) video games in education or the constructionist approach, both of which limit the need to create bespoke instructional games by professional game developers.

Instructionist Games for Higher Education. In higher education, the use of games is not only focused on learning a particular subject, such as using a bespoke serious game for learning a foreign language [27] and modding an existing game NeverWinter Nights to teach Structured Query Language (SQL) [29] etc., but also on the ability of the instrument to develop learning in general, e.g. to develop strategies for reading three-dimensional images, to develop learning through observation and hypothesis testing, to broaden the understanding of scientific simulations, and develop divided visual attention [12].

Using COTS Games for Higher Education. COTS games are designed for entertainment, not for learning. However, they can be incorporated into the curriculum, enable educators from multiple disciplines to engage students in learning and to reduce the costs of developing bespoke, custom-made instructional games.

Novak and Nackerud [20] proposed an adoption model for evaluating COTS games, particularly massively multiplayer role-playing games, for learning and teaching, and investigated the approach on a range of courses including history, English or literature, business, and physical science. The majority of research on using COTS games for education is aimed at students below the higher education level [9]. In higher education, educators tend to use virtual environments such as Second Life [5], [16] or modify COTS games (a.k.a. *modding*) [9], [29] in an educational setting.

Constructionist Games for Higher Education. Based on the constructionist learning philosophy, Smith [28] discussed three *domains of learning* for computer science students and lecturers in the process of the students developing their own serious games. As illustrated in Figure 1, students learned not only discipline-specific content of the serious games they created (Domain 1), but also more importantly, computing skills (Domain 2) when they go through the software (game) development process. As a by-product, since they create the game from the educator's perspective, they also learned assessment, rewards, feedback, and various approaches in game-based learning. In addition, the teacher/lecturer is learning of teaching computing undergraduates (Domain 3) by reflecting on his/her own practice.

Gamification in Higher Education. Instead of using, modding, or making games for education, teachers can also adapt and facilitate gaming experience to the learning process. Gamification is a newly coined term referring to the application of game mechanics, e.g. points, badges, levels, and league tables, to non-gaming processes. It focuses on sociological approach in which the main goal is the use of games effects on specific areas such as marketing promotion and education. Gamification does not require huge investment in technology.

The use of gamification in higher education is wide ranging from economics [8], psychology [14], to computer science [7]. For instance, in an economics course at Pennsylvania State University, the course content is integrated in 'Who wants to be a millionaire?' game play. The students are notified that grades are for sale and that the primary way to acquire capital is by answering multiple-choice questions correctly [8].

3.2   Serious Games for Anatomy Education

Instructionist Anatomy Games. There are a few instructionist anatomy education systems available online. Some of them are not really 'games' [19], [30], [36] since they are lack of certain game features like goals, rewards, and winning conditions, etc. In terms of presentation, most of them are two-dimensional [18], [19], [30], others are three-dimensional [1], [36] or pseudo-3D [4]. They fall into four categories:

- Games/quiz: BBC Human Body & Mind [4] and Artificial Anatomy [19]
- Simulations: there are a number of anatomy and surgery simulations for medical education. Some not only provide a photorealistic look but also feel real and allow the user to touch and manipulate using haptic interfaces [2].
- Browsers: Google's body browser [36] and eSkeletons [30],
- Education tools: Anatronica Interactive Anatomy 3D [1] and MEDtropolis' Virtual Body [18]. The Anatronica Interactive Anatomy 3D includes a quiz component as well.

BBC Human Body & Mind [4] is a series of drag-and-drop jigsaw games for learning human anatomy. The games include internal organs game, skeleton game, muscle game, nervous system game, and senses challenge quiz. The games are designed and involve drag-and-dropping a body part onto a transparent human figure. When the player is rotating a body part, the games use a series of images to fake a three-dimensional view. Artificial Anatomy Body Parts [19] is a short 10-question quiz on body parts. The player needs to identify a thumbnail image of a body part and match it with its location on a skeletal structure named *Jerome*, which is a paper mache anatomical model. The player can turn Jerome around for front view and back views. Anatronica Interactive Anatomy 3D [1] and Google body browser [36] are among the best instructionist anatomy education applications so far in terms of the level of details and anatomical and functional completeness. There are a number of anatomy applications available on smart phones, ranging from two-dimensional illustration, e.g. SusaSoftX Human Anatomy for both iPhone and Android, to three-dimensional models, e.g. Anatomy 3D-Anatronica for Android phones.

Constructionist Anatomy Games. Constructionists suggest that learning is more effective when a student is actively engaged in the learning process rather than attempting to receive knowledge passively.

Murray and Stewart [37] use the constructionist approach in a non-digital form. Their students used coloured electrical wires to model the somatic peripheral nervous system. The modelling of nerves is overlain onto a life sized plastic articulated skeleton (Fig. 1). This method helps students understand the origins of the nerves, the pathways that they take to reach the structures that they innervate; and it provides an indication of the spinal nerves which contribute to each peripheral nerve and the way they come together to supply particular structures or body compartments.

We adopt the constructionist approach in a digital form to encourages learners creating their own anatomy games like [1], [4] and [19]. The teacher facilitates the process of learning in which students are encouraged to be responsible and autonomous. Figure 2 illustrates the five domains of learning in constructionist anatomy games from both learners and educators perspectives. Instructionist anatomy games only cover the first domain of learning (D1) and are for those at the receiving end of serious games, i.e. the players. From the perspective of students who are engaged in the game development process, i.e. the game designers (and developers), the constructionist games also cover D2 and D3 learning domains (software development and human anatomy). The learner is involved in all the design decisions and develops technological skills, which are essential to implement his/her game design. These consist of 3D modelling, texturing, rigging, animation, game engine scripting, game mechanics, and agile project management etc. From the tutor's perspective they include two additional domains of learning, which are teaching non-computing students software development and teaching human anatomy using constructionist serious games.

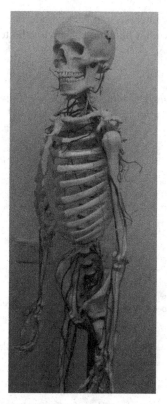

Fig. 1. Using coloured wires to model nervous system [37]

4   Course Design

We tested the constructionist approach in the learning and teaching practice of the MSc Medical Visualisation and Human Anatomy at the Glasgow School of Art and University of Glasgow. The students on the Masters course come from life sciences or medical/ biomedical related subjects, e.g. immunology, anatomy, and biomedical engineering.

They spend their first semester at the Digital Design Studio, Glasgow School of Art learning 3D modelling and animation, computer graphics and applications in medicine, software development, and volumetric visualization of medical data. In semester two, students take three modules at the Laboratory of Human Anatomy, University of Glasgow: introduction to anatomy, structure and function of the human body, and cadaveric dissection techniques. There is a logical progression from an introduction to anatomy and imaging through to examining key regions of gross anatomy, followed by dissection of a focal region. Nowadays, anatomy degrees do not focus enough on gross anatomy and cadaveric dissection, which means that this component is uniquely placed in delivering actual cadaveric dissection and related training. In the third semester, students undertake a Masters research project.

Dependent on the students' interests and background, the project can either be undertaken in a specialist field within human anatomy or the technological applications of medical visualisation.

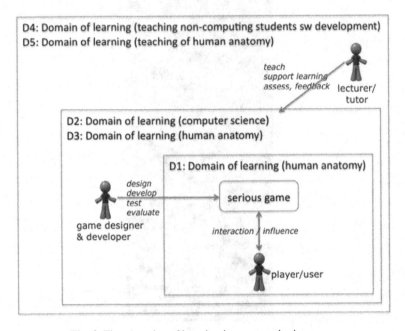

Fig. 2. Five domains of learning in constructionist games

The study was conducted in the first semester. Although the modules in this semester did not teach human anatomy in particular, students learned it from their mini-projects which required them to develop anatomy games using commercial software such as Maya and the Unity 3D engine. The assignments were designed to teach students not only about their chosen anatomical subject, e.g. dentistry (names of human teeth and dental treatment), upper body muscles, bones and orthopaedics (four-corner arthrodesis in wrist), but also about the basics of software development. Along with the anatomy games, students were required to submit a reflective development journal detailing each step of the process, discussion of the final game, and future aspects.

5   Software Selection

Since the majority of the students enrolled on the course have little to no formal training in computer programming, the focus of the course was to provide an introduction to building interactive anatomical applications rather than about the complexities of game development. The rise in popularity of computer games over the past decade has caused a wide range of game engines to enter the market in order to support their development. The role of modern game engines is to streamline and simplify the process of game development by providing the developer with common functionality and visual development tools from which to build an application. However, the types of features and functionality that each engine offers and the ease of interaction can vary widely. Due to these differences it was decided to outline a set of requirements upon which to base the decision on. Firstly, the game engine should provide a graphical user interface which students can use to put together the bulk of the functionality. Secondarily, any code that is required to provide game logic should use a simple scripting language rather than complex strongly typed languages such as C++ or Java. Finally, the game engine should provide common functions such as model loading, window creation and graphical user interface elements. Given these broad requirements the following game engines were highlighted for further consideration.

5.1   Unreal Development Kit

The Unreal Development Kit (UDK) from Epic Games [32] is perhaps one of the most well-known games engines currently on the market. It has been widely used in commercial development and has been responsible for some of the best-selling games of recent years. In early 2011, Epic Games made the decision to make their toolset free to use for non-commercial projects, enabling schools and universities to use it for teaching without cost. The UDK is a fully fledged game engine providing all of the latest shader effects, network capabilities and gameplay functionality required to make commercial quality games. The UDKs user interface combines the use of graph based visual programming and their custom scripting language called 'UnrealScript' to provide game logic. Epic's toolset is clearly designed to seamlessly integrate into the complex workflows of a functioning game studio and therefore assumes some level of expertise from its users. Consequently, the sheer amount of options and functionality that are available to the user make initial interactions a daunting task. Whilst there is a strong community of support around the toolset it was felt that the UDK was perhaps over-specified for our application.

5.2   Quest 3D

Quest 3D [24] presents itself as a graphical programming environment for generating interactive three-dimensional environments. It offers a comprehensive set of model loaders, effects and graphical user interface components and is targeted to users without any programming skills. Applications are constructed using a visual programming language whereby users can drag and drop components onto a workspace and connect them together in order to produce the desired visual output. Additional components and more complex functionality can be added using an API or alternatively using a scripting language. Quest 3D's simple interface makes constructing an interactive 3D scene straight forward. The graphical programming approach is beneficial for students as it requires very little programming, thereby allowing them to focus on content creation rather than solving the numerous potential pitfalls involved in traditional programming. However, whilst it does exhibit many of the features of a game engine, it is targeted more as a general visualisation tool. This is not necessarily a bad thing since students will only be capable of using a very limited subset of a more fully featured game engine all of which are well within the scope of Quest3D's feature sets.

5.3   Unity

Unity [31] is a multi-platform game engine that allows users to create applications on desktop operating systems such as MacOS and Windows, as well as mobile platforms and games consoles. This flexibility in deployment and its easy to use interface has made Unity a very attractive development tool for independent games developers. As with the other engines, Unity offers a comprehensive graphical user interface to use in building an application but relies on JavaScript to provide the game logic. The use of scripting to bind graphical elements together means that students have the flexibility to be creative with their ideas and are not constrained by the limitations of the software. However, this does pose potential problems for students that have no experience of programming as basic programming concepts will have to be learnt before they are able to start creating their applications.

5.4   Evaluation

All the engines above were considered perfectly capable of providing students with the tools that they would need to create their application. However, given the limited time that is available in the first semester, the choice came down to ease of use and cost. Whilst the UDK is arguably the most fully featured of the three, it was felt that flooding the students with options would only serve to confuse them. Consequently UDK was ruled out due to the unnecessarily steep learning curve for this application. Quest 3D on the other hand takes a much simpler route, its graphical programming interface makes it far more approachable for students without any traditional programming experience. However, given that students on the course were expected to gain some knowledge of how to build an application it was felt that Unity, with its mixture of visual and traditional programming, was the best candidate for the course.

5.5   Other Game Development Tools

There are a few other game development tools, which are not suitable for this specific application, but may be considered when adopting the game constructionist approach to other disciplines.

GameMaker and Scratch. GameMaker [21] and Scratch [26] are 2D game development tools that are oriented towards beginners and amateurs that know little about how to program. They allow users to design and create their own games using easy-to-learn drag-and-drop actions and a scripting language. Provided that users are supplied with high quality graphics, the user can create professional-quality games in a short period of time. Both engines support fundamental game features, such as animated graphics, pathfinding, particle effects, and GUI elements. It is also possible to use GameMaker to create pseudo-3D games which actually are two-dimensional. Both games engines are supported by large communities of amateur and indie game developers from around the world.

However, due to the geometric and spatial complexities of human anatomy, it was felt that the use of three-dimensional graphics was essential for the process of memorisation, understanding and visualisation tasks in anatomy education. Given this requirement, GameMaker and Scratch were deemed to be unsuitable for use in our study. However, they have successfully been used in other subjects, which do not require three-dimensional presentation. For example, Penta [23] evaluated five game development tools, including GameMaker and Scratch, for the use of game construction for mathematical learning in secondary education.

Game Modding. Many commercial video games provide level and character editors to extend the life-cycle of the games, for example, Valve's Half Life, World of Warcraft, Everquest II, NeverWinter Nights, Cilvilisation, and Second Life, etc. UDK is actually one of them, originally for the *Unreal Tournament*. These development tools could be very useful to lower the bar for the constructionist learning approach for students or for tutors to make instructionist games. Successful case studies include using a NeverWinter Nights mod to teach SQL [29] and using Garry's Mod, which was originally a Half-Life 2 mod, to teach molecular chemistry [10]. The game provides a physics sandbox and allows the lecturer to create a virtual object to represent a molecule structure that he can duplicate, pick up, move, connect them to one another and play around with.

6   Results

In this section the results of the taught module are described and discussed. The work of three students is used to illustrate the type of applications that were created as coursework over a two-month period. Each student chose a different subset of anatomical structures from which to create their game and was provided with three-dimensional models of their chosen areas which they were free to alter if they wished. These are highlighted in Figures 2 – 4.

Student A designed a game based around the muscles of the upper torso (Figure 3). The goal of the game was to identify a specified muscle on the body, by clicking on the associated muscle. Some of the muscles are located on the posterior aspect of the model. To gain access to these, the user can use a rotating button to turn the model and use arrow keys to control the view (virtual camera). A scoring system was implemented to keep track of the number of correct answers and the user was able to review their answers at the end of the game. Using Unity the student was able to load in a model of muscles in the upper torso with texture maps and provide visual and audio feedback during the game play. An animation sequence of the muscle man applause with clapping audio is played at the end of the game.

The student identified future improvements in her development journal. For instance, "to make the game more educational and less one dimensional, after correct identification the function of that muscle would be displayed"; the game could provide two modes– learning mode and assessment mode. In the learning mode, the correct muscle is highlighted/flashes, or name of the selected muscle and its function could be displayed on the screen, to assist learning.

Student B created a dental game (Figure 4) for assisting learning tooth notation and anatomy. The game shows a dental model consisting adult teeth, maxilla, and mandible. It allows the player to select (highlight) any tooth (or maxilla/mandible) and enter its number and name. The player can use a rotating button to turn the model and use arrow keys to control the virtual camera to gain access to individual tooth. A scoring system was implemented to keep track of the number of correct answers and the user was able to review the results at the end of the game. An animation sequence of teeth chattering with accompany audio is played on completion of the game.

Student C made a game to aid the learning of the anatomy of the forearm, wrist and hand bones. The game is based on a multiple choices quiz. For each question, a bone is highlighted on the screen and the player can choose one of the four answers. The scoring system and camera/model manoeuvring are similar to the above two games. For the 3D modelling and animation assignment, the student created an animation of four-corner arthrodesis in wrist, showing the range of movement before and after the operation.

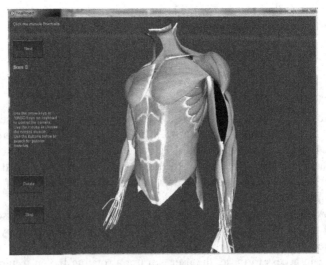

Fig. 3. Upper body muscles game

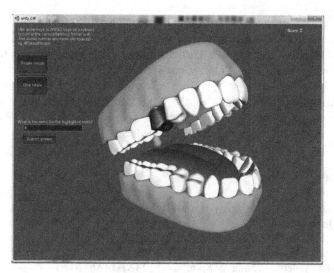

Fig. 4. A dental anatomy game

Below is student feedback on the game construct learning approach. It shows that students welcome this novel and active learning approach.

- "I think that using the computer programs to gain a better understanding of anatomy was a great way to cement the structure and names of the various parts being modeled and animated into your memory. Teaching and learning anatomy are both hard in themselves, but I believe that using the programs help a lot with remembering the multitude of detail required for understanding the bodies form and function."
- "I actually felt I learned some anatomy whilst working on the project. Probably due to the nature of the length of time it takes to model. I found when it came to the lower limb this term I actually had a good base knowledge of the bone structure and the spatial relationship between the bones of the foot after having sourced many reference pictures throughout that project."
- A student whose first degree was anatomy commented: "The first semester provided an opportunity for me to revise some of the anatomy I covered as an undergraduate anatomy student, for example the names and morphology of the carpal and metacarpal bones. However, I feel that I did not learn new anatomy during this period although I feel that this is because of my background knowledge of anatomy."

7   Conclusions

This novel approach of constructionist learning in anatomy education, whereby students are involved in the creation of the specimen, and the questions and answers, encourages greater engagement with both the computer software and also the anatomy of that region used. Design of this type of material could be used across many higher education disciplines to encourage participation in the learning process from a more active role, rather than from a didactic, passive role.

Acknowledgments. Our thanks to the MSc Medical Visualisation and Human Anatomy students at the Glasgow School of Art and University of Glasgow, who participated in this study and provided their feedback.

References

1. Anatronica Interactive Anatomy 3D (2011), http://www.anatronica.com (last accessed June 14, 2012)
2. Arango, F., Aziz, E.S., Esche, S.K., Chassapis, C.: A Review of Applications of Computer Games in Education and Training. In: Proceedings of the 38th ASEE/IEEE Frontiers in Education Conference, Saratoga Springs, NY, T4A1-T4A6 (2008)
3. Ashwell, K.W., Halasz, P.: An Acrobat-based program for gross anatomy revision. Medical Education 38, 1185–1186 (2004)
4. BBC Science: Human Body & Mind. Interactive Body, http://www.bbc.co.uk/science/humanbody/body/ (last accessed April 13, 2012)
5. Bloomfield, P.R.: Expanding a VLE-based integration framework supporting education in Second Life. In: Ma, M., et al. (eds.) Serious Games and Edutainment Applications, pp. 369–396. Springer, London (2001)
6. Carter, A.: Using Dungeons and Dragons to integrate curricula in an elementary classroom. In: Ma, M., et al. (eds.) Serious Games and Edutainment Applications, pp. 329–346. Springer, London (2011)
7. Charles, T., Bustard, D., Black, M.: Experiences of promoting student engagement through game-enhanced learning. In: Ma, M., et al. (eds.) Serious Games and Edutainment Applications, pp. 425–446. Springer, London (2011)
8. EDUCAUSE Learning Initiative. 7 Things You Should Know About Gamification. EDUCAUSE Learning Initiative (August 2011), http://net.educause.edu/ir/library/pdf/ELI7075.pdf (last accessed April 05, 2012)
9. Flynn, R.: Modifying Commercial Off-The-Shelf (COTS) Games for Use in Education. In: Felicia, P. (ed.) Handbook of Research on Improving Learning and Motivation through Educational Games: Multidisciplinary Approaches, pp. 876–894. IGI Global, Hershey (2011)
10. Garry's Mod. Describe and explain optical isomerism in simple organic molecules IB Chemistry, http://www.youtube.com/watch?v=ujOgXeT-11A&feature=player_embedded (last accessed April 14, 2012)
11. GMC, Tomorrow's Doctors (2009), http://www.gmc-uk.org/TomorrowsDoctors_2009.pdf_39260971.pdf (last accessed: March 29, 2012)
12. Gros, B.: Digital games in education: The design of Game-based Learning environments. Journal of Research on Technology in Education 40(1), 23–38 (2007)
13. Kafai, Y.B.: Playing and Making Games for Learning–Instructionist and Constructionist Perspectives for Game Studies. Games and Culture 1(1), 36–40 (2006)

14. Landers, R.N., Callan, R.C.: Casual social games as serious games: The psychology of gamification in undergraduate education and employee training. In: Ma, M., et al. (eds.) Serious Games and Edutainment Applications, pp. 399–424. Springer, London (2011)

15. Ma, M., Oikonomou, A., Jain, L. (eds.): Serious Games and Edutainment Applications. Springer, UK (2011)

16. Ma, M., Oikonomou, A., Zheng, H.: Second Life as a Learning and Teaching Environment for Digital Games Education. In: Lombard, M., et al. (eds.) Proceedings of the 12th Annual International Workshop on Presence (PRESENCE 2009), Los Angeles, California, USA, November 11-13 (2009)

17. Marsh, T., Li, Z.N., Klopfer, E., Chuang, X., Osterweil, S., Hass, J.: Fun and Learning: Blending Design and Development Dimensions in Serious Games through Narrative and Characters. In: Ma, M., et al. (eds.) Serious Games and Edutainment Applications, pp. 273–288. Springer, London (2011)

18. MEDtropolis. Virtual Body, http://www.medtropolis.com/virtual-body/ (last accessed April 13, 2012)

19. National Museum of American History. Artificial Anatomy: Papier-Mâché Anatomical Models, http://americanhistory.si.edu/anatomy/bodyparts/nma03_bodyparts.html (last accessed April 13, 2012)

20. Novak, K., Nackerud, R.: Choosing a serious game for the classroom: An adoption model for educators. In: Ma, M., et al. (eds.) Serious Games and Edutainment Applications, pp. 291–308. Springer, London (2011)

21. Overmars, M.: GameMaker, http://www.yoyogames.com/ (last accessed April 14, 2012)

22. Patel, K.M., Moxham, B.J.: The relationships between learning outcomes and methods of teaching anatomy as perceived by professional anatomists. Clinical Anatomy 21, 182–189 (2008)

23. Penta, M.K.: Video Game Creation as a Platform for Mathematical Learning. M.S. thesis. University of Massachusetts Lowell (2011)

24. Quest, Quest 3D (2012), http://www.quest3d.com (last accessed March 29, 2012)

25. Sawyer, B., Rejeski, D.: Serious Games: Improving Public Policy Through Game-based Learning and Simulation. Woodrow Wilson International Center for Scholars (2002)

26. Scratch, http://scratch.mit.edu/ (last accessed April 14, 2012)

27. Silva, A., Mamede, N., Ferreira, A., Baptista, J., Fernandes, J.: Towards a Serious Game for Portuguese Learning. In: Ma, M., Fradinho Oliveira, M., Madeiras Pereira, J. (eds.) SGDA 2011. LNCS, vol. 6944, pp. 83–94. Springer, Heidelberg (2011)

28. Smith, M.: What computing students can learn by developing their own serious games. In: Ma, M., et al. (eds.) Serious Games and Edutainment Applications, pp. 447–480. Springer, London (2011)

29. Soflano, M.: Modding in serious games: Teaching Structured Query Language (SQL) Using NeverWinter Nights. In: Ma, M., et al. (eds.) Serious Games and Edutainment Applications, pp. 347–368. Springer, London (2011)

30. University of Texas at Austin. eSkeletons, http://www.eskeletons.org/ (last accessed April 13, 2012)

31. Unity, Unity (2012), http://unity.com (last accessed March 29, 2012)

32. Unreal, Unreal Development Kit (2012), http://udk.com/ (last accessed March 29, 2012)

33. Verhoeven, B.H., Verwijnen, G.M., Scherpbier, A.J., van der Vleuten, C.P.: Growth of medical knowledge. Medical Education 36, 711–717 (2002)

34. Whitton, N.: Learning with Digital Games: A Practical Guide to Engaging Students in Higher Education. Routledge (2009)
35. Yan, F.: A SUNNY DAY: Ann and Ron's World an iPad Application for Children with Autism. In: Ma, M., Fradinho Oliveira, M., Madeiras Pereira, J. (eds.) SGDA 2011. LNCS, vol. 6944, pp. 129–138. Springer, Heidelberg (2011)
36. Zygote. Google body browser, http://bodybrowser.googlelabs.com/body. html# (last accessed 05, 2012)
37. Murray, R., Stewart, I.: Modelling the Somatic Peripheral Nervous System. In: The Proceedings of the 125th Anniversary Meeting of the Anatomical Society, July 10-12, The Royal College of Surgeons of Edinburgh, Scotland (2012)

Interdisciplinary and International Adaption and Personalization of the MetaVals Serious Games

Margarida Romero[1], Mireia Usart[1], Maria Popescu[2], and Elizabeth Boyle[3]

[1] ESADE Business & Law School – Universitat Ramon Llull, Spain
[2] Carol I National Defence University, Bucharest, Rumania
[3] University of the West of Scotland, UK
{Margarida.Romero,Mireia.Usart}@esade.edu, MPopescu03@gmail.com,
Liz.Boyle@uws.ac.uk

Abstract. Serious Games (SG) in Higher Education should be able to be adapted to particular learning needs and different university contexts in a sustainable way. In this respect, this study aims to describe the adaptation and personalization mechanism through the analysis of a case study developed in three countries and learning contexts. The adaptation is analyzed through the perspective of the perceived usability, utility and ease of use of the game in Spain, the UK and Romania. First results point to a positive evaluation by users of adaptable games, in the particular field of SGs for adult formal education. Future releases of the MetaVals game will be addressed towards the implementation of a complete and multi-language management interface, together with an improvement of the present static design.

Keywords: Serious Games, Adaption, Personalization, Higher Education.

1 Introduction

In recent years, active learning methodologies such as Serious Games have been promoted in European Higher Education through the European Higher Education Area and corresponding national policies. The development of ICT in European universities has contributed to the use of a higher number of computer-based learning activities. Most of these activities correspond to basic uses of learning technologies, such as the publication of learning materials in the Learning Management Systems (LMS) and the use of asynchronous communication tools such as forums. As observed by Selwyn (2007) the use of ICT for teaching and learning in the University exploits only a part of the potential of ICT. As a consequence, the active learning uses of ICT are limited and learning methodologies such as digital Game Based Learning (GBL) are used only by a small part of faculty. Part of the reason that has been argued for the limited use of GBL by faculty is the lack of technological competence in developing their own games, or adapting and developing already existing games. Some authors and game developers have addressed this challenge by proposing dynamically self-adapting games (Peirce, Conlan, & Wade, 2008; Pivec, & Baumann, 2004). The cost of self-adapting games based on intelligent computer techniques

M. Ma et al. (Eds.): SGDA 2012, LNCS 7528, pp. 59–73, 2012.

could constrain the development of games and their use in Higher Education. For this reason, in this paper we describe a low-cost approach which allows teachers to personalize and adapt a SG, based on the interdisciplinary adaptation of the items played by the learners in the game, and the international adaptation by the language and graphic design personalization. The description of the case study is based on the MetaVals game developed by the ESADE E-learning innovation unit (Romero, Usart, & Almirall, 2011; Usart, Romero, & Almirall, 2011) with a budget of €5000. We start analysing the relevance of personalisation in the context of Serious Games, and then we describe the game dynamics and architecture of the MetaVals Serious Game and the interdisciplinary and international adaptation capabilities that have been included in the game. After describing the personalisation and adaptation capabilities of MetaVals, the quality of the adaptation is analysed through the perspective of the perceived usability, utility and ease of use of the game.

2   Personalisation in Serious Games

High quality education requires a certain degree of adaptation to learners in terms of socio-cultural aspects, prior knowledge and the Zone of Proximal Development (ZDP, Vygotsky, 1978) as a potential capability of learning in a certain moment, but also as an adaptation to the learners' preferences and interests to promote a certain level of engagement. Personalizing games could be a key aspect in the field of SG (de Freitas, & Jarvis, 2006). According to these authors, SGs require specific levels of engagement in order to be effective, as learners demand fidelity and interactivity integrated into the game application. Therefore, higher levels of engagement and immersion with realistic graphical interfaces are important aspects to be addressed when implementing a SG. Other studies in this field have focused on different aspects of adaptation. Charski (2010) outlined the impact of adapted avatars on higher engagement. In their study on collaborative and SGs, concretely in online virtual worlds, Anderson and colleagues (2009) point to the fact that the use of personalized avatars could help in the creation of effective distance and online learning opportunities. Concerning the adaption of content in the game, Gunter, Kenny and Vick (2006) affirm that players are not simply motivated to learn because of the content placed inside the game. The authors stress the need for the correct use of practical instructional theories when trying to decrease the risk of the game failing to meet its intended educational goals.

3   MetaVals Game Dynamics and the Architecture
for Personalisation

MetaVals is a classification game. It can be considered as a decision-making activity initially developed with the pedagogical objective of practicing assets and liabilities in the field of finance. The design of MetaVals is based on Human Computer Interaction user-centered methodologies based on iterative prototyping (Lambropoulos, Romero, & Culwin, 2010). The first release of this SG was called *eFinance Game* and supported students in distinguishing whether a financial item was an asset or a liability (Padrós,

Romero, & Usart, 2011; Romero, Usart, & Almirall, 2011). Despite its initial use in the field of finance, the game was designed with a view to its future potential in adapting the decision-making dynamics involved in classification to other fields of knowledge. Some months after the first uses of the *eFinance Game*, there was an opportunity to play the game in the context of social sciences in the University of West of Scotland (UWS). This new release was used to rename the game as MetaVals and utilise the possibilities for computer adaptation allowing the personalization of knowledge items presented to the students and the look and feel of the game.

3.1   MetaVals Management Interface

In order to facilitate the management of the MetaVals game in different contexts, a management interface has been developed to allow easier management of the different contexts, groups, users and domain-specific knowledge settings. The interface is available online (http://www.metavals.eu) and has been designed to allow teachers and non-experts to manage the implementation of users, contexts, groups, knowledge items and their personalization. While the game is adaptable to different languages, the managing interface is only in Spanish because ESADE is managing the different contexts of use of the MetaVals SG. Nevertheless, the interface has been conceived to include other languages in case the MetaVals should be managed in other linguistic contexts.

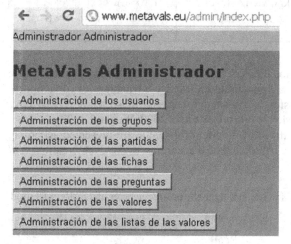

MetaVals Management

- Users' management
- Dyads' management
- Game play management
- Knowledge items grid management
- Knowledge questions management
- Answer values management
- Answer values dataset management

Fig. 1. MetaVals management interface

3.2   MetaVals Playing Modalities

The MetaVals game can be played in different modalities, depending on the characteristics of the course where the game is to be implemented. Firstly, MetaVals can be played by different types of dyad: *real dyads*, integrated by two real students interacting in real time (in face-to-face or in online learning) or *virtual dyads*: students playing together with a virtual peer. In the first scenario, the instructor should define, using the MetaVals management interface, the members of each*real dyad*. The instructor can define the dyads according to the criteria he considers the most relevant. This real dyads scenario demands peers to play synchronously. In the second scenario, the instructor can define the dyads matching each real student with a virtual player. This could allow students to play at any time the instructor or the learner decides. In this second context, the MetaVals game could be played asynchronously, a modality that is specially created to meet the demand of online activities that are self-regulated by the learners. In this *virtual dyads* modality, the instructor could decide the level of previous knowledge and experience of the virtual peer assigned to each real learner. In this way, the level of knowledge asymmetry within the dyad could be personalised. The instructor could assign an expert or non-expert virtual peer to the learner. This feature allows instructional designers and teachers to develop different modalities of dyads according to the learners' prior knowledge.

Table 1. Modalities of the prior knowledge symmetries within the learners in the dyad

		Virtual Learner #2	
		Low level	High level
Learner #1	Low level	Prior knowledge level symmetry (Low knowledge level)	Prior knowledge level asymmetry (Low/High)
	High level	Prior knowledge level asymmetry (High/Low)	Prior knowledge level symmetry (High knowledge level)

Table 1 shows the different modalities of prior knowledge symmetries that could be created by using MetaVals. The asymmetrical knowledge advantages of collaborative learning are argued as the transfer of knowledge between those learners who have different levels of previous knowledge (Ogata, & Yano, 2000; Wegerif, 1998).

In Table 2 the different modalities of the MetaVals game are presented according to the release: board or computer based, and also according to the dyad creation: *real dyad* or *virtual dyad*.

Table 2. Modalities of the MetaVals SG according to the board/computer and real/virtual dyad

Modality	Paper / Computer	Dyad Peer	Recommended use
Onsite	Paper	Real	✓ ✓
	Computer	Real	✓ ✓ ✓
		Virtual	✓
Distance	Computer	Real	✓
		Virtual	✓ ✓ ✓

3.3   MetaVals Personalization through the Different Stages of the Game

The game dynamics in MetaVals is structured in six potential stages as shown in figure 2. The first and last stages are related to the prior knowledge and intra-psychological diagnostics through the Pre-Test and the immediate or delayed knowledge gain measured through the Post-Test. These initial and final stages can be enabled or not, depending on the learning context and objectives set by the instructional designers. We describe below the personalization possibilities ascribed to each of these stages.

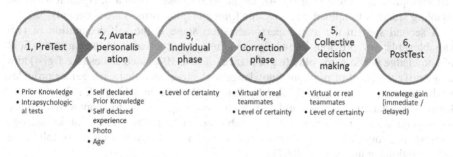

Fig. 2. Stages in the MetaVals game play

Stage 1. The Pre-Test is an optional phase aiming to identify the student in two aspects. Firstly, the Pre-Test includes an identification of prior knowledge of the student. Prior knowledge is defined as the amount of domain-specific knowledge acquired through experience or training (Spence, & Brucks, 1997). The personalisation of prior knowledge Pre-Test is achieved by the creation of a specific survey with a domain expert professor. This stage allows the integration of a link to web based surveys in a specific area of the MetaVals database that allows personalisation of the link for each implementation of the game. A second area allows integrating a second link to another test, also in the Pre-Test stage. This second link is generally used for the analysis of intra-psychological factors of the students, e.g. the temporal perspectives of students with the Zimbardo Time Perspective Inventory (Zimbardo, & Boyd, 1999). In figure 3, there is a screenshot of the groups management interface, including the personalisation features for the prior knowledge test (link Test 1) and the additional pre-test (link Test 2). The third link that could be personalised in this screen is used for the post-test questionnaire (see Stage 6).

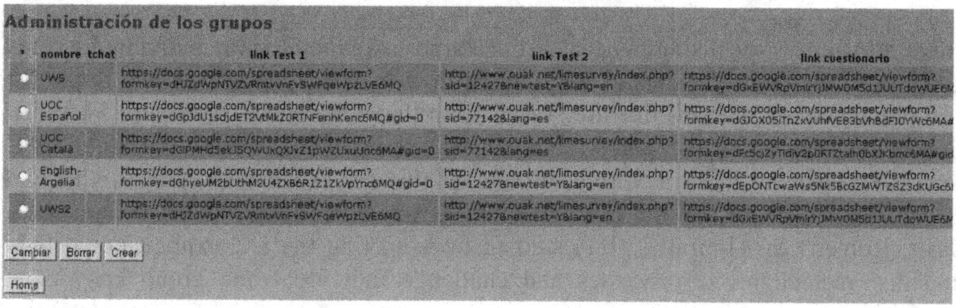

Fig. 3. Group management interface including the pre-test and post-test links

Stage 2. This stage allows students to enter four different kinds of personal data once they enter the MetaVals game. The first interactive screen allows students to personalise their avatar before starting the game play. Studies focusing on the use of avatars in games (Yee, 2006) have shown that allowing gamers to choose some aspects of their own avatar particularly in SGs could lead to higher empathy and more pride in the success of their avatar while playing (Gee, 2003; Charski, 2010). Players in Metavals can decide whether a standard avatar or a personalized picture represents them during the game play. If a player decides to upload an image by clicking on the "Change picture" button (see fig. 4), the game interface opens a navigation window, enabling students to upload an image file (*.jpg* and *.png* formats are accepted).

A second step in the avatar personalization stage is the self-declaration of two variables: players' previous knowledge and previous experience, in the particular field of knowledge of the game play (e.g. Finance). These 10-graded scales (see fig. 4) aim to quantify the level of previous knowledge and experience that each gamer provides to the learning context. As studied by Padrós, Romero and Usart (2012), the prior knowledge characterisation could be relevant as a requirement to adapt a SG activity to the end user. Furthermore, this variable could help the process of knowledge convergence, defined as an increase in common knowledge among peers following collaboration (Jeong, & Chi, 2007).

Finally, players can also write in their age in this second stage. This variable is especially important when MetaVals is implemented for research, as being part of the basic statistical data to study. Nevertheless, there are also some studies that highlight that being aware of their peers' personal information (age, gender and appearance) may provide gamers a rich and more realistic game experience (Monahan, McArdle, & Bertolotto, 2008).

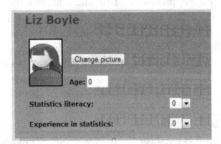

Fig. 4. MetaVals screen allowing the avatar personalisation

Stage 3. After personalising his avatar, the learner is invited to play individually. This first part of the game consists of deciding on their own the correct answers to the list of 6 domain-specific items that are presented in the game panel (see figure 5). When classifying each item, the player should also fill in the "Level of Certainty" (LC hereinafter) panel, placed next to each item. In this last column, the player is invited to indicate her/his LC on the classified item (from 0 "not sure" to 10 "very sure"). Usart, Romero & Almirall (2011) studied how making the LC explicit could help students' metacognitive processes and challenge individual and group knowledge acquisition.

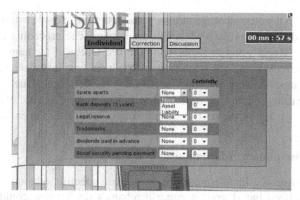

Fig. 5. Individual decision on assets / liabilities and Level of Certainty declaration

Stage 4. In the next part of the game, namely correction, each dyad accesses a screen which shows 6 items previously answered by his/her (virtual or real) peer as well as his/her peer's LC. This information is shown when the gamer classifies each of this second group of 6 items. The items for Player 1 and Player 2 are different; therefore, there is a total of 12 items for each game play. Following Nickerson (1999), individuals tend to misjudge others' degree of knowledge. Therefore, the use of awareness tools, in particular, those facilitating players with their peers' previous answers and LC levels, could help gamers in the judgement of peer's real knowledge (Nova et al., 2007).

Stage 5. Hence, both players have to go through 12 items all together in order to finish the game. In this second part of the game (see figure 6), Player 1 must decide whether to agree or disagree with Player 2's answers and vice versa. The aim of the discussion stage is to reach consensus among both members of the dyad, and correctly classify the 12 items. Player 1 and Player 2 work together and collaborate to get better grades than other dyads also playing the same game play. If the MetaVals is played in the *real dyad* modality, the management panel gives the teacher the chance to enter a link to a chat tool, in order to allow dyads to reach consensus on the final answer.

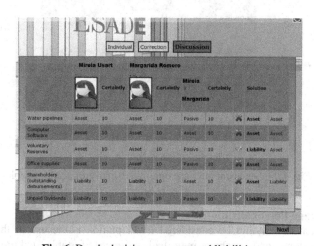

Fig. 6. Dyads decision on assets and liabilities

Stage 6. The final potential stage allows game setters to include a link to a post-test, which can be different for each MetaVals game play. The procedure is similar to the one detailed in Stage 1, and is displayed in the last screen of the game, where players access the final ranking. The inclusion of the post-test was designed in order to facilitate the measurement of knowledge gain in MetaVals. Due to the fact that meaningful learning cannot be measured via one unique measure after the learning activity (Ausubel, 1963), the post-test can be run months after the end of MetaVals.

3.4   Interdisciplinary Adaptation

In order to ensure the interdisciplinary, or domain-specific, adaptation of the game, MetaVals has been based upon a game mechanics design that could be applied to different disciplines. The main mechanism of the game is based on a classification activity for a list of items. The items are presented to the player in a gradual sequence. First, 6 items have to be classified individually by each student, second, the student can correct the 6 next different items that a virtual peer has classified, and finally, all 12 items must be arranged after discussion with the virtual peer. The team that correctly classifies the highest number of items in the least time wins the game.

3.5   International Adaptation

The MetaVals game also aims to address the concrete demands of each learning context where the SG may be implemented. This goal is realised by adapting both the graphical design and the language displayed in the game (see figure 7). Through the use of personalization, the sense of credibility of the SG could be enhanced. For example using a tailored graphic design allows students to identify more easily with the learning activity (Shapiro *et al.*, 2006).

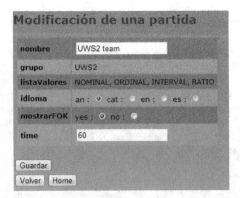

Fig. 7. Management interface options settings group and gameplay

3.5.1 Language Personalization
A first element that should be considered in adaptation is the use of the appropriate language. Students and teachers may feel more comfortable and develop deeper

understanding if the SG activity is displayed in their own language. MetaVals can accomplish this objective as it presents an accessible database, which has been designed in order to facilitate the insertion of new languages in a two-step process. First, text can be introduced screen by screen; second, this text can be recorded in a unique sequence, stored as language. Due to this simple process, when adapting the game activity to a new context, the designer or teacher should only enter the database and choose the language of the game play. Furthermore, if changes in concrete words or expressions have to be made, the text is totally available in the language database option.

3.5.2 Graphic Design Personalization

A second level of adaptation, considered in MetaVals, is the personalized graphic design. The designers pursued the identification of players with the SG context, as it

Fig. 8. Adaptation of MetaVals for the UWS (outdoor scenario)

Fig. 9. Adaptation of MetaVals in ESADE, with an inside scenario and virtual professor avatar

has been stated that it could facilitate different factors of motivation. Following Viau (1994), contextualization of learning objects and concepts is a core aspect of this process in MetaVals. With the aim of facilitating the personalization of the graphic context, a low cost process was defined. To adapt the SG, only three 2D images are needed. The design of the different scenarios is constructed with an outdoor image, an interior stage image, and a virtual representation of a game guide or teacher. The combination of these three elements gives enough flexibility to create the welcome screen, the introduction of data, and all the game stages, as well as the feedback or ranking screen, as can be observed in figures 8 and 9.

4   Use of MetaVals in Spain, UK and Romania

Since MetaVals was first created in the first term of 2011 by the ESADE DIPQA team, it has been tested and implemented as an active and adaptive learning tool in different learning contexts.

4.1   Use of MetaVals in Spain for Post Graduate Finance Students

The first uses of MetaVals, both in Spanish and English languages. were conducted in ESADE, a Spanish business school with more than 50 years of experience in training management students. It was adapted for a basic finance course where students had to classify items into assets or liabilities. A total of 181 students in 6 different postgraduate courses have used and evaluated the MetaVals game (Padrós, Romero, & Usart, 2011) and they provided valuable data for the continuous improvement of the SG. One of the key aspects in e-learning activities, such as Serious Games, is the consideration of the usability, ease of use and perceived usefulness for learning (Fuentes, Romero, & Serrano, 2011). The students' evaluation of the usability, ease of use and perceived usefulness was developed through the Technology Acceptance Model (TAM) developed by Davis (1989). The aggregated results of the MetaVals' TAM evaluation can be seen in figure 9, according to the different courses where the MetaVals was used in ESADE.

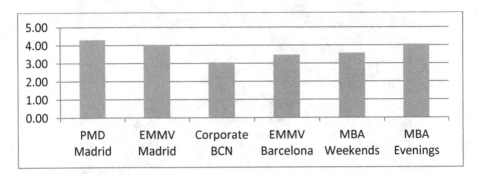

Fig. 10. Students' MetaVals TAM evaluation

4.2   Use of MetaVals in UK for Statistics Support for Undergraduate Psychology Students

The MetaVals adaptation for the University of the West of Scotland (UWS) involved both the implementation of a tailored graphical design (see figure 8) and interdisciplinary adaptation. The content of the SG play was statistics; therefore, both the pre- and post-questionnaires, together with the items of the game, were redesigned. The designing team implemented, together with the statistics lecturer, two questionnaires and twelve items, to the MetaVals database.

The context of MetaVals in UWS was designed in English, and the images of the game were adapted (as seen in the previous section). The game used *virtual dyads* and the learning context was online. Students had to classify 12 items as nominal, ordinal, interval and ratio.

Modern views about the effective teaching of statistics suggest that understanding statistical concepts and developing statistical reasoning would benefit from using appropriate technological tools and providing opportunities to explore and analyze data (Garfield, & Ben-Zvi, 2007). Metavals was thought to be suitable for application to statistics because students typically find many statistical concepts difficult to grasp and Metavals could offer an appropriate means of supporting their learning.

For the initial implementation the knowledge area selected was levels of measurement. Data in statistics have different characteristics and can be categorised according to how they should be measured in terms of four different kinds of measurement scale: nominal, ordinal, interval or ratio. In implementing this version of Metavals, the two previous response categories used in classification items of the ESADE version were increased to a total of four to accommodate the four possible categories for levels of measurement. Measurement scales are hierarchical in that data types higher in the sequence assume all the properties of types lower than them. Knowledge of levels of measurement is basic statistical knowledge which underlies subsequent choices of appropriate graphical representations and statistical tests in data analysis.

Nominal data is also called categorical because the variable which is being measured falls into distinct categories or groups. For example gender is a categorical variable since people are either male or female. Students' degree choice, such as Chemistry, History, Maths, English or Politics is another example of a categorical variable. With categorical data the categories are qualitatively different and there is no suggestion that one category is preferable to another.

Ordinal data can also be categorised but they have the further property of having an implicit order or rank. An example would be the position of 10 runners running a race as first, second, third, fourth etc. where clearly it is better to be first than tenth. Another example of interval data frequently used in research is the Likert scale, where attitudes for example are measured on a 1-5 scale where 1 means that an individual strongly agrees with the view that for example cannabis should be a legal drug and 5 means that they strongly disagree. Ordinal measurements do not imply differences in magnitude between two measurement points.

The next category is interval data which inherits the characteristics of the other two levels of measurement but also has the property that the differences in values on the measurement scale have meaning and consist of a series of equal intervals. The ratio between numbers on the interval scale is not meaningful. An example is temperature. The last scale, the ratio scale, is similar to the interval scale but the ratio between numbers on the scale is meaningful. Examples are weight, time and height.

Students typically find it difficult to categorise data with respect to levels of measurement because for many it is a relatively novel way of thinking. The examples are difficult, because the answer is not always self-evident to students and, although there is typically a correct answer for each example, students may have different levels of understanding and would benefit from discussion. There are many other concepts in statistics, such as variables and statistical tests, which could potentially benefit from presentation via Metavals.

The pilot study for the UWS Statistics course consisted of a sample of four students (M= 31.75; SD=13.50), with a self-reported previous knowledge of statistics of M= 3.50 (/10) and SD=3.70.

The pilot of Metavals in the content area of statistics will be extended in October 2012 when it will be used with a group of 70 3rd year psychology students at UWS.

4.3   Use of MetaVals in Romania for Post-Graduate Finance Students

MetaVals was adapted for the Financial English course in the Carol I National Defence University, Romania. The SG aimed to help students practice Financial English terminology in the module of English for Special Purposes. Due to this aim, the English version of the game on finance was activated, together with a graphical adaptation. For this adaptation and further implementation of MetaVals, the items set were the same as in the ESADE context, although the pedagogical aim was different. The professor aimed to measure the level of knowledge in English financial terminology as the students were attending a Postgraduate Finance & economy management course. In this case, also a *virtual dyads* scenario was designed. The sample from the Carol I University was composed of five adult students (M= 44.40; SD=1.82), playing in a face-to-face context, with a self-reported previous knowledge of English Financial terminology of M=3.50 (/10); SD=3.70.

The purpose of implementing the case study of MetaVals within the English for Specific Purposes- Financial terminology in a postgraduate Finance and Economy Management programme, was to reveal the effectiveness of using serious games in adult education, and to analyze the possibility of aligning this type of activity with the curriculum, as well as the feasibility of introducing this element in the syllabus. As a learning outcome our goal was to reinforce knowledge on some previously taught terminology and encourage debate that would stir the desire for new concept acquisition. The interesting parts were to be noticed both in the management of the activity itself from the teacher's point of view and in each student's participation to this activity, given their age and background. This game was meant to both test and reinforce knowledge on specific terminology in finance, after the input had been done in a face-to-face group work activity, within discussions where students had to find the correspondence between the English term and the financial concept as they knew it based on experience and professional knowledge. Hence, the MetaVals came both as self-evaluation, correction, and knowledge transfer with respect to the terminology lesson itself; on the other hand, the MetaVals gave them feedback on the self-esteem level, boosting self-confidence or revealing individualistic behaviours. The personalization aspects played a positive role in leveraging engagement especially when they received a personally addressed message giving them the password and also instructions to the game. What they lacked though were the real opponents; the engagement with virtual dyads brought the feeling of a biased self-evaluation as a real competition would have brought a greater sense of authenticity and satisfaction, irrespective of the results.

Another thing worth mentioning was that when students heard the word "competition" (the winner would be the first team completing the consensus over the dyads) – they suddenly lost interest in teacher's guidance over the game, preoccupied with the time frame. They also ignored the quality over quantity factor by being under the pressure of finishing in the shortest time possible.

Moreover, the competition factor focusing on time hindered them from allowing quality time on cooperating and debating over reaching consensus for the best choice of the term in the dyad.

When discussed at the end, students admitted time prevailed over quality. It is more interesting though to see this, as they are all in leading positions at their place of work and moreover the time factor is an important metric in their activity. As far as the TAM model is concerned, the students received the game well, even though they are part of the digital immigrant generation, and even suggested more interactivity for future releases of the same game. Looking at the chart below, it is interesting to see almost the same TAM values for the UWS and Carol I NDU, even though students' ages are so different. This aspect sheds a positive light on the mature students and their acceptance of Technology Enhanced Learning approach, SG based learning specifically.

As far as the use of the MetaVals game and its integration into the academic environment is concerned, it has not been difficult to adapt the game for different

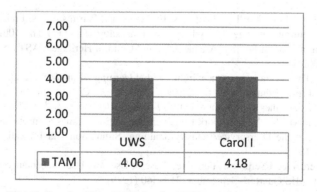

Fig. 11. Results of the TAM for the UWS and Carol I contexts

contexts and contents. In addition the game has been very well received by students. The course coordinators could easily see how activities in the game fitted with the topics being studied in the syllabus. However it would be a strenuous process to officially introduce serious games into curricula routinely since many professors are not yet convinced of the effectiveness of games in learning. This attitude is mainly explained by the reluctance of "digital immigrants", by the bureaucratic process and by the lack of technological advancement at all levels inside a university. For financial reasons, the same game would need endless repurposing to meet various objectives and adaptations for each and every tutor's perspective over the same subject matter. Hence, until we have a game-object repository with easily repurposable objects, uptake of serious games in Higher Education Areas may be limited.

5   Prospective Uses of MetaVals and Research Perspectives

In this study we have analysed the personalisation and adaptation components of the Serious Game MetaVals. After analysing these components, the quality of this adaptation is analyzed through the perspective of perceived usability, utility and ease of use of the game in each of the three countries participating in the case study. The results obtained in the Spanish, UK and Romanian context will be analysed to evaluate the MetaVals' ease of use, usability and perceived usefulness in these different contexts. The analysis of the results and their coherence in the different contexts will allow improvements to the next MetaVals release and analyses the level of the adaptation and personalization of the current release, before extending the use of MetaVals to other learning contexts in other countries, disciplines and educational levels. Further studies in the use of MetaVals will analyse the ease of use, usability and perceived usefulness in relation to the students' performance in each of the contexts of study.

References

Anderson, E.F., McLoughlin, L., Liarokapis, F., Peters, C., Petridis, P., de Freitas, S.: Serious Games in Cultural Heritage. In: Ashley, M., Liarokapis, F. (eds.) The 10th International Symposium on Virtual Reality, Archaeology and Cultural Heritage VAST - State of the Art Reports (2009)
Ausubel, D.P.: The psychology of meaningful verbal learning. Grune& Stratton, Oxford (1963)
Charski, D.: From Edutainment to Serious Games: A Change in the Use of Game Characteristics. Games and Culture 5(2), 177–198 (2010)
De Freitas, S., Jarvis, S.: A Framework for developing serious games to meet learner needs. In: Proceedings of the Interservice/Industry Training, Simulation and Education Conference, Florida (2006)
Davis, F.D.: Perceived Usefulness, Perceived Ease of Use, and User Acceptance of Information Technology. MIS QuarterlySeptember, 318–340 (1989)

Fuentes, M., Romero, M., Serrano, M.J.: E-Learning: Psycho-Pedagogical Utility, Usability and Accessibility Criteria from a Learner Centred Perspective. In: Lazarinis, F., Green, S., Pearson, E. (eds.) Handbook of Research on E-Learning Standards and Interoperability: Frameworks and Issues, pp. 419–434 (2011)

Garfield, J., Ben-Zvi, D.: How students learn statistics revisited: a current review of research on teaching and learning statistics. International Statistical Review 75(3), 372–396 (2007)

Gunter, G.A., Kenny, R.F., Vick, E.H.: A case for a formal design paradigm for serious games. The Journal of the International Digital Media and Arts Association 3(1), 93–105 (2006)

Jeong, H., Chi, M.T.H.: Knowledge convergence and collaborative learning. Instructional Science 35, 287–315 (2007)

Lambropoulos, N., Romero, M., Culwin, F.: HCI Education to Support Collaborative e-Learning Systems Design. eLearn Mag., 9 (2010)

Monahan, T., McArdle, G., Bertolotto, M.: Virtual reality for collaborative e-learning. Computers & Education 50, 1339–1353 (2008)

Nickerson, R.: How we know – and sometimes misjudge – what others know: Imputing one's own knowledge to others. Psychological Bulletin 125(6), 737–759 (1999)

Nova, N., Wehrle, T., Goslin, J., Bourquin, Y., Dillenbourg, P.: Collaboration in a multi-user game: impacts of an awareness tool on mutual modelling. Multimedia Tools Applications 32, 161–183 (2007)

Padrós, A., Romero, M., Usart, M.: Developing serious Games: Form Face-to-Face to a Computer-based Modality. E-learning Papers 25 (July 15, 2011)

Peirce, N., Conlan, O., Wade, V.: Adaptive Educational Games: Providing Non-invasive Personalised Learning Experiences. In: Proceedings of the Second IEEE International Conference DIGITEL, Banff, Canada, pp. 17–19 (2008)

Pivec, M., Baumann, K.: The Role of Adaptation and Personalisation in Classroom-Based Learning and in e-Learning. J. UCS 10(1), 63–79 (2004)

Romero, M., Usart, M., Almirall, E.: Serious games in a finance course promoting the knowledge group awareness. In: EDULEARN 2011 Proceedings, pp. 3490–3492 (2011)

Selwyn, N.: The use of computer technology in university teaching and learning: a critical perspective. Journal of Computer Assisted Learning 23(2), 83–94 (2007)

Shapiro, M.A., Pena-Herborn, J., Bryant, J.: &Hancock, J. T.Realism, imagination and narrative video games. In: Vorderer, P., Bryant, J.M. (eds.) Playing Video Games: Motives, Responses, and Consequences. Lawrence Erlbaum Associates, NJ (2006)

Spence, M., Brucks, M.: The moderating effects of problem characteristics on experts' and novices judgments. Journal of Marketing Research 34, 233–247 (1997)

Usart, M., Romero, M., Almirall, E.: Impact of the Feeling of Knowledge Explicitness in the Learners' Participation and Performance in a Collaborative Game Based Learning Activity. In: Ma, M., Fradinho Oliveira, M., Madeiras Pereira, J. (eds.) SGDA 2011. LNCS, vol. 6944, pp. 23–35. Springer, Heidelberg (2011)

Viau, R.: La motivation en contextescolaire. De BoeckUniversité, Bruxelles (1994)

Vygotsky, L.S.: Mind in Society: The Development of Higher Psychological Processes. Harvard University Press (1978)

Yee, N.: The Psychology of MMORPGs: Emotional Investment, Motivations, Relationship Formation, and Problematic Usage. In: Schroeder, R., Axelsson, A. (eds.) Avatars at Work and Play: Collaboration and Interaction in Shared Virtual Environments, pp. 187–207. Springer, London (2006)

Serious Games Adoption in Corporate Training

Aida Azadegan[1], Johann C.K.H. Riedel[1], and Jannicke Baalsrud Hauge[2]

[1] Nottingham University Business School, Nottingham, UK
{aida.azadegan,johann.riedel}@nottingham.ac.uk
[2] University of Bremen, Bremen, Germany
baa@biba.uni-bremen.de

Abstract. Corporate managers are constantly looking for more effective and efficient ways to deliver training to their employees. Traditional classroom methods have been used for a long time. However, in the last decade electronic learning technology has gained in significance. Serious Games are games that educate, train and inform using entertainment principles, creativity, and technology. Serious Games are proven as a learning method for conveying skills on complex tasks by incorporating sound learning and pedagogical principles into their design and structure. Therefore, it is believed that Serious Games have got the potential to be used to meet government or corporate training objectives. However, the awareness and adoption level of serious games by industry is not known.

In this research we designed and conducted a pilot survey among UK-based companies. We used the survey in order to assess the level of awareness and adoption of Serious Games in companies for corporate training. We aim to understand what kinds of skills development Serious Games-based trainings are desired by companies and to know what they perceive the benefits and barriers of using Serious Games are in companies. This paper describes the stages of the design of the survey questionnaire, presents and analyses the results and ends with conclusions and a discussion about the future research work.

Keywords: Serious Games, Innovation Adoption, Awareness, Corporate Training.

1 Introduction

Game-based learning is one of the issues under debate today. A **serious game** is a game designed for a primary purpose other than pure entertainment. Serious games can be applied to a broad spectrum of application areas, e.g. military, government, educational, corporate, and healthcare. Zyda [1] argues that serious games have more than just story, art, and software. It is the addition of *pedagogy* (activities that educate or instruct, thereby imparting knowledge or skill) that makes games serious. However, he also stresses that pedagogy must be subordinate to story and that the entertainment component comes first.

M. Ma et al. (Eds.): SGDA 2012, LNCS 7528, pp. 74–85, 2012.
© Springer-Verlag Berlin Heidelberg 2012

The use of *Serious Games* in *corporate training* is not extensively studied and investigated by researchers. Today's corporate training market is a large industry. Corporations need to train their employees to improve their skills and knowledge. When the learning material is technical or boring, or the learning objectives are difficult, Serious Games can play an important role in training [2]. Serious Games offer a paradigm shift in training as it changes the role of the trainee from passive to active [2].

Serious games have proven to be an important tool in supporting the education and training at schools and universities as well as vocational training in industry [3], but still they are not often in use. In our research we are interested in understanding two key questions - how extensively Serious Games are being used in corporate training and what the level of awareness of serious games for training is. We look at Serious Games as an innovation and try to understand the current organizations' behaviour in terms of the adoption of such new and emerging technology for corporate training. We are interested in understanding the needs and requirements for the use of serious games for training purposes in companies. Also we aim to investigate how the potential adopters will respond to the use of this technology and whether or not it will be adopted on a large scale.

To satisfy these aims a pilot questionnaire survey of 300 companies in the UK was designed and conducted: The sample included the 100 best companies to work for, the 100 most profitable companies and the 100 fastest growing technology companies in the year 2011.

2   Background

One field that is constantly evolved through adoption of new techniques and technologies, especially by incorporation of IT frameworks and techniques is corporate training [4, 5]. Companies spend large amounts of money on employee training. Traditional methods of training turn out to be costly for organizations. Hall and LeCavalier [6] describe some economic advantages of converting their traditional training delivery methods to the use of IT-based methods. Using a blend of Web-based (80 percent) and classroom (20 percent) instruction, Ernst & Young reduced training costs by 35 percent while improving consistency and scalability. Rockwell Collins reduced training expenditures by 40 percent with only a 25 percent conversion rate to Web-based training. Other success stories also exist in addition to generally positive economic benefits. For instance advantages such as convenience, standardized delivery, self-paced learning, and variety of available content, have made IT-based technology a high priority for many corporations [7].

Serious Games, uses IT-based techniques, is allowing corporations to improve their training of employees, both by engaging them more actively and by testing their comprehension of the information conveyed. Games can be used as training tools for basic corporate situations, or they can be tailored for a particular industry. Video games have created more productive workers demographics. Gaming teaches employees to solve problems in a non-traditional way, using trial and error. Gamers also develop marketable business skills. Beck and Wade show that compared to non-gamers, employees who train with video games are good at "multi-tasking, good at making decisions and evaluating risks, flexible in the face of change and inclined to treat setbacks as chances to try again [9].

3   Methodology

The aim of the survey was to assess the degree of awareness of serious games for training in UK companies and to assess the level of adoption and the barriers to adoption. In this research we seek to ascertain companies' attitudes on the use of Serious Games in corporate training. We anticipated that the awareness level and adoption of Serious Games would be low. Therefore, to pursue our aim we used the *Descriptive Survey method*. A Descriptive Survey [10, 11] is aimed at understanding the relevance and distribution of a phenomenon, which in the case of this research is Serious Games adoption, in a population. Using a Descriptive Survey, we are not aiming for theory building but for gaining some hints for future research, for theory development and refinement.

The survey was conducted by Nottingham University Business School during the months of May and June 2011. The survey questionnaire was posted to a sample of 300 UK-based organizations as compiled by the Sunday Times - a UK weekly newspaper. The companies were mainly small, mid-size and some big workplaces in the UK and categorized as the 100 best companies to work for, the 100 most profitable companies and the 100 fastest growing technology companies. The companies were representing diverse industry sectors such as consumer goods, manufacturing, wholesale or retail, transport, computers and electronics, business services, healthcare and leisure, etc.

The 100 best companies to work for were selected by the Sunday Times mainly based on an organisation's commitment to its most important assets - its workforce. Focusing on employees brings real benefits such as, improved workplace engagement, better staff retention, reduced recruitment costs and greater financial performance. Having a main stress on staff development, the list of 100 best companies to work for can be a good candidate to satisfy the purpose for the survey, which contributes to corporate training. The list of 100 most profitable companies is well respected in the business sector and ranks companies according to their average profits over the last three years. The fastest growing technology companies are ranked as Britain's top one hundred technology companies with the fastest-growing sales over the last three years [12].

The companies were asked to post the response back using an enclosed Freepost envelope. The questionnaires were sent to the "HR Manager" in the companies, rather than the training manager – as small companies may not have training managers.

After receiving the responses back from 11 companies, we calculated the response rate, which resulted in 3%. The response rate is disappointingly small. Further Steps were taken to try to improve the response rate and to understand why the response rate was so low. This was done by telephoning a sample of the non-respondents.

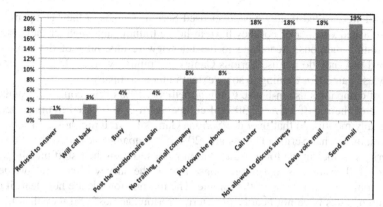

Fig. 1. Reasons given for Negative Reponses (n=190)

To try to improve the response rate for 200 of the companies, the 100 best companies to work for and the 100 fastest growing companies, were contacted by telephone for a follow up conversation and short interview regarding aspects of adoption and awareness of Serious Games for corporate training. It was chosen to contact the companies by phone rather than sending them reminders by post. Making phone calls to companies could allow us to make sure that the interview is directed to the appropriate respondent within the company – the HR manager or the Head of Training.

A considerable number of companies showed a low level of interest to participate in the telephone follow up interviews. A number of reasons were given based on the negative responses given by the company managers, see Figure 1. Almost 20% of the companies asked for sending them follow up e-mails since they were not interested in answering interviews or questions over the phone. 18% of the companies mentioned that they are not legally allowed to discuss surveys over the phone. 18% of the companies referred the interviewee to leave a message on the manager's voice mail for further follow up conversations. Other reasons were given, such as, being busy, being a small company without specific training methods, hanging up the phone and some other reasons were given by the companies in order not to answer the short interview over the phone. Figure 1 presents the reasons given for negative responses. None of the reasons given related to serious games.

3.1   Characteristics of Respondents

According to the survey results, 64% of the respondents were large companies and consequently 36% were SMEs with less than 250 employees. 27% of the companies that responded to the survey belonged to the Business Services sector. Companies belonging to the IT Services sector were 27% of the companies. 18% of the companies that responded to the survey belonged to the Manufacturing Sector and the rest of the companies belonged to the Voluntary, Leisure and Transport Services sector.

We could successfully interview the HR managers of 10 companies or 5% of the companies that we telephoned. Firstly, we asked them to try returning the questionnaire back to us and they were offered to have the questionnaire sent to them again. If they did not wish to complete the questionnaire, the HR managers were interviewed briefly and were asked if they have ever used Serious Games in their company. They were also asked whether or not they have in-house training and whether they use web-based training methods. According to the interview results, 80% of the respondents mentioned that they do not use Serious Games for training while only 20% mentioned that they use games for training to some extent in their company.

90% of companies use in-house training methods. 10% of the companies outsource all or part of their staff training. 30% of companies use web-based training methods. No company mentioned that they use Serious Games for training, however, after they were explained what Serious Games are, 20% of companies admitted that they have used Serious Games in the form of simulation games to train their staff members.

The overall result was that the response rate to the survey remained low, despite the telephoning of two thirds of the sample. The reasons for this are not clear. It could be that companies have not heard of the term "serious games" and they thus have no interest in completing a survey on the topic.

3.2   Design of the Survey Questions

The first part of the questionnaire seeks to understand the level of awareness of serious games and to compare the company's innovation approach to see if they would be likely to adopt new technologies like serious games. Then the question of the level of adoption is investigated – any or no adoption, test or pilot adoptions or wide scale adoption (we anticipate the latter to be unlikely). Then we examine the barriers to adoption: knowledge/information deficit, practical/ facilities barriers, cost/ business case barriers, low familiarity with electronic training means/ IT, lack of staff, and perception problems (that games are not serious). We then ask what the perceived benefits of serious games are. If companies perceive the benefits to be good they will be more likely to adopt them and conversely.

Finally, we ask about the types of skills that companies want to address using serious games. The question of what types of skill do industry need to be mediated by serious games is key. A question on skills mediated was thus included in the questionnaire. It divides skills into hard and soft skills – hard skills are those associated with knowledge required to carry out one's job, eg. knowledge of the product being manufactured/sold, customer service, project management, etc. Soft skills are those associated with working with other people – team working, communication, inter-personal skills, etc. It has often been pointed out that soft skills are actually very difficult to acquire and develop – in fact more so than hard skills. And it has been further observed that soft skills are more easily mediated by serous games [19].

4   Survey Results

This section focuses on the results of the survey and interpretation of the results.

4.1   Serious Games Awareness

According to our survey almost 29% of companies responded that they have heard about the use of Serious Games for corporate training. However, 15 out of 21 companies have never heard of using Serious Games for corporate training. The results received from the companies indicate a considerable low level of awareness about the use of Serious Games for corporate training among a range of different companies in the UK.

4.2   Serious Games Adoption

The result for the rate of adoption was 10% (one company stated that they used serious games). To ascertain why this might be, we asked about their attitude to adoption of serious games. It might be that companies are risk averse when it comes to the use of new technologies like serious games for training. 60% of the respondents believe that they are *slow adopters,* which means they are cautious in taking up new technology and are only interested in adopting new technology when the market is mature and the benefits are clear. 20% of the respondents say they are *first followers* and they will take the risk of deploying Serious Games relatively early if they are promising. The remaining 20% of the respondents say they are *early adopters* and are willing to use the Serious Games, and taking the risk of unprofitability or uncertainty. According to the responses to the survey, it can be interpreted that there is not much hope for 60% of the companies to adopt Serious Games until a wide scale adoption of Serious Games in industry is seen. The rest of the respondents, 40% of the companies, are either first followers or early adopters. This is a promising outcome and reveals that 40% of the companies are nearly ready to nearly adopt Serious Games. Further investigation is required to understand what would make these two groups of companies adopt Serious Games. Follow up interviews with these companies would be beneficial to understand the requirements for such companies to fully adopt Serious Games.

4.3   Serious Games Adoption/ Use

Regarding Serious Games adoption/ use, most of the respondents (82%) have never investigated their applicability. Only one respondent has already adopted Serious Games in their company to some extent and one other respondent is investigating the possibility of the application of Serious Games for Corporate Training. Both of these companies have mentioned that they have already heard of Serious Games for corporate training. The number of respondents in this survey is not sufficient to analyse the reason for why they have not fully adopted Serious Games for corporate training purposes.

4.4   Use of Different Training Methods

Regarding the investigation about the use of different training methods used in companies, almost 80% of the respondents say that Coaching and Mentoring methods are used in their organization for corporate training purposes. Simulation methods are used by almost 55% of the respondents. This relatively high adoption level of Simulation methods for training can imply that the use of Serious Games for corporate training has got the potential to be more widely used. Similarly, Business Games are also used at the rate of 30% in organizations. These two responses indicate that there is interest in companies for using simulations and games for training – and hence serious games.

4.5   Application of Serious Games for Skills Training

The questionnaire also focused on understanding in what specific type of skills different companies are interested in using Serious Games. Two business areas of soft skills and hard skills were identified as the basis of the investigation. Hard skills are technical or administrative procedures related to an organization's core business. Hard skills refer to the knowledge about professional theory and skills. These skills are typically easy to observe, quantify and measure. They are also easy to train, because most of the time the skill sets are brand new to the learner and no unlearning is involved. Harrison suggests that hard skills are those relating to the operation of any technology, new or old [20]. Hard skills are those that refer to a set of well-defined skills possible for unambiguous testing. Clearly any technical effort (such as the operation of machinery) falls into this category. The output from such processes based on hard skills can be predicted based on the inputs and the rules. Hard skills have a high knowledge and technical content, and it is essential that an incumbent has achieved a high level of competence in the particular knowledge domain if they are to be allowed to practice the skill [21]. On the other hand, Soft skills represent generic skills that support any discipline, and that can be transmitted to a range of work contexts. Such soft skill competencies represent what is often referred to as emotional intelligence and are predictive of superior performance in work roles. Soft-skills training programmes are usually arranged in groups with intensive involvement of teachers/facilitators for analysing and discussing the demonstrated behaviours of learners. Accordingly such training programmes are quite costly, and there is a consensus that soft skills training is a lifelong affair needing a lot of guided practice. Therefore,serious games show promises for delivering soft-skills training.

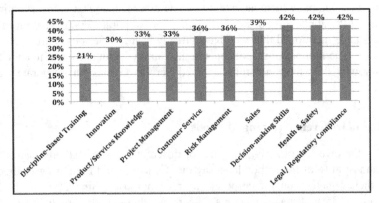

Fig. 2. Interest in Using Serious Games for Hard Skills Training

In terms of hard skills, the respondents are interested at the rate of 42% to use Serious Games for improving the legal compliance, Health and Safety and Decision making Skills. The respondents believe Serious Games can be used the least (21%) for integration with or improvement of Discipline-Based training.

The level of interest in using Serious Games to improve soft skills in companies varies between 36% to 48%, whereas in hard skills the level of interest varies at a lower level of 21% to 42%. The difference between interest levels indicates that potentially Serious Games can improve staff soft skills more compared to hard skills in organizations.

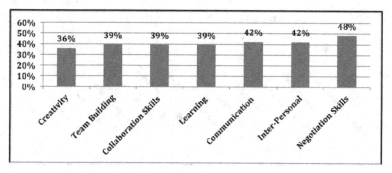

Fig. 3. Interest in Using Serious Games for Soft Skills Training

In terms of soft skills, the respondents show the most interest, at the rate of 48%, in using Serious Games to apply it to Negotiation Skills that they use in their company. The next highest interest is towards the use of Serious Games for developing interpersonal and communication skills at the rate of 42%. Respondents are equally interested at the rate of 39% in using Serious Games for developing learning skills as well as collaboration and team building skills. Serious Games are expected to be used at the lowest level of interest for improving creativity among the staff in companies. Overall the companies show more interest in using Serious Games for developing soft skills rather than for hard skills, with the most interest being in using Serious Games for developing Negotiation Skills.

4.6   Benefits of Using Serious Games

The respondents were asked for their opinion about the benefits that Serious Games can bring into their company. 39% say that they want Serious Games to help the company to be more efficient. The respondents would like Serous Games to improve their staff competence (36%) and become more flexible (30%). This indicates that companies see the benefits of Serious Games to help staff improve their flexibility and competence. It is believed that Serious Games can help at the least level, only 9%, to be helpful for reducing the cost of physical training provision. Reducing training costs also achieved a low rate of 15% according to the analysis of the survey responses. According to the results, reducing the cost of different aspects of training is believed not to be a strong benefit of using Serious Games. This means organizations do not see cost as a barrier – this could be because they genuinely do not see them as costly or because they are unaware of the cost. Given the low level of Serious Games awareness the latter explanation is more likely, however, interviews with companies would help to clarify this issue.

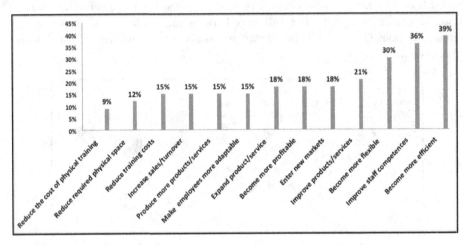

Fig. 4. Perceived Benefits for of using Serious Games in Organizations

4.7   Barriers towards Using the Games

Barriers towards adopting Serious Games in companies are analyzed in five main categories: financial barriers, barriers with familiarity about Serious Games, barriers in terms of the practicality of Serious Games, and finally the level of IT knowledge and support.

According to the results, in terms of financial barriers the majority of respondents, 81%, are not convinced of the business case; and 54% are concerned about the cost as the main financial barrier towards the adoption of Serious Games. 45% of the respondents believe that low familiarity with virtual worlds is a main barrier. This is followed by low familiarity with 3D environments which is agreed by 36% respondents. This means that almost half the companies believe that high technology solutions using 3D/ virtual worlds are a barrier – so lower technology solutions should be proposed. Regarding serious games 27% of the respondents pointed out that not being sure about the reliability of Serous Games was a concern and 27% mentioned that the staff perception about Serous Games training is that it is easy and not seen as valuable. 82% respondents replied that there is not enough known about the practicality of Serous Games use and finally 27% of respondents mentioned that they have problems with the lack of IT support which can be a barrier towards the adoption of Serious Games in their company.

Table 1. Barriers towards using Serious Games

Financial Barriers		Information Barriers	
Unconvinced of the business case	81%	Lack of knowledge (self, company) about Serious Games	63%
Cost of Serious Games	54%	Lack of awareness of the benefits of Serious Games	63%
Difficult to estimate the Return On Investment	36%	Not sure of the reliability of the technology	27%
Unwilling to invest in developing Serious Games	27%	Staff and employee perception that playing games is easy and not valuable	27%
IT Familiarity Barriers		Worries about serious games not satisfying the company's purpose	18%
Low Familiarity with using Virtual Worlds	45%	Not understanding the mechanism in the games that makes them educational	18%
Low Familiarity with using 3D Environments	36%	**Practicality Barriers**	
Low Familiarity with using Web-based Conferencing	27%	Not enough is known about their practical application	72%
Low Familiarity with using Online Training	18%	Lack of good quality information about Serious Games use in training	54%
Low Familiarity with using Skype	18%	Difficulty to measure the learning outcome	45%
Low Familiarity with using Video Conferencing	18%	Not enough time to use serious games in our company	27%
IT Support/Facilities Barriers		It is not easy, or practical, in our business to develop serious games	27%
Lack of IT Support	27%	Lack of training staff who are willing/ experienced in using serious games	18%
Lack of IT/ technical facilities for using serious games	18%	Worries about the integration of Serious Games in to existing training	9%

5   Conclusions and Future Work

This paper has described the research work undertaken on serious games awareness and adoption by companies as part of the GALA network of excellence on Serious Games. The pilot survey described in this paper focused on the assessment of the level of awareness and adoption of Serious Games in a sample of UK based companies for corporate training purposes. The survey was posted to 300 top performing companies. Although, the response rate achieved was low (3%), there are a number of interesting insights that emerged. First, the level of awareness was low – 36%. Second, the level of adoption was very low, 10%. However, 40% of companies are willing to be early adopters or first followers of new technologies and this is promising for serious games adoption.

In terms of the types of training methods in use there is also some promise. Although 80% of companies use coaching/ mentoring, with 60% using traditional classroom-based methods, role play was in use by 45%, simulation by 55%, and business games by 30%. This means companies show a good disposition towards using gaming based methods for training. Companies are more inclined to consider using Serious

Games for soft skills training rather than for hard skills. Companies showed more interest in using Serious Games for improving their employees' negotiation skills, inter-personal skills and communication. For hard skills, the main interests are for legal/regulatory compliance, health and safety and decision-making skills. The main perceived benefits of using Serious Games for corporate training are to help companies become more efficient, to improve staff competencies and to make the company more flexible. Companies do not show much interest in using Serious Games to reduce the cost of training, or to reduce the cost of the physical space required for training, or to reduce the cost of training facilities. The main barriers towards using Serious Games in corporate training were that the companies are not convinced of the business case and then the cost of incorporating Serious Games into their settings.

The response rate achieved for the pilot survey was low. One reason for this could be that the term "serious games" is not well disseminated and established in the Human Resources profession, in industry publications or in corporate settings in general in the UK. The result from the survey showed that more than half of the companies have already used simulation methods, therefore, companies might be already using games for training but not yet learnt the term Serious Games and the definition used. To try to establish this reason future work can be to conduct a survey at a larger scale and posting it to a larger number of companies across a number of European countries to possibly increase the number of responses and the response rate. Further, sending the survey out to members of industry associations (such as training or human resources associations) that are likely to use Serious Games would also be a solution for achieving a higher response rate.

Further study could be carried out in order to understand how to increase the awareness and adoption level of Serious Games as an innovation in companies. According to the survey result 40% of the companies are already willing to take risk of unprofitability or uncertainty of using very latest technology or to deploy new technology relatively early if they are promising. Further research should focus on understanding what criteria need to be taken into consideration and what requirements should be provided in order for these groups of companies to adopt Serious Games in their companies. Further research can be carried out to compare the level of adoption of serious games and e-learning technologies. We would expect the adoption of elearning to be higher as it has been around for more than a decade and has become fairly well standardised as a training approach. The comparison could help to understand the required stages that organizations need to go through to adopt Serious Games and use them in practice for corporate training purposes. Future work can focus on using case studies and interviewing managers in companies, who already have used Serious Games in their corporate settings. This could help to understand how they became aware of, and how, they adopted Serious Games and what factors motivated them.

Obviously users, technology and the market are constantly in a process of change. Users lack infrastructures depending on their needs at each period of time, therefore user requirements are constantly changing and users follow the change in technology to satisfy their requirements. Marketing for serious games strategies should be focused on the changing needs of the users and the change of technology to respond to evolving developments. Desktop learning, mobile learning and social gaming (eg. Farmville) have increased in significance in recent years. Technology providers and serious game researchers need to work on these emerging techniques to develop compelling serious games that can be delivered anywhere, anytime, anyhow. Understanding the serious game value and researching into how it should be managed to satisfy both users (companies) and technology (Serious Games) providers, is part of the GALA serious games network mandate and will direct the research in the future.

Acknowledgements. The research reported in this paper has been supported partially supported by the European Union, particularly through the project GaLA: The European Network of Excellence on Serious Games (FP7-ICT) www.galanoe.eu.

References

1. Zyda, M.: From Visual Simulation to Virtual Reality to Games. Computer 38(9), 25–32 (2005)
2. Michael, D., Chen, S.: Serious Games: Games that educate, train, and inform. Thomson Course Technology, Boston (2006)
3. Windhoff, G.: Planspiele für die verteilte Produktion. Entwicklung und Einsatz von Trainingsmodulen für das aktive Erleben charakteristischer Arbeitssituationen in arbeitsteiligen, verteilten Produktionssystemen auf Basis der Planspielmethodik. Dissertation. Bremen (2001)
4. Srother, J.B.: An Assessment of the Effectiveness of e-learning in Corporate Training Programs. International Review of Research in Open and Distance Learning 3(1) (2002)
5. Beck, J., Wade, M.: Got Game shows how growing up immersed in video games has profoundly shaped the attitudes and abilities of this new generation. Harvard Business Press, Boston (2004)
6. Crandall, R.W., Sidak, J.G.: Video Games: Serious Business for America's Economy. Entertainment Software Association Report, Available at SSRN (2006), http://ssrn.com/abstract=969728 (last accessed: November 29, 2011)
7. Malhorta, M.K., Grover, V.: An assessment of survey research in POM: from constructs to theory. Journal of Operations Management 16, 407–425 (1998)
8. Wacker, J.G.: A definition of theory: research guidelines for different theory-building research methods in operations management. Journal of Operations Management 16(4), 361–385 (1998)
9. Best Companies The workplace engagement specialist (2011), http://www.bestcompanies.co.uk/ (last accessed: July 13, 2012)
10. Scholz-Reiter, B., Gavirey, S., Echelmeyer, W., Hamann, T., Doberenz, R.: Developing a virtual tutorial system for online simulation games. In: Proceedings of the 30th SEFI Annual Conference, Firenze, Italy (2002)
11. Siddiqui, M.H.: Distance Learning Technologies, p. 321. APH Publishing Corporation, New Delhi (2004)
12. Chell, E., Athayde, E.: Planning for uncertainty: soft skills, hard skills and innovation. Reflective Practice 12(5) (2011)

Towards Participative and Knowledge-Intensive Serious Games

Nour El Mawas and Jean-Pierre Cahier

ICD/ Tech-CICO
University of Technology of Troyes (UTT) Troyes, France
{nour.el_mawas,cahier@utt.fr}@utt.fr

Abstract. We propose the "Architecture for Representations, Games, Interactions, and Learning among Experts" (ARGILE) for participatory and knowledge -intensive serious games. Faced with the problem of training on professional practices in areas of advanced expertise, reference knowledge are neither stabilized nor unanimous, but rather dynamic and continuously evolving. Moreover, the practicioner does not make decisions based on pre-established recipes, but it is brought to trial and error, to discuss with peers and to discover solutions in complex situations that are proposed. That's why the rules and the game objects must be easily annotated, discussed and modified by trainers and players themselves. We present in this paper a methodology, tools and technical architecture to design, use and evaluate such serious games. ARGILE allows ensuring the participatory design of rules of the game and involving debate among designers. We illustrate concretely the ideas presented on an example related to "Aidcrisis" an ongoing project which uses this architecture for training in action in a crisis situation (Aidcrisis project).

Keywords: participation architecture, e-training, serious games, Knowledge Engineering, cooperation, discussion forum.

1   Introduction

Our approach aims to the training of professionals or a wide public, in domains where the transmitted knowledge are complex and "expert" [1]. These knowledge are neither stabilized nor unanimous, but on the contrary dynamics and in continuous evolution. The actor does not make his decisions according to pre-established recipes, but it is brought to mobilize all his intelligence, to proceed by trial and error, to communicate with his peers and to discover continuously the suitable solutions in complex situations proposed to him. In this context, we are thus interested in a type of serious game which we name " participative and knowledge-intensive ", from which we wait in a correlated way i) for a better learning of the domain knowledge by learners and ii) a relevance and a greater learnability of the knowledge inserted into the game by designers.

The proposed approach allows in particular a co-conception of rules and certain objects of the game by the actors and the trainers of the domain. We speak generally

M. Ma et al. (Eds.): SGDA 2012, LNCS 7528, pp. 86–97, 2012.

in this paper, in a equivalent way, about player, about participant or about learner; and we will use indifferently, for our proposed system, the terms of game, useful game, serious game or learning system, by adding to these terms - participative, intensive in knowledge - characteristics which we will define and illustrate gradually in the article.

Numerous and diversified, the objects and the rules of the serious games will result, in the system we propose, from a decentralized and participative design: it's an user centered design on the one hand and on the other it confronts several designers, teachers, actors of the domain, local partners, experts or scientists of diverse disciplines, who know and consider the game, the territories and the knowledge domain (also the problems and the evaluations) in complementary or crossed approaches. Rules and objects of the game can be commented, discussed easily and modified by the trainers and the actors of the domain, without the intermediary of IT specialists. The context of the game, aimed by our architecture, is the multi-players game (and even massively multi-players), opening the way to the training in team activities, for example.

The rest of this paper is organized as follows. From some readings, the section II proposes preliminary centering elements on the notion of serious game. The section III details our scientific positioning and defines our approach of serious games «participative and intensive in knowledge ", with several models intended to illustrate the key concepts. The section IV illustrates the interest and the application of our approach on a project in crisis management, by detailing the main lines of scenes or scenarios designed for these projects. The section V specifies how we envisage the scientific validation of our proposal, by the experimentation and the evaluation of the impact of our architecture on the players learning. The section VI summarizes the conclusions of this paper.

2   Pedagogy and Serious Game, Some Preliminary Considerations

The idea that the serious games facilitate the learning is confirmed in numerous domains like languages and health, economy and management [2] The educational games can offer many learning benefits such as motivation, engagement and fun [3].These "serious games" would rather be named "useful games", as suggests it Stéphane Natkin [4], because if they contribute to serious learning in complex domains knowledge, they haven't to be, however, serious or boring.

But on the contrary, no need to add "funny" dimensions. It is enough so that there is "game", useful or not, that deploys all the tension of the associated personal investment. The player is not the spectator of a show, he is interactive, nor a "user" or a consumer of an application conveyed by an Human-Computer Interface, he does not behave towards the game as towards an object; What defines the player, and what defines the playful character, is that he/she is inside the game and takes seriously the purposes of his/her game, whatever is this game. The game is not thus characterized by a factor of joke, whim or surprise, which it would be necessary to strengthen by subtleties, but, thus according to the philosopher H.G. Gadamer, the game is characterized by the implication of the player subjectivity *"which forgets himself (...)* *in and out of the game movement. (...) The player is in a world which is determined* *by the seriousness of his purposes"* (ibid). Subjectively, this definition of the playful character seems completely to characterize the serious games intended for the professionals, as for the emergency doctors training with possible operations in case of disaster (§4): the professional mission (in this particular case, to limit the number of victims) is amply the enough element for making exist the playful dimension and, the priority objective of designers will be to analyze in closer the real situations lived by the professionals, to identify and model the playful elements.

The situations being arrested by actors through their activities and their knowledge, asks the question of knowledge. Several authors explain clearly the relation between the playful and fascinating game character on one hand and the learning on the other hand, in other words, between to play and to learn. By considering the serious games as characterized by a learning aspects (memorization, personalization) and a playful aspect (motivation, interaction), the objective for [5] is to integrate the contents of learning into the playful aspect. Fabricatore [6] differentiate two ways to design the serious games by speaking about " extrinsic metaphor " - Where the playful aspect is an overlayer without relationship with the didactic contents - and about " intrinsic metaphor " - Where the learning is in the heart of the playability. Because the game is a subjective implication, we have to consider the participation as a complementary and sometimes essential vector of the learning: " I learn because I participate, because I make a commitment in an activity which offers me information elements, knowledge transformation or practices, as well by being conscious or no of educational effects of the process" [7].

The transformation of knowledge, considered as "knowledge for the action" [8] includes the contribution of knowledge through the player. The knowledge through the player brings to the collective his "added value" to know, to know-how, to comment or to initiative and to facilitate contribution when the participative and knowledge-intensive game, as we propose it, allows to collect and to capitalize these contributions. The use of the serious games presents a big interest in the development of the students' psychomotricity, the improvement of their concentration, their motivation and their self-respect. The games allow developing at player's the "skills of the XXIth century" such as innovation, critical and systematic thought, and teamwork, to have knowledge producers and not only consumers [9]. It is about the informal strategic learning, between the formal learning and the informal learning of daily life [10].

In our works, where we want in particular to evaluate the improvement of players learning when the game contains a discussion forum for players, we can lean for example on [11], which had already deduced that the conversations in the forum will contribute to return the learners masters of their learning and to favor the passage of the transmissive model of knowledge towards the collaborative model of learners communities.

From the view point of serious games evaluation, [12] notes the difficulty of the operation, the evaluations of educational objectives achievement which cannot be totally reliable, because of the numerous ways that the players can understand and learn from the educational scenario: the risk (or the luck!) exist that they learn things others than planned and this author prefers to speak about " educational intentions " rather than about " educational objectives ". Frasca [13] explain that "designer can suggest a set of rules, but it is always players who have the last word".

Le Marc [14] note that in the games, based on the players actions and their decisions, the players are not passive and do not undergo the situation. They act and are in the center of the game. The game exists with the help of players, who create their own values according to their choices and actions. This context allows them to rely on their own appreciations and to build, themselves, their own experiences and knowledge.

3   Participative, Knowledge-Intensive Games

3.1   The Game as a Participative Space

In agreement with Computer Supported Cooperative Work [8][19], and "Social Semantic Web" approaches [15][16] the co-design must be also accompanied by the construction of semantic structures of actors such as "maps" of their knowledge in connection with their practices. It allows actors themselves to map the shared items and to organize their space of cooperation even "to appear" this organization in continuous process.

The space of "participative" serious game is for us a co-designed space and which has to propose rich functions. He has to allow not only confronting massively multiple players that use existing objects of this space, but also that the space of the game can be easily co-built by a wide group, by an addition, a modification and a discussion of new objects, knowledge and rules. The space of the game is thus participative at the same time for the group of players and for that of designers. These two groups are not divided up moreover totally: certain players, for example most experimented or creative, having the idea of improvements or new services, could be urged to join the group of designers or tend to press on him to obtain changes.

The possibility of "participation architectures", ambitious for the virtual universes, was consolidated by the success of applications like Wikipedia or more generally Web 2.0 applications [17]. But the realization of similar architectures for serious games still raises numerous problems, because it is necessary at the level of infrastructure to take into account the large number of players, to introduce a certain flexibility to take into account contributions of the multiple actors (players and designers). Furthermore, the actors have to cross their skills in situations for which knowledge and data are very numerous and strongly evolutionary, that is the case in games, where scenes and their items are numerous.

The figure 1 illustrates the infrastructure and the participative aspects at the level of both communities: co-designers and players. At the infrastructure level, Knowledge Organization System records the game items, the exchanged messages by actors, etc. The authorized actors can look, add, catalog, discuss, comment items. Intermediate plan is the one of the game. From the game, players can look and comment items.

We propose that designers and players share a permanent unique discussion forum, with possibility of filtering the messages (see Fig.3 and Fig.5) and with differentiated rights (see Fig.4) because designers and players do not have always the same priorities. But in the Serious Game contexts, it is possible to use "Open Source" Communities' well-established principles, by considering that designers' and gamers' communities as mature ones.

The actors must be able to discuss on any object of the game or every rule connected to an object, in particular when the game is used, because at this moment the differences of interpretation, opinions and approaches are the easiest to express and to discuss. The game has to base, on one hand, on a database cataloging and returning easily accessible and editable game items (including rules, designed as editable contents elements) and on the other hand the forum.

If we consider a game scene, this one is going to be constituted at first by knowledge elements and rules specified by trainers and designers, for example rules governing the penalty of an action on an object in terms of "points". Then, the scene is going to be played and the rules instantiated. The designers have to specify on one hand rules and items of the game, and on the other hand rules of the educational evaluation included in this game (in particular values such as the number of won or lost points, which are visible to the learner, facilitating in particular his motivation in game, his auto training, etc.).

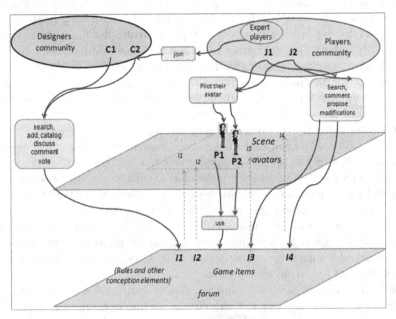

Fig. 1. Actors' participation in game and in knowledge organization system

The architecture of the software platform we want to propose to the designers has to allow editing these diverse specifications, finding easily knowledge, discussing them item by item, reaching the moderate values of attributes, etc. From their part, the players also can look for items and use them to treat assimilate and comment them - for example to confront their experiences, exchange hints and tips. It will be interesting that the players can reach certain parts of the designers' forum.

Via the forum, the learners can discuss, between them and with the designers, in an asynchronous way, on the rules of an action, the won and the loss of points, know and criticize the reason of this rule, etc. In the forum a mark allows to spot if messages are posted by a player or by a designer; the designers can, if they wish it, mask some of their exchanges to the players.

4   Illustration on the "Aidcrisis" Project

Our architecture, for the participative and knowledge-intensive serious games design, is developed in the perspective of a project Aidcrisis, described below.

4.1   Scientific Approach

Started in 2011, the Aidcrisis project [18], led by the University of Technology of Troyes in association with the Emergency service of Troyes Hospital (see Fig.2a), concerns the management of NRBCE[1] crisis situations on the territory of the Aube department (France). One of the modules of this project concerns e-training of the emergency staffs (doctors, ambulance drivers, nurses etc.) and joins in the approach described in this paper. In the Aidcrisis project, the experiences of accident treatment case or disaster are the object of a collection and an analysis leading, through the architecture we propose, in the specification of scenes facilitating the training of emergency staffs in the decisions and in the operations in the crisis cases.

In Aidcrisis, numerous factors plead for the use of the approach of participative and knowledge-intensive serious game: the cases of possible disasters although unlikely (but requiring for the emergency staffs to get ready for it) are very numerous, especially if we consider the conjunction of unforeseen factors or crossed causes of NRBCE / natural disasters. The real exercises are very expensive and difficult to organize. And even if we want to proceed to virtual exercises with a classic approach of serious game, because of the current cost of the development of the game sequences, we could treat only some tens or hundreds of scenarios, what would not allow facing real stakes in the preparation for real risk.

The answer is to co-design the details specifications with and by the persons in charge of training at the emergency medical service, to benefit from the proposed interaction systems (sharing of specifications, designers forum, game forum), to give the system, master to persons in charge of the emergency trainings so they can develop easily any new scenario. Our objective is to prepare these professionals to be auto-

---

[1] NRBCE: Nuclear Radioactive Biological Chemical Explosive.

nomous in the imagination of new cases and in the production of the new associated scenes (or variants of the existing scenes) based on their fine knowledge of the domain and their educational priorities.

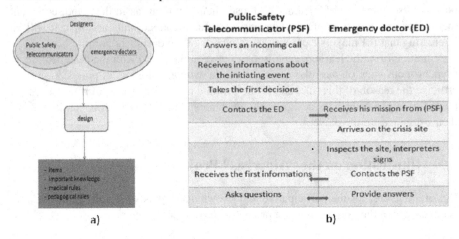

Public Safety Telecommunicator (PSF)	Emergency doctor (ED)
Answers an incoming call	
Receives informations about the initiating event	
Takes the first decisions	
Contacts the ED	Receives his mission from (PSF)
	Arrives on the crisis site
	Inspects the site, interpreters signs
Receives the first informations	Contacts the PSF
Asks questions	Provide answers

a)   b)

Fig. 2. A serious game for the Aidcrisis project a) Actors of the design, b)Example of scenario

4.2   Usage of the Forum by the Co-designers

The proposed architecture is going to offer to the designers a working system which articulates:

- A specification system directed to a teamwork susceptible to associate skills resulting from several disciplines (jobs of expertise field, trainers of the field, pedagogy specialists, graphic designers and scriptwriters),
- A navigation system in the game objects (this point is particularly crucial in the applications of knowledge-intensive in game, which contain numerous objects and rules),
- A discussion forum type (see mock-up below, Fig.4).

In the complex domains (sustainability, crisis management…) actors think and act locally according to rules which can depend on places, on seasons or on other factors. That is why for a designer who builds objects and rules of a scene, it is important to have design forum for the discussion between peers.

In the Aidcrisis project, designers are Emergency Doctors (ED) and Public Safety Telecommunicators (PSF). They co-design rules for every item. Each rule consists of an important knowledge, a medical and pedagogical rules in the game's scene (see Fig.2b).

For example if the community adopts the principle that a rule must not have "veto" of any other designer, all designers will be invited to join the " design forum " to discuss new rules and find the necessary compromise for their implementation in the game.

The figure 3, for example, shows the rule discussion corresponding to the item "Overturned truck" (training doctors in a given crisis situation). The initial designer suggests for this item:

- On knowledge level: search if the track has danger signs like "flammable liquids stored here".
- On medical rule level: danger signs --> safety perimeter
- On pedagogical rule level: if a player thinks of danger signs, he will win 5 points.

Other designers comment, vote and give their view points during 20 days before the implementation of the first version of the rule in the game (Fig.4). After this deadline, the designers, who participated in the design forum of the current rule, form a group to discuss all the proposed modifications before the team leader confirms the first version of the rule to implement it in the game. The figure 4 shows the activity model related to the co-design of the rule.

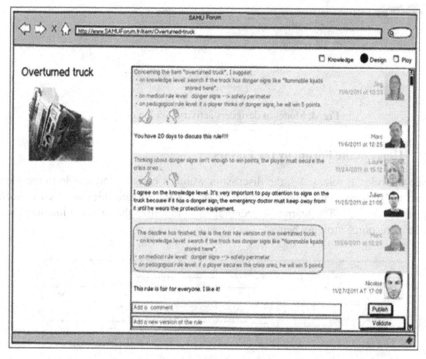

Fig. 3. Usage of the forum by designers for a participative rule (circled) concerning an "Overturned truck" *(mock-up)*

A SeeMe [19] diagram (Fig.4) is used for the roles, the activities and the entities presentation. We distinguish several roles in this model: the initial designer, the group of designers (with possibly a team leader) and the player. To note that designers have on the forum a discussion thread for every object or rule. Every time that an initial designer implements the first version of the rule, a discussion thread is opened in the forum, and actors are notified.

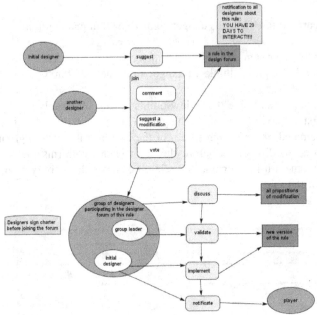

Fig. 4. Model of designers activity (SeeMe diagram)

4.3   Usage of the Forum by the Players

When the rule "is released ", the discussion which it caused is available in the game scene: we suggest to the player-learner the he can investigate rules attached to scene objects (cf. Fig. 5). The learner is encouraged to mobilize the rule and his discussion thread as resource "to play better".

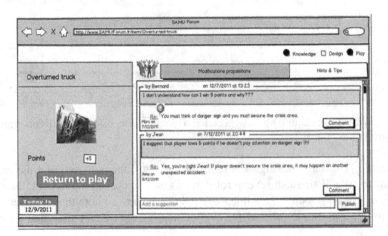

Fig. 5. Usage of the forum by players for the rule concerning an "Overturned truck" *(mock-up)*

Beyond the game rules, the learner can discover illustrated knowledge as well as related experts debates. Around the rule, the players are invited to exchange between them; "hints and tips". Complementary to the use of statistics, these "narratives" give designers more qualitative and richer returns. Finally, players can suggest improvement ideas for the game, introducing them, little by little, into the universe of designers and experts.

A designer appreciating a player proposal for changing a rule cannot alone modify this rule, because changing a rule depends on the discussion between the designers groups participating to the design forum of this rule.

To encourage players to contribute and to improve the game, they have to feel that their proposals are examined and lead to improvements in the game. That is why, regularly, the group of designers should discuss new players' proposals to decide if they reject, adopt or postpone the proposed modification of the rule.

5   Evaluation

Our objective is to evaluate our approach of the participative and knowledge-intensive serious game, by observing more particularly results concerning knowledge learned by the player-learner. We consider the hypothesis that this learning is going to be strengthened by the participative proposed forms (the game forum at the level of each of its objects). The hypotheses which we wish to confirm come, in a lineage of theoretical works, signaled in §2 on the evaluation of serious game. It considers that the conversations space of the forum helps to return learners more masters of their learning and favors the passage from transmissive model of the knowledge towards the collaborative model of communities of learners.

The proposed platform allows designing the educational evaluation elements, for example the number of points sanctioning a progress or an educational regression. Quantitatively, the evaluator can know at which moment, after which cogitation delay, with which use level of the forum, etc., the player wins or loses points, acquires an object, succeeds or fails a mission or a sub-task, etc. We wish to complete then qualitatively these measures, by the analysis of messages exchanged by the player on the forum (by using software of qualitative analysis such as Cassandre and Lasuli[2]).

In a first experience (envisaged at the end of 2012), we are interested in the learner's learning and his/her progress through the forum of game and not only through the game itself. For that purpose, the learning will be estimated by placing the learners in two configurations, without and with the discussion forum, and the results will be compared to evaluate our hypothesis: by using the game forum, we have a better learning (we will interest after in the advantages that can also present the forums for designers).

To interpret the experience, we will base on different variables got by the software platform that we are presently building. The platform will constitute the players trac-

---

[2] See http://www.hypertopic.org

es, as the time spent by the player on each task, the won / lost points for every action according to the designers' rules and the discussion threads in the game forum. The participants will play and, for those of the second group (only who wish it) they can use the available time to express themselves and discuss (in their group) via the forum. The analysis of these traces allows the control and the regulation of the learning activity [20]. The observation based on traces will also be an important factor to estimate the quality of the learning scenario [21] and to evaluate the influence of the scene components in the players disturbance or in the help to achieve their objectives.

The output data of this evaluation interest us as researchers confronted with the first necessity of evaluating our proposal of "participative and knowledge-intensive serious game ". But, in a continuous improvement approach of contents and quality, these outputs interest as well, designers and trainers to specify the game, to develop it and to increase continuously the relevance for a given public.

6   Conclusion and Perspectives

In this paper, we specified the notion of massively participative and knowledge-intensive serious games, we proposed to experiment hypotheses such as the improvement of leaning when using gamers' forums. We indicated on an example how rules and game objects could be discussed by stakeholders, and why this solution is the most suitable to build such advanced games services

To complete our project, we are presently designing the experimental software platform ARGILE (Architecture for Representations, Games, Interactions, and Learning among Experts) including especially the Forum and the Knowledge Organisation System. This work plan for the architecture implementation will allows us to validate gradually certain underlying hypotheses in our proposal. The current stages include in particular the setting-up of the mock-ups of forum solutions presented in the present paper, and of the graphical editor. We wish as soon as possible to realize the experience proposed in §5. We also want to imply groups of non-IT specialists' co-designers - within the framework of the Aidcrisis project, - , so they define scenes, create and modify them continuously, according to the proposed rapid prototyping and co-building method.

References

1. Cahier, J.P., El Mawas, N., Bénel, A., Zhou, C.: Web 2.0 & Serious Game: Structuring knowledge for participative and educative representations of the City. In: International Conference on Smart and Sustainable City, Shanghai, July 6-8 (2011)
2. Blunt, R.: Do serious games work? Results from three studies. eLearn Magazine (December 1, 2009)
3. Ibrahim, R., Jaafar, A.: Using educationnal games in learning introductory programming: A pilot study on students' perceptions. In: Conf. IADIS "Game and Entertainment Technologies 2010", Freiburg, Germany, July 27 (2010)

4. Natkin, S., Dupire, J.K.: Proceedings of 8th International Conference Entertainment Computing - ICEC 2009, Paris, France, September 3-5. Springer (2009)
5. Gadamer, H.G.: Truth and method (2nd rev. ed.) (J. Weinsheimer & D. G. Marshal, Trans.). Continuum, New York (original work published 1975) (1989)
6. Fabricatore, C.: Learning and Videogames: an Unexploited Synergy. In: 2000 AECT National Convention - a Recap. 2000 AECT National Convention. Springer Science + Business Media, Long Beach, Secaucus (2000)
7. Brougère, G.: "Using the Concept of Participation to Understand Intercultural Experience and Learning", communication au séminaire international "Research on peace education in multilingual and intercultural contexts: the CISV case". Université de Modène, Italie (mars 27, 2009)
8. Zacklad, M.: Communities of Action: a Cognitive and Social Approach to the design of CSCW Systems. In: Proceedings of GROUP 2003, Sanibel Island, Florida, USA, pp. 190–197 (2003)
9. Gee, J.P., Schaffer, D.W.: "Looking where the light is bad: Video games and the future of assessment", Epistemic Group Working Paper, no 2010-02. University of Wisconsin-Madison (April 2010)
10. Protopsaltis, A., Pannese, L., Pappa, D., Hetzner, S.: Serious Games and Formal and Informal Learning. eLearning Papers (25) (juillet 2011)
11. Riel, M.: Cross-classroom collaboration in global learning circles. In: Star, D.S. (ed.) The Cultures of Computing, Blackwell, Oxford (1995)
12. Alvarez, J., Djaouti, D., Michaud, L.: Serious Games: Training & Teaching - Healthcare - Defence & security - Information & Communication. IDATE (juin 2010)
13. Frasca: Videogames of the oppressed: Videogames as a means for critical thinking and debate. Communication and culture. Georgia, School of Literature. Master of Information Design and Technology (2001)
14. Le Marc, C., Mathieu, J., Pallot, M., Richir, S.: Serious Gaming: From Learning Experience towards User Experience. In: ICE 2011 Conference (juillet 28, 2010)
15. Bénel, A., Zhou, C., Cahier, J.P.: Beyond Web 2.0... And Beyond the Semantic Web. In: Randall, D., Salembier, P. (eds.) From CSCW to Web 2.0: European Developments in Collaborative Design, Computer Supported Cooperative Work, pp. 155–171. Springer (2010)
16. Cahier, J.P., Ma, X., Zaher, L.H.: Document and Item-based Modeling: a Hybrid Method for Socio-Semantic Web. In: ACM Symposium on Document Engineering DocEng (2010)
17. O'Reilly, T.: What is web 2.0: Design patterns and business models for the next generation of software. Social Science Research Network (2005)
18. Matta, M., Loriette, S., Sediri, M., Nigro, J.M., Barloy, Y., Cahier, J.P., Hugerot, A.: Representing experience on Road accident Management. In: IEEE 21st International WETICE Conference, 2nd CT2CM Track (Collaborative Technology for Coordinating Crisis Management), Toulouse, France, June 25-27 (2012)
19. Herrmann, T., Hoffmann, M., Loser, K.-U., Moysich, K.: Semistructured models are surprisingly useful for user-centered design. In: Dieng, R., Giboin, A., Karsenty, L., De Michelis, G. (Hrsg.) Designing Cooperative Systems. IOC Press, Amsterdam (2000)
20. Heraud, J.-M., Marty, J.-C., France, L., Carron, T.: Helping the Interpretation of Web Logs: Application to Learning Scenario Improvement. In: Workshop AIED 2005, Amsterdam, July 18-22 (2005)
21. Marty, J.-C., Heraud, J.-M., Carron, T., France, L.: A quality approach for collaborative learning scenarios. Learning Technology Newsletter of IEEE Computer Society 6(4), 46–48 (2004)

Towards Designing for Competence and Engagement in Serious Games

Erik D. van der Spek

Department of Industrial Design, Eindhoven University of Technology, The Netherlands
e.d.vanderspek@tue.nl

Abstract. Through a series of game design experiments evidence was found signifying the importance of feeling competence as a driver for engagement during gameplay. Engagement during gameplay is important both as a motivation to play games, as well as for serious games to improve cognitive interest and thereby the learning efficacy of the game. Consequently, a number of design guidelines are proposed, both on the local and global level of the game, to enhance the feeling of competence and thereby engagement of the game.

Keywords: game design, designing for competence, engagement, serious games, experiential learning, self-determination theory.

1   Introduction

Little is known scientifically on how to design a serious gametomake it more efficacious in reaching its learning goals, or how design decisions impact the experienced engagement of a game. In order to shed more light on the matter I created a serious game, systematically changed things in the game design based on theories from cognitive psychology, and subsequently empirically tested the effects of these game design techniques on learning and engagement.

The game, Code Red Triage [1], was a total conversion mod of Half Life 2. In it, the player is a medical first responder that has to learn how to perform a primary triage, a prioritization procedure to categorize the victims of a mass casualty event according to urgency of needed medical attention. In the game, the player arrives at a train station and has to find the way to a subway platform, where the victims of a terrorist strike can be found scattered about. Approaching a victim, one can conjure up a triage menu with eight triage action buttons and four triage categories. The player then has to iteratively triage nineteen victims and, according to the feedback he or she gets upon selecting an action button or after triaging a victim, has to determine what the correct triage procedure is.

In total five experiments were performed with the game: one media comparison study, where the game was comparedwith a PowerPoint of the same instructional content,on learning gains and enjoyment; and four game design studies, where the effects of the introduction of game design techniques on learning and enjoyment were measured. For the game design experiments these were: the introduction of visual and

M. Ma et al. (Eds.): SGDA 2012, LNCS 7528, pp. 98–109, 2012.

auditory cues to improve the selection of relevant over irrelevant information; a comparison of different ways to introduce the instructional complexity; an adaptivity engine that let better learners progress through the game faster; and the introduction of surprising events in the game narrative to stimulate the integration of new information into prior knowledge structures [2]. Screenshots of the game can be seen in figures 1 through 3.

Fig. 1. Train station in the game

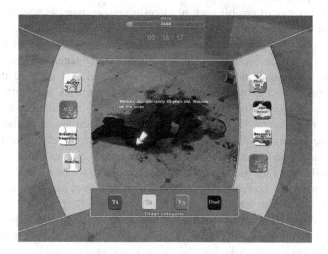

Fig. 2. Triage menu in the game with visual cue to aid the player

Fig. 3. Example of one of the experimental conditions where surprising events (in this case an explosion in a power box causing the lights to go out) were introduced

2   Engagement in Games

The purpose of the experiments was to see if simple interventions in a game's design could be discovered that, when implemented, improved the learning efficacy of the game without harming the engaging qualities thereof. This was generally successful. Visual cues were found to improve learning, but only for experienced gamers. When the game adapts to the performance of the player, determined by the in-game score, the total amount of time needed to learn the material could be significantly reduced. Lastly, the introduction of surprising events around the time something important has to be learned led to an improvement in deep learning. Curiously, none of the aforementioned experiments saw a significant effect of condition on the reported engagement (measured with the ITC-Sense of Presence Inventory [3]), or enjoyment (a single item, 10-point scale) of the game, nor was this the case for the comparison with a PowerPoint procedure.

The reason for this ostensible lack of effect on engagement is unclear. While for the purpose of the research this outcome was quite desirable, after all the main reason was to improve learning efficacy while not hindering engagement, all three of the value-added experiments were expected to influence the engagement in some way. In one experiment auditory and visual cues were provided that directed the player's attention to the correct answer (see figure 2). Guidance cues may infringe on the player's sense of agency or ownership of the game[4] and feeling in control is important for engagement [5].In addition, the bright green arrow of the visual cue could harm the feelings of presence, which in turn may negatively influence engagement [6].However, no effect on engagement was found. Nor in another experiment where the challenge of the game automatically adapted to the proficiency of the player, in that players that scored well on a certain victim case, could proceed faster to more difficult cases. The hypothesis was that this would keep players in a sense of Flow [7], but again to no avail. Similarly,it was expected that the surprising events condition (see figure 3) would be more exciting, as it was more eventful by e.g. introducing an explosion. Additionally, the serious game provided a much richer multimodal experience as well as more interaction, but was not rated as being more enjoyable than the static PowerPoint presentation. A number of explanations may be given for the lack of effect on rated engagement and enjoyment. Primarily, the participants only saw one condition and lacked a clear referent to compare it to, but the interventions could also be too subtle or the post intervention measurement scales ill-suited for measuring the effects of serious game design considerations on engagement during gameplay.

Curiously, the only experiment that did show a significant effect of the interventions on engagement and enjoyment was the one where no a priori effect was expected. This experiment was more of a pedagogical investigation into the best way of presenting the instruction. The experiment was a 2x2 design, where the introduction of *problem complexity* was contrasted with the introduction of the *option complexity* needed to overcome these problems. In colloquial terms, the victims were either presented in a progressive manner from easy to difficult (massed), or with a high variability in encountered difficulty (spaced). This was then offset to a version where the triage action buttons were introduced gradually and just-in-time, or where the player had all the buttons from the start (just-in-case).

There was a significant main effect on enjoyment for option complexity in favor of the just-in-case option complexity presentation, but more importantly, there was a significant interaction effect showing that players particularly enjoyed the combination of a just-in-case option complexity with a gradual increase in victim complexity ($F(1,51) = 4.78$, $p < 0.05$, $\eta^2 = 0.08$). See figure 4 for the graph of the enjoyment ratings over the different conditions. These results probably corroborate Self-Determination Theory [8] in games and more particular the findings of Przybylski, Rigby and Ryan [9], who found that the feeling of autonomy and competence (and to a slightly lesser extent, and less applicable when it comes to singleplayer games, relatedness) were important predictors for the enjoyment of a game. More so than the other conditions, this condition seemed to support players to feel autonomous, as they were less restricted in choosing their actions, while gradually building up a feeling of competence, as victim cases could be practiced before moving on to a more complex victim case.

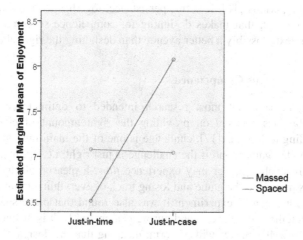

Fig. 4. The effect of option complexity x problem complexity on enjoyment ratings

Designing for autonomy in a serious game is a difficult problem; on the one hand all games provide some degree of autonomy as good games are quintessentially about experiential learning [4], on the other hand too much autonomy will infringe on the game designer's authorship of the experience [10]. This is especially relevant for serious game designers, whose main objective is to ensure that learners experience the right (educational) content in order to reach the (learning) goals of the game.True sandbox-style autonomy is subsequently impossible for most serious games and serious game designers should therefore strife to create the *illusion* of autonomy (see also [10]). With the aforementioned game Code Red Triage, it was shown that this can partially be realized by giving the player more options than necessary to overcome a problem. Another approach is to create an ostensibly open world, or open problem, but lure the player into the intended direction by making him (or her) curious for the right answer. In such a way the player will feel that his actions are his own, but still receive the intended relevant educational content.Research on how to foster curiosity through game design is for instance done in [11] and [12]. Here, I will instead focus on game design to foster a feeling of competence.

3   Designing Engagement through Competence

Engagement in games is important, for both entertainment and serious games, because it is the reason people play games and players will afford more attention to learning when optimally engaged [1], [5], [13]. Given the evidence stated in the introduction, and in line with Self-Determination Theory [8], [9], I contend that building competenceof something is one of the main reasons why people play games. In addition, feeling competent is closely related to self-efficacy, in that a person experiences personal agency and mastery over a situation [14]. Improving self-efficacy too has been linked to themotivation to play video games [15], and, like engagement, leads students to undertake challenging tasks more readily, as well as promotingpersistence over longer time periods [16]. It is this persistence, together with an increased effort and cognitive interest, that makes designing for competence so compelling. And,as will be posited next, possibly a better avenue than designing the right challenge.

3.1   Challenge versus Competence

Until now, it appears that most research intended to optimally engage players during gameplay has focused on providing the right amount of challenge to the player. According to Malone [17], challenge is one of the main intrinsically motivating factors of video games, and if the challenge is just right, i.e. optimally adjusted to a person's skill level, a player may experience *flow*, a pleasurable feeling of being completely absorbed into the game and losing track of everything around you [7].

However, in a previous experiment it was also found that players are at different skill levels when they start a game and during gameplay [2]. It is difficult to ascertain beforehand how well a player will perform, meaning that the design of a game often caters to the greatest common denominator, leading to a game that may be too difficult for some, and too easy for others. A game that is too difficult rapidly leads to disengagement from the game [17], and thereby less cognitive interest in the subject matter. A game that is too easy may lead to passive fatigue and therebydistractibility and disengagement from the task, degrading performance in the game [18].In order to counter this, various researchers and game companies have experimented with a dynamic difficulty adjustment (DDA) [19] that adapts the difficulty and challenge of the game to the proficiency of the player, with the purpose to keep players in theaforementioned sense of flow [7], [20].

There are multiple ways in which the desired flow state in games has been depicted as a measure of a player's skill in relationship to the challenge of the game [21], but most take the approach of figure 5, where one can also see that a challenge that is too great leads to anxiety in the player and a challenge that is too small to boredom. The added benefit of this approach is that it can be used as a way to show a game's ideal difficulty progression; something that has been done by McGinnis et al. [22]. As games are about learning and practicing new skills to overcome challenges, most games will lead to the player improving in skill as the game progresses; therefore the game's difficulty should increase accordingly, to keep the player from becoming bored or anxious. The graph showing the ideal game difficulty progression as hypothesized by [22] can be seen in figure 6.

While the approach of using DDA to keep players optimally challenged and within the hypothetical flow channel definitely has merit, there are a number of problems with it. For instance, not only are some game genres more conducive to flow than others, the personality of the player moderates the effect as well, where e.g. low-skilled but playfully minded players do not experience flow when confronted with a high challenge, whereas players that have a low level of playfulness do [24]. This is something a game designer has little control over.

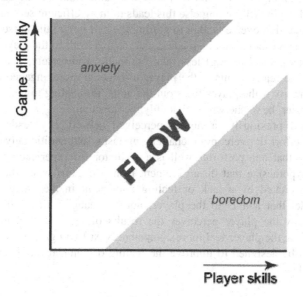

Fig. 5. Flow as a measure of player skills and game difficulty, adapted from [23]

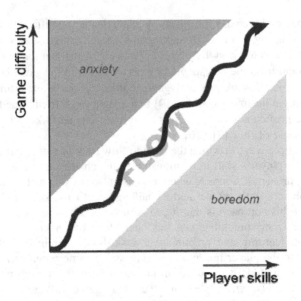

Fig. 6. Ideal game difficulty progression adapted from [22], superimposed on the flow model

Even if one factors out flow and just wishes to adjust the challenge to a player's skill level to create a more fun experience, this may not be the best way to approach the problem. Firstly, the idea that difficulty governs whether players become engaged or not, does not explain why some difficult games are considered highly frustrating while other, perhaps even more difficult games are applauded for this characteristic. Secondly, while an argument could be made that games that are too easy should be made more challenging (if nothing else this leads to more efficient serious games [2]), I would argue that the reverse is akin to putting the cart before the horse. If the game is too hard, the game should not be made easier, as this leads to the player performing (and in a serious game learning) less than optimally. Conversely, if a game is too difficult, what one really wants is the player to become more engaged at these moments. What's more, if the player finds out the game is adapting to his or her failures and becomes easier, he or she will feel doubly incompetent.

As mentioned previously, a higher perceived self-efficacy leads to someone investing more effort in overcoming challenging tasks, and additionally it was found that discovering that one performs well is a predictor for experiencing flow [24]. I consequently hypothesize that disengagement from the game when the challenge is too highis precipitated by a lack of feeling competent in the game. Therefore, I propose a model that adapts to the player, not by changing the challenge, but by changing the way the player perceives the results of his or her actions, with the purpose of making the player feel more competent.Next I will give a few examples of how games can be designed to improve the feeling of competence, both on thelocal and global level.

3.2   Competence on the Local Level

A recent commercial-off-the-shelf(COTS) entertainment game that is notorious for being extremely difficult, but without deterring players and in fact receiving accolades for it [25], is the game *Dark Souls*.In this game the player is an undead knight in a gothic fantasy world who ventures out to perform quests, and has to defeat many very difficult adversaries on the way. The player typically starts from a bonfire area, which is also his last save location. Should the player die during an encounter with a monster, he is transported back to this bonfire area. Other bonfire spots can be found along the way and upon lighting the fire, the game saves the player's progress, making this the next 'respawn' point. It is not unusual for the player to die before reaching the next bonfire however, and dying many times over. Sometimes a player can spend hours playing the game and then turn off the game console without having progressed in the game world. While this may be enough to never touch a game again, Dark Souls does something interesting. As the player defeats enemies, he is awarded experience points that make his character stronger, and the enemies occasionally drop 'loot', i.e. new weapons and items. Unlike other games, dying and being reverted to the last save state does not make the player lose these things. So in effect, while the game is punishing the player for not performing well enough, which should negatively impact his competence, it also rewards the player with things that should make him feel stronger and thereby more competent. The secret to Dark Souls success may well be in part explained by this mechanic.A solution to mitigate a possible decrease of perceived competence when a player dies (and thereby disengage the player) could therefore be to reward them with something that increases the competence of the player character.

In an experiment on course design for learning division problems, Schunk found that if you gave children rewards that were linked to attaining preset proximal performance goals, the children performed better and reported a higher degree of self-efficacy than conditions where they only received rewards for completion, or when they were only given the goals [26]. At some moments in a game it may be advisable to delayrewards or feedback to a player action because it allows for learning strategies [27] or to improve curiosity [28], but in cases where the player might feel incompetent due to failing, it may be prudent to adaptively shorten the timing for rewards and increase the value of the reward. In this way, the player still suffers fail states but cansimultaneously still experience that his actions do have a desired outcome. Likewise, negative feedback can stimulate people with high self-efficacy to perform well, but if a player's feeling of competence is negatively affected by a game due to high challenge, the game should switch to more positive feedback in order to improve the player's self-efficacy and thereby engagement during the game [29].

3.3   Competence on the Global Level

In figure 6 it was shown that a game should ideally adapt the challenge to the skills of the player, to facilitate optimal engagement and flow. This notion was implemented in the COTS entertainment game *The Elder Scrolls: Oblivion*. In this game, the player is a hero that is free to explore a vast medieval fantasy world with cities and dungeons. As the game progresses and the player defeats enemies, his character will increase in experience and strength. The player will typically encounter enemies in the dungeons, but because the player is free to roam the world in any direction, it is likely that he encounters enemies that are too strong for him at that moment in the game. Therefore the game had an adaptation engine where the enemies' strengthwas always automatically set at around the same level of strength as the player. This should have led to an optimal challenge level throughout the game, but after the game was released this adaptation engine was widely criticized by gamers [30]. The rationale behind the criticism was that players no longer felt a sense of increasing competence as the game progressed. After many hours of playing the game, they felt little sense of achievement, as they were still as competent in defeating enemies as when they started out playing.

Therefore, when one looks at the game as a whole, an improvement in perceived competence may be facilitated by adjusting the game difficulty in such a way that the game becomes easier near the end, perhaps even venturing in what according to flow theory would lead to boredom (although not for too long). The ideal difficulty progression graph may subsequently look more closely to the one in figure 7.

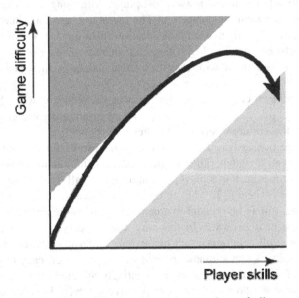

Fig. 7. Hypothetical ideal difficulty progression to enhance feeling competence

The difficulty progression in figure 7 should still be seen as very much hypothetical. It could be that the feeling of competence is boosted stronger if the game starts out easy, then suddenly spikes and subsequently levels out. On the other hand it should be noted that the peak in the difficulty progression curve could coincide narratively with an ending epiphany or feeling of catharsis. Such narrative structures not only increase self-efficacy, but also enhance constructivist learning and internalization [31].

4   Conclusion

In this paper I argued for a paradigm shift in how to design games to be more engaging, not based on providing the optimal challenge level, but based on the feeling of competence in players. An increase in the feeling of competence additionally has the added benefit of improving persistence of play and possibly multiple playthroughs of the same game.

Two levels were identified on which one can design for competence. On the local level, whenever a game is highly challenging and the player is likely to fail often, a decrease in the player's feeling of competence can be expected, which may be a main cause for players to become disengaged. Therefore the perceived competence of the player has to be boosted, for instance by (1) rewarding the player despite of death, (2) rewarding the player quicker and more often, or (3) by switching from negative to positive feedback. On the global level, the overall feeling of competence improvement as a result of playing the game may be enhanced by making the final part of the game relatively easy, for instance as a result of a narrative epiphany.

These examples of game design guidelines should by no means be considered exhaustive, nor even factual, as they are mostly still hypotheses. Rather, they are meant as new ways of thinking about (serious) game design and avenues for future research.

References

1. Van der Spek, E.D., Wouters, P., Van Oostendorp, H.: Code Red: Triage or COgnition-based DEsign Rules Enhancing DecisionmakingTRaining In A Game Environment. British Journal of Educational Technology 42, 441–455 (2011)
2. Van der Spek, E.D.: Experiments in serious game design: a cognitive approach. Doctoral dissertation. Utrecht University. SIKS Dissertation Series, vol. 2011-36 (2011)
3. Lessiter, J., Freeman, J., Keogh, E., Davidoff, J.: A Cross-Media Presence Questionnaire: The ITC-Sense of Presence Inventory. Presence: Teleoperators and Virtual Environments 10, 282–297 (2001)
4. Gee, J.P.: Learning and Games. In: Salen, K. (ed.) The Ecology of Games: Connecting Youth, Games, and Learning, pp. 21–40. MIT Press, Cambridge (2008)
5. Garris, R., Ahlers, R., Driskell, J.E.: Games, Motivation, and Learning: A Research and Practice Model. Simulation & Gaming 33, 441–467 (2002)
6. Tamborini, R., Skalski, P.: The Role of Presence in the Experience of Electronic Games. In: Vorderer, P., Bryant, J. (eds.) Playing Video Games Motives Responses and Consequences, pp. 225–240. Lawrence Erlbaum Associates (2006)
7. Sweetser, P., Wyeth, P.: GameFlow: A Model for Evaluating Player Enjoyment in Games. Computers in Entertainment 3, 1–24 (2005)
8. Ryan, R.M., Deci, E.L.: Self-determination theory and the facilitation of intrinsic motivation, social development, and well-being. American Psychologist 55, 68–78 (2000)

9. Przybylski, A.K., Rigby, C.S., Ryan, R.M.: A motivational model of video game engagement. Review of General Psychology 14, 154–166 (2010)
10. Tanenbaum, K., Tanenbaum, J.: Agency as commitment to meaning: communicative competence in games. Digital Creativity 21, 11–17 (2010)
11. Wouters, P., Oostendorp, H.V., Boonekamp, R., Van der Spek, E.D.: The role of Game Discourse Analysis and curiosity in creating engaging and effective serious games by implementing a back story and foreshadowing. Interacting with Computers 23, 329–336 (2011)
12. Habgood, M.P.J.: Endogenous fantasy and learning in digital games. Simulation & Gaming 36, 483–498 (2005)
13. Dickey, M.D.: Engaging By Design: How Engagement Strategies in Popular Computer and Video Games Can Inform Instructional Design. Educational Technology Research and Development 53, 67–83 (2005)
14. Gecas, V.: The social psychology of self-efficacy. Annual Review of Social Psychology 15, 291–316 (1989)
15. Klimmt, C., Hartmann, T.: Effectance, self-efficacy, and the motivation to play video games. In: Vorderer, P., Bryant, J. (eds.) Playing Video Games: Motives, Responses, and Consequences, pp. 133–145. Lawrence Erlbaum Associates, Mahwah (2006)
16. Zimmerman, B.: Self-Efficacy: An Essential Motive to Learn. Contemporary Educational Psychology 25, 82–91 (2000)
17. Yun, C., Shastri, D., Pavlidis, I., Deng, Z.: O' Game, Can You Feel My Frustration?: Improving User' s Gaming Experience via StressCam. In: Proceedings of the CHI Conference, pp. 2195–2204 (2009)
18. Matthews, G., Warm, J.S., Reinerman, L.E., Langheim, L.K.: Task Engagement, Attention, and Executive Control. In: Gruszka, A., Matthews, G., Szymura, B. (eds.) Handbook of Individual Differences in Cognition, pp. 205–230. Springer, New York (2010)
19. Lopes, R., Bidarra, R.: Adaptivity Challenges in Games and Simulations: a Survey. IEEE Transactions on Computational Intelligence and AI in Games 3, 85–99 (2011)
20. Shute, V.J., Ventura, M., Bauer, M., Zapata-Rivera, D.: Melding the Power of Serious Games and Embedded Assessment to Monitor and Foster Learning: Flow and Grow. In: Ritterfeld, U., Cody, M., Vorderer, P. (eds.) Serious Games: Mechanisms and Effects, pp. 295–321. Routledge, New York (2009)
21. Nakatsu, R., Rauterberg, M., Vorderer, P.: A New Framework for Entertainment Computing: From Passive to Active Experience. In: Kishino, F., Kitamura, Y., Kato, H., Nagata, N. (eds.) ICEC 2005. LNCS, vol. 3711, pp. 1–12. Springer, Heidelberg (2005)
22. McGinnis, T., Bustard, D.W., Black, M., Charles, D.: Enhancing E-Learning Engagement Using Design Patterns from Computer Games. In: First International Conference on Advances in Computer-Human Interaction, pp. 124–130. IEEE (2008)
23. Chanel, G., Rebetez, C., Bétrancourt, M., Pun, T.: Boredom, engagement and anxiety as indicators for adaptation to difficulty in games. In: Proceedings of the 12th International Conference on Entertainment and Media in the Ubiquitous Era, pp. 13–17. ACM, New York (2008)
24. Jin, S.-A.A.: "Toward Integrative Models of Flow": Effects of Performance, Skill, Challenge, Playfulness, and Presence on Flow in Video Games. Journal of Broadcasting & Electronic Media 56, 169–186 (2012)
25. Metacritic: Dark Souls, http://www.metacritic.com/game/xbox-360/dark-souls
26. Schunk, D.H.: Enhancing self-efficacy and achievement through rewards and goals: Motivational and informational effects. Journal of Educational Research 78, 29–34 (1984)

27. Butler, D.L., Winne, P.H.: Feedback and self-regulated learning: A theoretical synthesis. Review of Educational Research 65, 245–281 (1995)
28. Loewenstein, G.: The psychology of curiosity: A review and reinterpretation. Psychological Bulletin 116, 75–98 (1994)
29. Hattie, J., Timperley, H.: The Power of Feedback. Review of Educational Research 77, 81–112 (2007)
30. Bostan, B., Ogut, S.: Game challenges and difficulty levels: lessons learned From RPGs. In: Proceedings of the International Simulation and Gaming Association Conference (2009)
31. Dede, C.: The Evolution of Constructivist Learning Environments: Immersion in Distributed, Virtual Worlds. Educational Technology 35, 46–52 (1995)

Blended In-Game and Off-Game Learning: Assimilating Serious Games in the Classroom and Curriculum

Tim Marsh[1], Li Zhiqiang Nickole[2], Eric Klopfer[3], and Jason Haas[3]

[1] James Cook University, QLD, Australia
`tim.marsh@jcu.edu.au`
[2] Ubisoft, Singapore
`fenris@singnet.com.sg`
[3] Massachusetts Institute of Technology, MA, USA
`{klopfer,jhaas}@MIT.edu`

Abstract. This paper describes a comparative study to investigate the efficacy of interactive games, non-interactive media and traditional instructional teaching on mathematics and science learning with high school students (aged 13-14). Utilizing a blended in-game (narrative and puzzle games) and off-game (machinima/animation and teacher) learning approach to assess the efficacy, together with survey of teachers' opinions on the introduction of serious games and blended learning approaches, the results shed some light on the integration / assimilate of serious games into the classroom and curriculum.

Keywords: Narrative, Puzzle, Games, Learning, Machinima, Analysis.

1 Introduction

We describe the final study of a two-year research and development project carried out as part of the Singapore-MIT GAMBIT Game Lab to investigate the role of narrative in puzzle-based learning games and their effect on students' engaged learning experience. In previous work we have described the development of our puzzle and narrative-based games, and results from studies to compare their effectiveness for students to learn about aspects of physics (displacement and velocity) and motion graphing [1, 2]. Building on this previous research the focus of this paper is in comparing our games with other teaching resources in typical classroom settings, and blending serious games with other teaching and learning resources in the classroom.

We describe a comparative study to investigate the efficacy of interactive games, non-interactive media and traditional teacher-led face-to-face instruction on mathematics and science learning with high school students. In addition, we describe qualitative results from a follow-up survey with teachers from the Singapore high school, to show their opinions and preferences about introducing serious games in the classroom and blending with other teaching materials and resources. Utilizing a blended in-game (narrative and puzzle games) and off-game (animation/machinima and teacher) learning approach, the learning results together with the teachers' opinions/preferences, help shed light on the integration and assimilation of serious games into the classroom and curriculum.

M. Ma et al. (Eds.): SGDA 2012, LNCS 7528, pp. 110–122, 2012.

This paper is organized as follows. We first describe the development of our puzzle and narrative-based games, the animation/machinima and teachers' lesson plan, each with identical learning objectives (to learn about aspects of displacement, velocity, and motion graphing) and similar content (constrained by media type). Next we describe the study conducted in a Singapore high school with 58 students and survey of 20 teachers, and present the results. This is followed by discussion and conclusion section. The research described herein helps shed some light on the very important but little investigated area to integrate and assimilate serious games into the classroom and curriculum. While our comparative studies can be considered as preliminary research in this direction, they provide interesting results and suggest directions for further empirical testing in this area.

2   Game, Animation/Machinima and Lesson Development

We first describe the development work carried out in order to investigate the efficacy of narrative and narrative in puzzle-based games, non-interactive media and traditional instructional teaching, both on their own and in blended learning set-ups/lesson plans in a Singapore High School.

2.1   Puzzle and Narrative in Puzzle-Based Learning Games

The learning games used in the study was based on the game Waker 1.0, developed for our research project through the Singapore-MIT GAMBIT Game Lab [3]. It is a platform-based puzzle game wrapped in a narrative. The narrative, told in cutscenes and voiceovers, largely at the beginning, in-between levels and at the end of the game, tells of a child's broken dream and provides the game objective to fix broken pathways and journey through levels of the dream world to release the child from her dream. The puzzle (2011) or abstract version of the game is essentially Waker 1.0 with the voiceover narrative and cutscenes removed [3]. In this version, the game starts immediately with no introduction or guidelines and players have to figure out the gameplay/game mechanics, with no clues about the connection to displacement or velocity (see figure 1).

 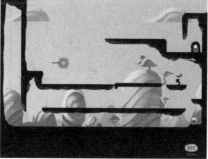

Fig. 1 & 2. Screenshot of puzzle & narrative in puzzle game

The core puzzle gameplay / game mechanic for both the puzzle and narrative versions of the game is to figure out how to construct appropriately inclined paths that will enable the player to move up through levels (in the y-axis) by moving a corresponding direction, distance and speed along the x-axis. Path construction is akin to a constructionist learning approach. Path construction also provides the learning goals – to learn about motion graphing and aspects associated with the physics concepts of displacement and velocity. After only short gameplay, path construction became intuitive for players and as the game proceeds gameplay becomes progressively more complex.

Shown in figure 2, is the narrative version of the game, referred to as Waker 2.0 (2011) [3]. This is essentially Waker 1.0 with extended instructional design features and in particular, the topic of learning was interwoven with an extended narrative/story and narrated by an off-screen character - the child trapped inside her dream. In this way the character's purpose is firstly, as part of the storyline and secondly, as learning partner/assistant. The extended Waker 2.0 version increased both the fun *and* learning in comparison to Waker 1.0 and the Puzzle only versions of the game. Refer to [1, 2] for more details of the comparative study results to test the efficacy of Waker 1.0, Waker 2.0 and Puzzle game.

2.2   Animation/Machinima

Figure 3 shows a screenshot of the time-based linear video presentation consisting of animated graphics and text superimposed onto captured sections/machinima of the Waker 2.0 game [4]. In addition, new animated sections were created in order to illustrate more difficult concepts. As shown in figure 4, in order to do this, storyboards and a script for the voiceover were first developed. The voiceover provided a description of how the game relates to the learning topics: motion graphing, displacement, velocity and acceleration. Music from Waker was dubbed over the entire video. Limited interactivity enabled students to view/review the machinima at their own pace using pause, stop, rewind and forward features. As a reminder, at the end of the video presentation, the voiceover encouraged students to go back and review the machinima.

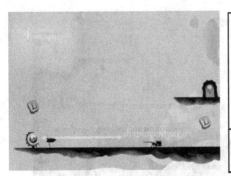

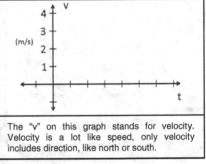

The "v" on this graph stands for velocity. Velocity is a lot like speed, only velocity includes direction, like north or south.

Fig. 3. Machinima Screenshot   **Fig. 4.** Machinima storyboards and script

2.3   Teacher-Led Instructional Lesson

Taken from the machinima storyboards and script, and based on sthe Waker 2.0 game, we developed a script and slides for the teacher-led sessions, as shown in figure 5. Teacher sessions were conducted just like regular instructional everyday classes (akin to a lecture) followed by short question and answer session between students and teacher. The topics covered in the teacher lecture session and machinima were as far as possible the same, based on the learning topics and objectives of the Waker 2.0 game but were constrained by characteristics of the teaching/learning approach.

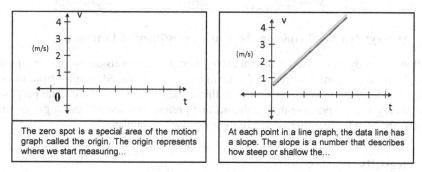

Fig. 5. Slides from teacher-led instructional session

3   Study

The study was conducted at the Hwa Chong Institution, High School, Singapore. A total of 58 students participated in the study, of which none had been previously exposed to the physics concepts of displacement, velocity and acceleration. Any understanding they acquired would be directly related to their experiences during exposure to the learning materials. Students were divided into 8 groups as shown in Table 1. In their various groups, the students were exposed to learning materials, followed by a questionnaire to assess their understanding of motion graphs, displacement, velocity and acceleration. In reference to table 1, four groups (1 to 4) were exposed to just one learning material followed by the questionnaire, and four groups (5 to 8) were exposed to a version of the game (puzzle or narrative), followed by off-game learning material (teacher-led or machinima/video) and then the questionnaire. The wording of questions was amended accordingly to fit with the teaching and learning material. For example, as seen in the results section, in the game versions students controlled a cat-like figure representing the Waker; and all questions related to its movement in the game and the resulting graphs. Likewise, in the machinima version, the cat-like figure was animated and all questions related to it and the resulting graphs. In the teacher session, the lecture talked about a creature called Waker and its movement and the resulting graphs.

Table 1. Group assignment of students

Group	Study Session Sequence		
1	Video	Questionnaire	
2	Waker 2.0	Questionnaire	
3	Teacher	Questionnaire	
4	Puzzle	Questionnaire	
5	Puzzle	Video	Questionnaire
6	Puzzle	Teacher	Questionnaire
7	Waker 2.0	Video	Questionnaire
8	Waker 2.0	Teacher	Questionnaire

3.1 Survey: Teachers' Opinions Serious Games/Blended Learning

A follow on study was conducted with 20 teachers from various disciplines from the Hwa Chong Institution. The years of teaching experience varied ranging from completely new teachers to veterans with over thirty years under their belts. The purpose of the survey was to evaluate their opinions and preferences towards using games for learning and blended learning as part of their regular lesson plan.

4   Results

4.1   Efficacy

Correct answers in the questionnaire were scored with a 1, while incorrect answers scored 0. In reference to Table 2 below, the results were then ranked according to highest mean percentage of correct answers. From Table 2, the Waker 2.0 (narrative in puzzle game) groups performed better on the whole than the puzzle game groups, with the Waker 2.0 groups clustering at the top 4 places. This suggests the efficacy of Waker 2.0 at improving students' understanding of the learning topics over students who used the puzzle game.

Table 2. Group Efficacy Ranked by Mean Percent (%)

Rank	Group	Study Session Sequence			Mean %
1	7	Waker 2.0	Video	Questionnaire	53.1%
2	2	Waker 2.0	Questionnaire		52.8%
3	1	Video	Questionnaire		44.9%
4	8	Waker 2.0	Teacher	Questionnaire	44.0%
5	6	Puzzle	Teacher	Questionnaire	43.9%
6	5	Puzzle	Video	Questionnaire	42.0%
7	4	Puzzle	Questionnaire		35.7%
8	3	Teacher	Questionnaire		35.7%

Table 3 below shows the results of the questionnaire. It comprises the breakdown of the 14 questions contributing to the final mean scores of each group as seen on the leftmost column of the table. A one-way ANOVA was carried out on the questionnaire results to evaluate differences between groups.

Table 3. Mean Percent (%) of Correct Responses Across Questions

Group	Questions														
	1	2	3	4	5	6	7	8	9	10	11	12	13	14	Mean
1	57	0	71	86	57	71	86	0	29	86	0	14	43	29	45
2	75	13	100	13	38	75	100	50	13	100	88	13	25	25	53
3	0	0	88	63	25	25	38	75	25	63	75	0	25	0	36
4	100	0	71	14	57	14	57	0	14	71	43	14	14	29	36
5	38	13	88	50	50	50	100	13	0	100	88	0	0	0	42
6	43	14	86	71	0	43	86	14	0	100	100	0	29	29	44
7	86	29	100	29	29	43	86	57	14	86	86	43	14	43	53
8	33	0	100	17	50	50	83	33	0	67	67	33	33	50	44

A one-way ANOVA was run on the results of the student questionnaire. The statistically significant results are included below. As can be seen, statistically different results were observed for questions 1, 4, 8 and 11. To further explore whether the differences between groups were statistically significant in any of the ANOVAS, the Games-Howell post-hoc test was applied to the results. The Games-Howell test was chosen because the group variances were found to be unequal, and the results are shown in table 4.

Table 4. Games-Howell test results (*mean difference significant at $p<0.05$ level)

Dependent Variable	(I) Group	(J) Group	Mean Difference (I-J)	Std. Error
Question 1	2	3	.750*	.164
	7	3	.857*	.143
Question 4	1	2	.732*	.190
Question 8	1	3	-.750*	.164
	3	4	.750*	.164
Question 11	1	2	-.875*	.125
	1	3	-.750*	.164
	1	5	-.875*	.125
	1	7	-.857*	.143

In Table 4, statistically significant results of the post-hoc test are shown, indicating significant differences at $p<0.05$ between the groups for questions 1, 4, 8 and 11 (see below). All example questions shown in charts 1 to 4 below are from the games questionnaire. As shown in Table 3, no one in Group 3 (teacher only) provided the correct answer for Question 1, while 75% of Group 2 (Waker 2.0), 86% of Group 7 (Waker 2.0, Video) and 100% of Group 4 (Waker 2.0, Teacher) gave the correct answer.

1) This path was probably produced using which orb?

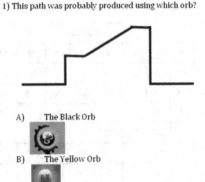

A)   The Black Orb

B)   The Yellow Orb

C)   This path is impossible to produce

Chart 1. Question 1 of questionnaire

For Question 4 below, 86% of Group 1 (Video only) answered correctly while only 13% of Group 2 (Waker 2.0) were right, as shown in Table 4.

4) Using the keyboard, a player does the following:
- Hold the left key for two seconds
- Hold the right key for two seconds

The Waker moves to the left for two seconds and then right for two seconds. If the Waker is holding the Yellow Orb, which graph is produced?

A)   B)

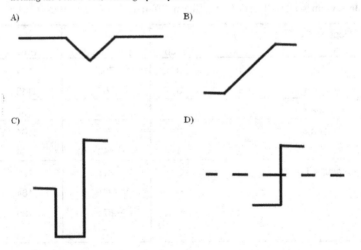

C)   D)

Chart 2. Question 4 of questionnaire

In Question 8, 75% of Group 3 (Teacher only) responded correctly while 0% of Groups 1 (Video only) and 4 (Puzzle only) were correct.

8) These paths are from a Waker holding a Yellow Orb. Which Waker reached the fastest speed while making the path?

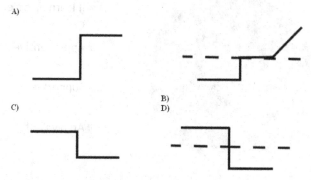

Chart 3. Question 8 of questionnaire

In Question 11, 0% of Group 1 (Video only) were correct while the other groups did much better: Group 2 (Waker 2.0 only) 88%, Group 3 (Teacher only) 75%, Group 5 (Puzzle only) 88%, Group 7 (Waker 2.0 and Video) 86%.

11) In which of the velocity graphs does the object change directions?

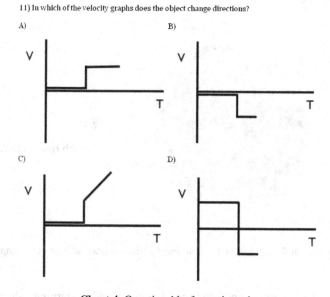

Chart 4. Question 11 of questionnaire

4.2   Survey: Teachers' Opinions

Opinions on Bringing Serious Games into the Classroom. As shown in Chart 5, most of the teachers were supportive about adopting the blended learning approach, again stating that as long as the learning objectives were met. Those who were ambivalent or apprehensive expressed concerns about the sustainability and suitability of the ICT materials.

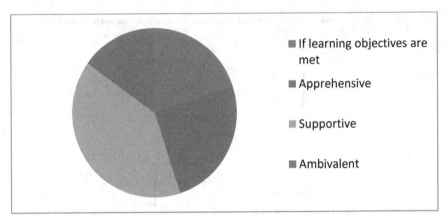

Chart 5. What are your feelings about introducing games for learning / serious games into the classroom?

Of those opposed, they were skeptical about the efficacy of games supported learning as opposed to traditional teaching methods. One response summed it up, saying, "good for starting a topic, not appropriate for depth and details".

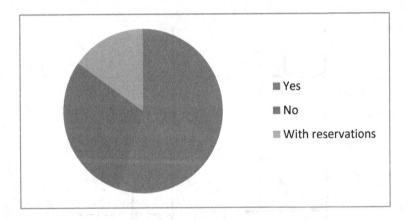

Chart 6. Do you think that games for learning / serious games will or can complement your teaching?

Again in Chart 6, most embraced the idea that blended learning can complement their teaching, but some felt that it was "...possible but have not seen a good one yet." The reservations were again about whether appropriate materials would be available for the purpose.

On Serious Games Working Alongside Traditional Teaching Methods. Just over half of the teachers (11) agreed that learning games can complement their teaching methods, while 3 had strong reservations. Concerns that were raised included whether games was suitable for learning and about whether games could lead to misconceptions.

Despite the reservations expressed, 18 of the 20 teachers thought that the students would prefer blended learning over regular teaching as shown in Chart 7.

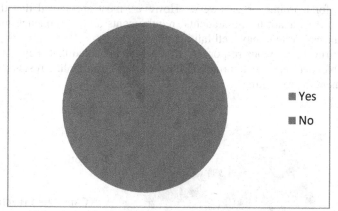

Chart 7. Do you think your students would enjoy a blended learning approach over teaching alone?

Almost all of the teachers felt students would enjoy blended learning, though one noted that not all students would be necessarily comfortable: "there are still some students that prefer traditional teaching and they mentioned that explicitly". Most also agreed that blended learning was by no means new and used fairly often in the classroom. For example, teachers specifically identified video, ICT, multi-media and the Internet being blended with the traditional teaching.

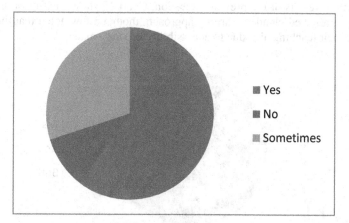

Chart 8. Do you already use a blended learning approach in your lessons? If not, do you hope to use a blended learning approach in the future and when do you hope to implement this?

Chart 8 shows that most of the respondents were already using blended learning in their lessons; those who responded that they wouldn't be using a blended learning approach did not elaborate on their reasons for not doing so.

Preferred Blended Teaching/Learning in Class. There was no general consensus on the preferred order of blended teaching methods, whether having teaching first before the games for learning, or vice versa. However, most are agreed that the teaching methods need to adapt to the students' requirements as one sequence may work in some instances, while it may well fail in others.

To confirm the previous responses, 15 teachers indicated that they did not have a preferred blended learning approach. Those who did used online resources or videos to supplement their teaching.

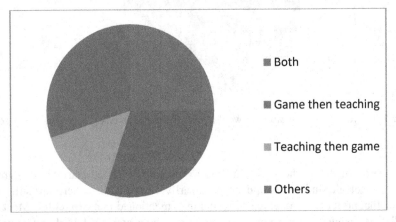

Chart 9. Of the following blended learning approaches, which do you think your students would prefer: (i) game followed by teaching or (ii) teaching followed by game? Please give reasons for your answer

To support results of the previous question, Chart 10 shows that most teachers did not have a preferred blended learning approach, though a few noted that they did use videos as their teaching aids due to accessibility of video materials.

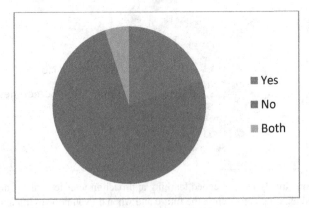

Chart 10. Do you have a preferred blended learning approach?

5   Discussion and Conclusion

Teaching experience of survey respondents varied considerably ranging from completely new teachers to veterans with over thirty years under their belts. They were generally supportive of the idea of using blended learning in their lesson and many already incorporate blended learning approach in their lessons; including blending traditional teaching with video, multi-media, the Internet and/or under the broad label ICT. One teacher summed up the advantages of blended learning by saying "the digital natives in classes can't get enough of ICT tools in class." To suggest that because students have grown up with ICT, media and computers, they are generally comfortable around and learning with/from technology. However, as one teacher indicated, we should not assume that all students have come to expect or prefer blended learning, saying that "...there are still some students that prefer traditional teaching and they mentioned that explicitly."

As far as the sequence of presentation of learning materials (e.g. game before teacher session or vice versa), there was no overall stated preference from teachers. But in general, they preferred to keep their lessons flexible, with sequences determined on a case by case basis or as one teacher stated, "[it] depends on the context". No effort was made in the study to alter the sequence of learning materials and so this is an interesting area for further investigation.

Corresponding with previous studies [1, 2], students playing Waker 2.0 (narrative in puzzle game) groups performed better on the whole than students in the puzzle game groups. Surprisingly, Waker 2.0 followed by teacher had the lowest mean percent with almost 10 percent less than Waker 2.0 followed by the video groups who were first. Even more surprising was that the teacher alone groups were in last position (almost 18% lower than Waker 2.0 with video) and that puzzle game followed by teacher group was the highest in the puzzle groups. This suggests that the two were complementary where the teacher perhaps was able to clarify or link the puzzle gameplay to learning. Of the groups that had just one teaching/learning material, Waker 2.0 had the highest percentage coming second overall, followed by the video group in third place, puzzle game and finally teacher.

Our initial expectations were that the teachers could elaborate and explain / clarify the learning better than a game or video. While this appears to be so for the puzzle game the results for Waker 2.0 groups suggest otherwise.

Indeed the mean percentage for both Waker 2.0 followed by teacher (Group 8) and Puzzle followed by teacher (Group 6) are almost identical. One possible explanation for this result is that Group 6 performed as expected, that is, the teacher's role was to further explain or link the learning with the gameplay activity and this piqued their interest in discovering what the game was about.

On the other hand, as the teacher sessions were based on the learning objectives in Waker 2.0, the students in the Waker 2.0 followed by teacher group (Group 8) could have viewed the teacher session as a summary or even repeated session, thus having the effect of dampening students' interest. However, this fails to explain why the Waker 2.0 followed by video and Waker 2.0 alone groups (Groups 7 and 2, respectively) performed better on the questionnaire.

It is possible that each teaching and learning material may be better suited to students learning different aspects about the topics. For example, the results of this study show that some groups scored 100% on some questions and zero on others. This shows that the teaching methods were highly successful in teaching the material in some instances, and fared poorly in others. One could argue that identifying dissimilar findings in the result and careful blending of materials would have better overall results.

Perhaps this could explain why Puzzle followed by teacher (Group 6) worked well: they complemented each other in some way. Follow on research should investigate this further.

While we acknowledge that group sizes are small and so our comparative studies should be considered as preliminary research in this direction, they provide interesting results and suggest directions for further empirical testing in this area.

Acknowledgements. Funding in-part provided by the Media Development Authority (MDA), Singapore through the Singapore-MIT Gambit Game Lab. Thanks to students and staff at Hwa Chong Institution, Singapore who took part in the study and survey and in particular, thanks to Ng-Ang Siew Hoon and Chan-Lim Yah Ling Rachel. Special thanks to Yeow An Gnin for help with animation/machinima development.

References

[1] Marsh, T., Li Zhiqiang, N., Klopfer, E., Chuang, X., Osterweil, S., Haas, J.: Fun and Learning: Blending Design and Development Dimensions in Serious Games Through Narrative and Characters. In: Serious Games and Edutainment Applications, ch. 14, pp. 273–287. Springer (2011a)

[2] Marsh, T., Li Zhiqiang, N., Klopfer, E., Chuang, X., Osterweil, S., Haas, J.: Fun and Learning: The Power of Narrative. In: Foundations of Digital Games 2011 (FDG 2011), Bordeaux, France (2011b)

[3] Waker 1.0 (2009); Waker 2.0 (2011) & Puzzle (2011) Game Versions. GAMBIT Game Lab, MIT: DOI=http://gambit.mit.edu/loadgame/waker.php

[4] Waker Machinima (2011), Youtube:
DOI=http://www.youtube.com/watch?v=vb0Kre0vm-I

A Computer Game Based Motivation System for Human Physiology Studies

Tintu Mathew[1], Jochen Zange[2], Joern Rittweger[2], and Rainer Herpers[1,3,4]

[1] Bonn-Rhein-Sieg University of Applied Sciences, Institute of Visual Computing,
Sankt Augustin, Germany
`tintu.mathew@smail.inf.h-brs.de`
[2] DLR Institute of Aerospace Medicine, Cologne, Germany
[3] York University, Faculty of Science and Engineering, Ontario, Canada
[4] University of New Brunswick, Faculty of Computer Science, NB, Canada

Abstract. Maximal strength testing of different muscle groups is a standard procedure in human physiology experiments. Test subjects have to exert maximum force voluntarily and are verbally encouraged by the investigator. The performance of the subjects is influenced by the verbal encouragement, but the encouragement procedure is not standardized or reproducible. To counter this problem a game-based motivation system prototype is developed to provide instant feedback to the subjects and also incentives to motivate them. The prototype was developed for the Biodex System 3 Isokinetic Dynamometer to improve the peak torque performance in an isometric knee extensor strength examination. Data analysis is performed on torque data from an existing study to understand torque response characteristics of different subjects. The parameters identified in the data analysis are used to design a shark-fish predator-prey game. The game depends on data obtained from the dynamometer in real time. A first evaluation shows that the game rewards and motivates the subject continuously over a repetition to reach the peak torque value. It also shows that the game rewards the user more if he overcomes a baseline torque value within the first second and then gradually increases the torque to reach the peak value.

Keywords: serious game, human physiology study, game based motivation system, visual encouragement.

1 Introduction

In human physiology studies subjects are often asked to perform certain exercises, eg. knee extension or flexion, hip extension or flexion etc. Those experiments are split into several repetitions which lasts just a few seconds. Therefore, subjects need to be motivated fast and reliably to perform a maximum extension or flexion. The standard procedure in those cases is verbal motivation by the investigator (in fact, the investigator is just yelling at the subject "Push harder, harder ...") . It has been shown that the performance of the subject is strongly correlated to verbal motivation by the investigator [3–8]. Therefore, it

M. Ma et al. (Eds.): SGDA 2012, LNCS 7528, pp. 123–134, 2012.

is possible that the reproducibility of the test is affected. In some cases even an investigator-dependent bias is introduced.

In the physiology laboratory at the DLR Institute of Aerospace Medicine, the Biodex System3 Isokinetic Dynamometer [1] is used for force and power diagnostics in different human muscle groups [2]. The different force and power diagnostic experiments conducted require the human subjects to exert maximum force voluntarily. The experiment heavily relies on the subject's voluntary effort as well as verbal motivation by investigator. To overcome the problems associated with the standard verbal motivation procedure a game based motivation system prototype has been designed. Computer games are known to engage people in game play for long durations and make it an enjoyable experience. It is possible to create new and interesting tasks using game- or virtual- reality-based systems. So computer games have been combined with exercising or rehabilitation equipments to provide motivation and customized training [9–15]. Taking a cue from this, a computer-game-based motivation system was developed for the dynamometer. A tailor-made game for the system can motivate the subject and also standardize the process. It will reduce the dependency on the investigator for encouragement as well as guide the subjects through the experiment.

The game-based system is expected to replace verbal encouragement by

- providing visual feedback to improve peak torque
- providing continuous motivation
- helping the user perform consistently over repetitions

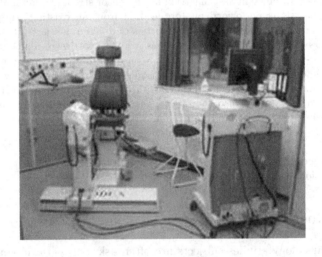

Fig. 1. Biodex Isokinetic Dynamometer

2   Game Concept and Design

The game was developed for one particular test on the dynamometer, the maximal isometric knee extension test. A test protocol will detail the specifics of the test, like the setup details of the dynamometer, the number of required visits by the subject, number of times the test is repeated in a visit (repetition) and the time between repetitions (relax interval). In the isometric mode of operation, the dynamometer maintains the velocity at zero. The subject can exert force at any selected point within the range of motion for any joint with zero velocity. For the knee extension test, a knee adapter is fixed to the dynamometer shaft. The range of motion of the leg is from 0° to 135°. The subject will push hard against the adapter. In an extension, the subject exerts force in a direction away from the dynamometer. The player controls the game by pushing on the knee adapter attached to the dynamometer. When the user pushes the knee adapter the torque exerted is obtained as a voltage signal. This signal is retrieved from the analog signal interface of the dynamometer and is transmitted to the game engine. The game engine uses this to control the movement of the characters in the game. The amount of time the player plays is lesser than conventional computer games since the studies used to estimate peak torque usually do not last more than five seconds. The player should be able to control the game effectively using the dynamometer and get immediate feedback for his actions.

The game identified for implementation is 'Bruce- The Shark'. A shark chases a school of fish in a deep sea environment (Fig. 2). The shark has to move fast and get closer to the fish using torque applied on the dynamometer. The shark must aim to catch the maximum number of fish. The game rewards the player, if he exceeds an expected level of torque, with an extra boost in speed. With this boost the shark will accelerate more and catch the last fish. After this catch the rest of the fish will move away and the shark again follows them. Every instant the user generates a desired level of torque, the action is reinforced by giving a speed boost to the shark, thereby enabling it to catch another fish. The number of fish caught reflects how well the player performed in the repetition and also in the complete visit.

Fig. 2. Game snapshot. The shark follows a school of fish. It catches the first fish when the torque exerted on the dynamometer meets an initial threshold. The threshold is increased after this. The shark will catch a fish whenever the torque meets the current threshold.

3 Data Analysis

Torque data for isometric knee extension from a previous study was analyzed to define control parameters for the game. The torque data from eight subjects over four visits was used for analysis. The data set consisted of isometric knee extension tests which lasted five seconds. In a visit, every test subject performed six contractions which lasted around five seconds with thirty second long rest intervals. The six contractions alternated between extensions and flexions.The torque response for a five second long isometric knee extension repetition is shown in Fig. 3. The torque data for extensions was considered for developing the prototype. The torque data was analyzed to find how rapidly the torque rose, how much time users took to reach peak torque in general and how the performance of the users across different repetitions was. In most repetitions subjects reached eighty percent of the peak torque within the first two seconds, since torque builds up rapidly within the first second. Subjects attained their peak torque within three to five seconds. A baseline torque value, initial threshold, is defined to compare different torque curves as well as to establish a reward system. For the data analysis step, the initial threshold is considered as eighty percent of the peak torque attained in the first repetition in the first visit of the subject. Based on the initial threshold, the torque curves were classified into the following cases.

1. Repetitions in which the subject exceeds the initial threshold.
   This case is further divided into the following three cases.
   (a) The subject goes above the initial threshold very late.
       The test subject must be motivated to cross the threshold sooner and attain higher peak torque.
   (b) The subject goes above the initial threshold and sustains it to reach the peak.
       The test subject should be motivated continuously and rewarded for the desired response.
   (c) The subject goes above the initial threshold early in the repetition but did not sustain it for long.
       The test subject should be motivated to keep pushing harder without giving up.
   (d) Repetition in which the subject crosses the initial threshold and reaches peak torque within the first two seconds.
       The subject's intrinsic motivation would have contributed more to the high peak torque. It will be challenging for the game to motivate the subject to reach peak within a short interval.
2. Repetitions in which the subject does not go above threshold.
   If the subject is not given any reward when he is exerting torque below the initial threshold, it will act as negative reinforcement which in turn encourages the subject.
3. Repetitions in which the subject goes above threshold but keeps varying the torque up and down frequently
   The game should motivate the user to continuously increase the effort without giving up in between.

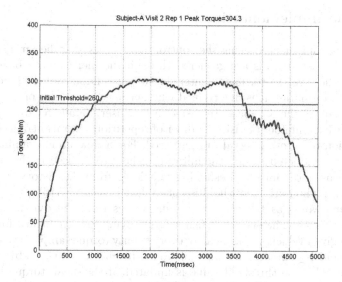

Fig. 3. Torque response for a five second long isometric knee extension test. The horizontal line indicates the initial threshold. The subject has to exert a torque above initial threshold to begin being rewarded in the game.

The control parameters identified for implementing the game are initial threshold, mean torque (mean of torque samples within a sampling interval), peak torque (maximum torque attained in a repetition) and threshold (initial threshold is adapted for every sampling interval). The initial threshold is calculated from a familiarization repetition for a new subject. For an existing subject it is calculated from the peak torques attained in previous visits. Within a visit the initial threshold is kept constant across repetitions. To understand the changes in the torque curve during, the curve is analyzed over small sampling intervals. The subject's torque response for a sampling interval will be analyzed and he will be encouraged to modify the response the next interval. The sampling interval was assumed to be 200 ms (equivalent to 20 samples). The torque values can have changing behaviors within an interval. It can have a positive gradient, a negative gradient or a mixture of both. The mean of the torque samples in the interval will reflect the torque response appropriately.

The initial threshold has to be adapted to keep the subject motivated. The current threshold was compared to the mean torque computed in the sampling intervals. The difference in mean torque of the current and previous interval is determined. The threshold can be adapted to a fraction of this value. If the mean value has increased over the intervals, the threshold can be increased to motivate the user to push harder. If the mean value has decreased, the threshold has not been reduced. In this case, the user ended up getting more rewards and it reduced the value of the rewards.

4   Game Implementation

The game is implemented using the control parameters identified from the data analysis. The user details are gathered through the menu at the beginning of the game. The investigator has to enter the subject's name and the study name. Using this information it is determined whether it is a new user or whether the user is already in the database. In case of a new user, details regarding the test protocol such as number of visits, number of repetitions, duration of a repetition and duration of a rest interval are gathered. For a new user a familiarization repetition is conducted to find the initial threshold to be used in the study. For an existing user, the initial threshold is calculated from the history available in the database. The initial threshold is not updated within a visit.

The game works as follows. The torque values from the dynamometer are read by the game. The school of fish starts moving and the shark follows the school at a given velocity. The mean of every twenty torque samples is calculated. The threshold is compared against this mean torque. Once the subject crosses initial threshold, the threshold value is updated. If the mean torque is greater than the current threshold, the threshold is updated and a catch flag is set to indicate that the user deserves a reward. Once the catch flag is set the reward algorithm is initiated. The reward algorithm compares the speed of the fish and

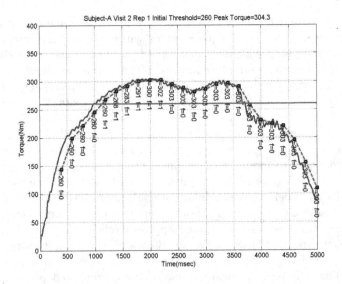

Fig. 4. Torque response for a five second long isometric knee extension test. The subject's performance is evaluated at constant time intervals (200ms), the mean torque is compared against current threshold (values next to square markers before the start of the interval). If the new mean torque is above current threshold, an eligibility for a reward is marked as f=1 and the threshold (values next to square markers at the end of the interval) is updated.

shark and gives the shark a speed boost to catch a fish. The catch flag is reset after the shark gets a fish. These steps are continued until the repetition time is over. Once the repetition time is over, the user can relax over a rest interval. A countdown is displayed during the rest interval. After the rest interval the threshold is re-initialized and the repetition continues as described above until all the repetitions for the current visit are over. Fig. 4 shows how the algorithm works for a sample torque curve.

5   Evaluation and Results

Two approaches were used for evaluation - retrospective analysis and online analysis. In retrospective analysis, the system was analyzed with existing data. i.e. The torque data from an existing study was used to run the game in offline mode. In online analysis, the subjects were asked to play the game with the dynamometer and the torque values were analyzed.

5.1   Retrospective Analysis

The behavior of the reward system was analyzed on a different existing data set from the same study. The data set contained isometric knee extension tests for eight subjects across four visits. Each visit had three five-second-long, knee extension repetitions. In the evaluation different parameters in the reward system are explored.

The game was played using the evaluation data set and the events were logged in a database. This data was later analyzed to evaluate the behavior of the

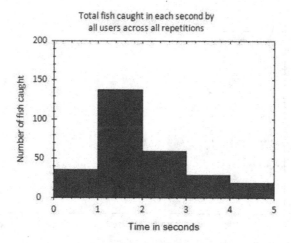

Fig. 5. Total fish caught in each second by all users across all repetitions in all visits. The number of fish caught is comparatively lesser in the first second since the first 200 to 300 ms is the torque build-up time.The user meets initial threshold towards the end of the first second.

program. A histogram was plotted to find the time duration in which more fish was caught. It showed that less number of fish is caught within the first second and the last two seconds. The relatively low number of fish caught within the first second is due to the fact that the first 200 to 300ms is the torque build-up time. The user meets the threshold and increases the torque after this. Because of the latency in reward, most of the rewards meant for the latter half of the first second is given in the next second. The lower number of fish caught in the last two seconds is because the subject is reducing the torque exerted after reaching his maximum.

Next, the influence of time taken to reach initial threshold on the total number of rewards is analyzed. A scatter plot (Fig. 6) was drawn with the time taken for a subject to meet the initial threshold against the number of fish caught. It shows that the subject is rewarded more if he meets the initial threshold within the first second. When the initial threshold is met after the second second, the rewards are lesser since the subject will not have much time to push harder and gain more rewards.

In this game relatively small number of fish was caught when the user reached peak torque fast, i.e. within the first second. A scatter plot (Fig. 7) was plotted to visualize the relation between the rewards and time taken to reach the peak. The scatter plot shows that relatively small number of fish is caught when the user reaches peak torque within the first second. This is because the threshold is adapted to the high peak torque and the user is not able to go higher than this. The scatter plot also shows an increase in the number of fish caught when the peak torque is attained after the 2 seconds. This is due to the fact that the

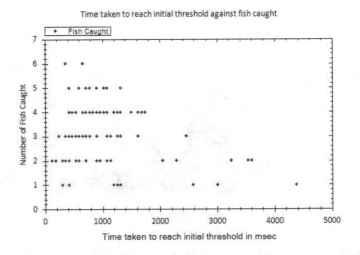

Fig. 6. Scatter plot for fish caught against time taken to reach initial threshold. The number of fish caught is greater if the user meets initial threshold early enough, here within two seconds.

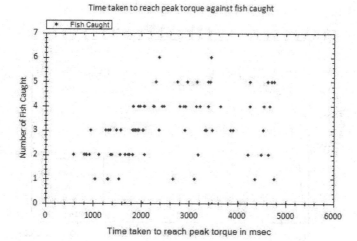

Fig. 7. Scatter plot for fish caught against time taken to reach peak torque. The number of fish caught is less when the user reached peak torque early, here within two seconds.

user increases the torque from initial threshold to peak torque gradually over a few seconds collecting rewards continuously.

The time difference between when the user deserves a reward and when he actually gets a reward is analyzed here. A histogram was plotted to show the latency across rewards in all repetitions. To be rewarded the user had to overcome the gap between the shark and fish after he was marked for a reward. This resulted in a latency in rewards. The latency is between 0 to 700ms, although in most cases it is between 100 to 400ms. There are a few events in which the user was marked for a reward but did not get it. This is because the user was marked for the reward towards the end of a repetition and the repetition ended before the user could be rewarded.

The evaluation of the game shows that the game encourages the user to improve his torque output by continuously rewarding him for any increase in torque exerted. The game also encourages a user to cross the initial threshold faster to gain more rewards. The analysis of game events shows that the game provides appropriate motivation for different torque responses, although the latency in rewards delayed the encouragement. The subject was rewarded more when he met initial threshold early in the repetition and reached peak torque towards the end. The rewards were not directly proportional to peak torque but to time taken to reach peak torque.

5.2   Online Analysis

The game was initially tested on real time data with five subjects for one visit. The subjects performed three consecutive five-second-long isometric knee extension tests. The subjects were rewarded for any increase in torque value. The

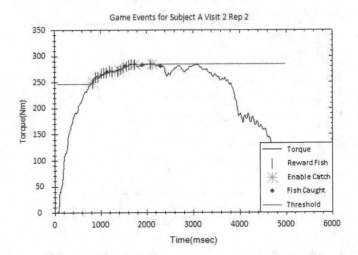

Fig. 8. Retrospective analysis - The events for a game played using torque data from an existing data set. In the game, the threshold is adapted continuously. When the user is eligible for a reward it is marked by a vertical dash symbol. Then the shark is given a speed boost at the point indicated by a star symbol. The shark catches the fish at the point marked by a diamond symbol.

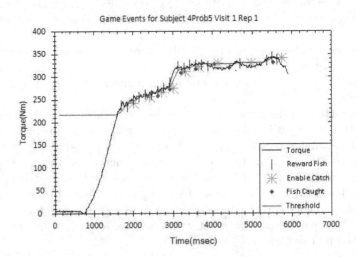

Fig. 9. Online Analysis - The events for a game played in real time is depicted above. The user is eligible for rewards at instances marked by the vertical dash symbols. The shark is given a speed boost at the instances indicated by the star symbols and rewarded at the instances denoted by the diamond symbols.

subjects were enthusiastic to participate in the game-based approach. The peak torque attained remained consistent over repetitions. There was no visible increase in torque so far due to the game. The game has to be tested further on more subjects over more than one visit and the performances in game-based and verbal approach has to be compared.

6 Conclusions and Future Work

The game-based approach provided standardized and reproducible motivation to the subjects performing an isometric knee extension test. The subject was motivated by being rewarded when any increase in torque was detected. The reward is not proportional to peak torque but rather to the time taken to attain it. The user will be able to perceive the results better if the peak torque is proportional to the score. The game can also be changed to improve the torque build-up time, i.e. the user must reach initial thresholds faster. For this, catching the fish can be made tougher as seconds go by. Usually, subjects play the game for around five seconds and has to rest for at least thirty seconds before they can start playing again. Since the rest intervals are longer than the play intervals, the story board of the game can be adapted to make the experience more enjoyable.

References

1. Biodex (April 2012), http://www.biodex.com
2. Physiology Laboratory at the Institute of Aerospace Medicine, German Aerospace Center (April 2012), http://www.dlr.de/me
3. Campenella, B., Mattacola, C.G., Kimura, I.F.: Effect of visual feedback and verbal encouragement on concentric quadriceps and hamstrings peak torque of males and females. Isokinetics and Exercise Science 8, 1–6 (2000)
4. Jung, M.C., Hallbeck, M.S.: Quantification of the effects of instruction type, verbal encouragement and visual feedback on static and peak handgrip strength. International Journal of Industrial Ergonomics 34, 367–374 (2004)
5. Hald, R.D., Bottjen, E.J.: Effect of Visual Feedback on Maximal and Submaximal Isokinetic Test Measurements of Normal Quadriceps and Hamstrings. The Journal of Orthopaedic and Sports Physical Therapy (1987)
6. Andreacci, J.L., Lemura, L.M., Cohen, S.L., Urbansky, E.A., Chelland, S.A., von Duvillard, S.P.: The effects of frequency of encouragement on performance during maximal exercise testing. Journal of Sports Sciences 20, 345–352 (2002)
7. McNair, P.J., Depledge, J., Brettkelly, M., Stanley, S.N.: Verbal encouragement: effects on maximum effort voluntary muscle: action. British Journal of Sports Medicine 30, 243–245 (1996)
8. Figoni, S.F., Morris, A.F.: Effects of Knowledge of Results on Reciprocal, Isokinetic Strength and Fatigue. The Journal of Orthopaedic and Sports Physical Therapy 6, 190 (1984)
9. Bogost, I.: The rhetoric of exergaming. In: Digital Arts and Cultures (DAC) Conference. IT University Copenhagen (December 2005)
10. Goebel, S., Hardy, S., Wendel, V., Mehm, F., Steinmetz, R.: Serious games for health: personalized exergames. In: Proceedings of the International Conference on Multimedia 2010, pp. 1663–1666. ACM (2010)

11. Lin, J.J., Mamykina, L., Lindtner, S., Delajoux, G., Strub, H.B.: Fish'n'Steps: Encouraging Physical Activity with an Interactive Computer Game. In: Dourish, P., Friday, A. (eds.) UbiComp 2006. LNCS, vol. 4206, pp. 261–278. Springer, Heidelberg (2006)
12. Merians, A.S., Jack, D., Boian, R., Tremaine, M., Burdea, G.C., Adamovich, S.V., Recce, M., Poizner, H.: Virtual reality–augmented rehabilitation for patients following stroke. Physical Therapy 82, 898–915 (2002)
13. Heidi, S.: Motor rehabilitation using virtual reality. Journal of NeuroEngineering and Rehabilitation
14. Yannakakis, G.N., Togelius, J.: Experience-driven procedural content generation. IEEE Transactions on Affective Computing 2, 147–161 (2011)
15. Burke, J.W., McNeill, M.D.J., Charles, D.K., Morrow, P.J., Crosbie, J.H., McDonough, S.M.: Serious games for upper limb rehabilitation following stroke. In: IEEE Conference on Games and Virtual Worlds for Serious Applications, VS-GAMES 2009, pp. 103–110 (2009)

Lessons Learnt from Contextualized Interactive Story Driven Development Methodology

Manuel Fradinho Oliveira[1] and Heiko Duin[2]

[1] Sintef, Technology and Society, S.P. Andersensv. 5, NO-7465 Trondheim, Norway
manuel.oliveira@sintef.no
[2] BIBA – Bremer Institut für Produktion und Logistik GmbH, Hochschulring 20, D-28359
Bremen, Germany
du@biba.uni-bremen.de

Abstract. The advances in innovative responsive educational and training delivery platforms has not cease, with serious games taking centre stage in new crop of solutions promising to deliver reduced time-to-competence of employees at anytime and anywhere. Irrespective of the technical and pedaogical merit of such solutions, the challenge remains the same, how to develop the required content that is grounded in the relevant learning domains (eg: project management) and provide effective learning experiences at good value. This paper presents the Contextualized Interactive Story Driven Development (CISD²) methodology to develop content for serious games aimed at providing situated contexts for the development of competences, relying on the contributions of a multidisciplinary team. The framework has two distinct strands, one focuses on the contextualization of situated contexts, whilst the other focuses on the desired competences to acquire and their model, leading to the observed behaviours that may be measured and calculated as performance of the desired competences. Both strands have four distinct layers, starting at conceptual level and finishing with the actual story implementation that provides the effective transformation of learners according to the intended learning outcomes and that such transformation can be measured. When progressing through the layers, CISD² recognizes the need of making decisions to reduce the scope and avoid feature creep.

Keywords: Game design, competence development, serious game.

1   Introduction

The importance of human capital is well recognized, which led McKinsey [1] to coin the term 'war for talent' to capture the ever competitive landscape for recruiting and then maintaining individuals of high worth to an organization. According to the study carried out in 1997, talented individuals have a direct impact on the profitability of an organization, but being a resource in short supply, corporations engage in a war to secure the resources. Even with the recession, the war for talent has not lessened [2] requiring innovative processes for talent management, where corporate training plays

M. Ma et al. (Eds.): SGDA 2012, LNCS 7528, pp. 135–149, 2012.

a fundamental role for success. In fact, according to Bersins & Co [3], the corporate training market was estimated to have been $67 billion USD in 2011, with a recent survey [4] stating 50% of those surveyed said that their company is consistently investing more time and money in staff development. Consequently, new strategies and solutions are sought to provide strategic advantage over the competition.

There is a growing acceptance in the corporate training world of using game based learning in the form of serious games. The landscape is littered with many failures whilst any success stories are closely guarded secrets to avoid disclosing a competitive advantage to the market. An analysis of those serious games that are on the market as a product/service for corporate training (eg: Virtual Leader from SimuLearn [5]) denotes the importance of getting the balance right between the game design and the learning, such that transfer is achieved. However, achieving an effective game design tailored to a particular learning domain is hard to achieve as designing a serious game remains an art, resembling a craft-like process that involves a high degree of creativity.

The aim of this paper is to present the Contextualized Interactive Story Driven Development (CISD^2) methodology, which relies on a step-by-step framework going from concept to actual implementation of interactive emerging digital storytelling scenarios. The paper also presents some lessons learnt from applying the methodology to the development of three distinct game scenarios, with two in project management and one in sustainable global manufacturing.

2   Challenges of Designing Serious Games

As pointed out by Gunter [6], packaging learning content into a game does not yield automatically an effective educational experience for learners. In addition, extracting the relevant domain knowledge to shape the game design is an onerous task, as exemplified by the case of the Virtual Leader serious game [5] where plans for close collaboration with domain experts in leadership were eventually dropped when it became clear that the insights yielded would be difficult to integrate into the game. In the end, the game design relied on a crafted approach confined to the ideas and experiences of the developers [7]. Consequently, there is a need to ensure that the design process of a serious game becomes more predictable, and to enhance the educational or instructional effect of games, it is necessary to devise a systematic approach to guide and organize game design.

One approach is to adopt techniques, as in the case of [8] which adopted Concur-TaskTrees (CCT) [9] to analyze and structure pedagogical content about the procedures within a particular task domain. The method is applied to the design of a serious game for training nurses in emergency medical procedures. Whilst promising, this approach incurs the limitation that it only elicits information about procedural task elements. It does not elicit information about the knowledge, thought processes and goal structures that underlie task performance. This method is very task oriented and not applicable for areas where high cognitive competences are required, such as in the case of sense-making, negotiation, etc.

3   Contextualized Interactive Story Driven Development

The Contextualized Interactive Story Driven Development (CISD^2) methodology was created within the Transformative, Adaptive, Responsive and enGaging EnvironmenT (TARGET) project [10] to create situated contexts where a learner engages in solving challenges and consequently acquiring the knowledge and developing the competences to be successful. The TARGET learning process draws heavily from Problem Based Learning (PBL) [11] and Action Learning (AL) [12], which implies that the associated game scenarios must be designed to harmonise the entertainment and education around the specifics of contextual competences.

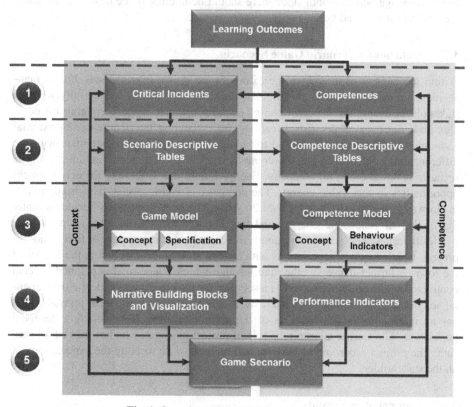

Fig. 1. Overview of the CISD2 methodology

An overview of the CISD^2 methodology is captured in Fig. 1, which depicts a total of five incremental steps, where a multidisciplinary team begins with the desired learning outcomes to arrive to the resulting game scenario that supports the development of the desired competences. There are two distinctive strands:

- **Contexts**: This strand is responsible for developing the situated context of the competence(s) and formalisation and refinements down to specifications for implementation of the actual game mechanics (programming of the game engine).
- **Competences**: This strand provides the theoretical basis for developing the models based on contextual factors, which contribute to the Contexts strand. The Organizational Knowledge Environment Individual (OKEI) [13] framework was designed to support the process.

At the end of each step, irrespective of the strand being considered, there is an analysis of the step and decisions are made concerning the scope, prioritization and how to proceed in the subsequent step. In some cases this may result in feedbacks and revisits to earlier steps. While the two strands can be executed in parallel, it needs to be assured a rich exchange between both since there should be nothing in the design of the game scenario that doesn't address a particular competence.

3.1   Stakeholder Scenario Game Scenario

Within the context of the paper, the examples are drawn from the stakeholder management scenario, which is to stimulate learning on how to successfully manage stakeholders during the different phases of the project. It supports training for complex and controversial decision situations, understanding the importance of external communication in projects exposed to public interest and how to negotiate with the different stakeholders taking into account their intrinsic motivations and interests. The scenario is based on an oil company, Energy Future that is looking for new business opportunities in renewable energy. The company is multinational, with headquarters in Norway being in existence for over 20 years. The management has decided to enter the market of renewable energy, and has initially focused its interest in onshore windmill farms. The scenario is about the launch of the company's first windmill project, which requires negotiations with several stakeholders including the Mayor of the town, a farmer that owns the land through which a new road is planned, a local contractor whom has placed a bid as a supplier for the project and a local environmental activist; each with their own interests. In addition, there is the local journalist that has an impact on the expectations of the remainder characters, including the local population. The learner takes on the role of project manager, who has the task of pursuing the project according to the plan and budget, while meeting the expectations of all the stakeholders

3.2   Competences Strand

The OKEI [13] framework, depicted in Fig 2, drives the Competences strand and it stipulates that maximizing work performance is the ultimate goal of competence development resulting form corporate training. The framework carries out the analysis beyond the individual alone and engages in a dialogue with various contextual factors, namely the organization (dimension represents the organizational aspects that influence the work performance and application of competences), environment (contextual factors external to the organization that have an impact on the work performances, such as competition, legislation, market, etc) and knowledge base (this dimension captures the external knowledge resources necessary to carry out the work).

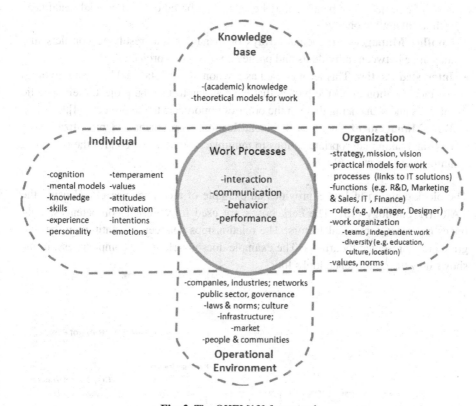

Fig. 2. The OKEI [13] framework

In the case of the stakeholder management scenario, the competences captured were:

- **Negotiation**: Negotiations are the means by which parties can resolve disagreements concerned with the project or programme to arrive at a mutually satisfactory solution [14].
- **Leadership**: involves providing direction and motivating others in their role or task to fulfil the project's objectives. It is a vital competence for a project manager [14].
- **Trust Building**: "Trust is a disposition and attitude concerning the willingness to rely upon the actions of or be vulnerable towards another party, under circumstances of contractual and social obligations, with the potential for collaboration." [16]

- **Decision Making**: is an important competence for project managers in leading the project, managing conflicts and ensuring good teamwork within the project.
- **Communication**: covers the effective exchange and understanding of information between parties. Effective communication is vital to the success of projects [14].
- **Cost/Benefit Analysis**: is the process for calculating and comparing benefits and costs of a project. The benefits may be calculated based on the financial benefits as well as intangible ones.
- **Conflict Management**: includes ways of managing and resolving conflicts that may arise between individuals and parties involved in a project.
- **Interested Parties**: This term is used as a synonym for "stakeholders" and involves the identification of all the parties that have an interest in the project, their specific interests and sequencing them in the order of importance to the project [14].
- **Risk Management**: includes the identification, assessment and prioritization of risks and taking appropriate actions to minimize, monitor and control the impact of unfortunate events [16]

The block diagram of Fig. 3 provides an example of a competence model using the TARGET ontology [13]. The dark boxes are used to represent competences, light boxes represent contextual factors. The relationships between the entities in the diagram are represented by arrows. The example does not claim for completeness, it just shows how the competence looks like.

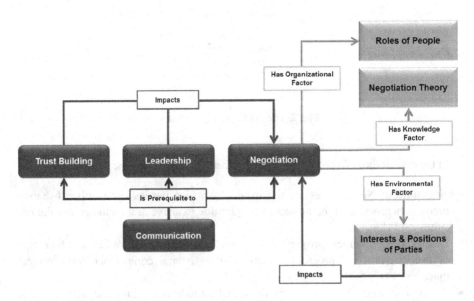

Fig. 3. Portion of the competence model for the stakeholder management scenario

Based on the competence mode, one then creates the behavior indicators and subsequently the formulas that calculate observable competence performance of an individual. As an illustrative example, Table 1 presents from of the Performance Indicators associated to the Stakeholder Management scenario.

Table 1. Example PIs taken from [17]

PI	Description	Formula
PI1	Use of professional vocabulary	$$\beta_1 = \frac{\sum N_L + \sum A_L}{\sum N_C + \sum A_C}$$ with: NL = Nouns used by the learner AL = Adjectives and Adverbs used by the learner NC = Content-Nouns used by the learner (see table below) AC = Content- Adjectives and Content- Adverbs used by the learner (see table below)
PI2	Phrasing / Verbalisation of Propositions	$$\beta_2 = \frac{\sum \text{Interrogative Sentences}}{\sum \text{Sentences}}$$ with: ∑InterrogativeSentences = Amount of sentences (= lines) with interrogative words like "Who", "Where", "How", etc.

The PIs are relevant for the TARGET learning process on two accounts. The first is that the measures are analyzed by the TARGET platform to calculate the probability that the learner has achieved the intended learning outcomes and the second is that the TARGET platform provides the learner with a video playback of what they did correlated to the competence performance over a timeline.

3.3   Context Strand

The Context Strand begins with the identification of Critical Incidents within the scope of the Story Outline (eg: the Stakeholder Management described in Section 3.1). The next step in the CISD2 methodology is the definition of critical incidents, which correspond to major decision points and events with significant impact on the unfolding of the Story, which in the stakeholder management scenario correspond to those outlined in Table 2.

Table 2. Overview of the critical incidents associated to the Stakeholder Management scenario

Num	Critical Incident
CI1	Decision of how and where to build the access road to the site where the windmill farm is to be built
CI2	Negotiate for the local land owned by the farmer
CI3	Participative planning
CI3a	Interviews with the journalist
CI3b	How many and when to plan information days
CI3c	Discussion with the activist
CI4	Decide on degree of local content
CI5	Timing of contract sensitive information (eg: disclosing the decision on tender has impact on behaviour of the local contractor)
CI6	Ordering the turbines

The Critical Incidents (CIs) are prioritized according to a 3 point scale, which are then cross referenced with the competences according to relevance. The prioritization of the Critical Incidents and competences was conducted in collaboration with the domain experts and pedagogues, where the domain experts, who also provided the scenario, validated the results of the analyses that were done by facilitators, and provided feedback for improvement. Based on this matrix, the relevant subset of critical incidents is chosen for defining a set of Scenario Descriptive Tables described in block diagram of Fig. 4.

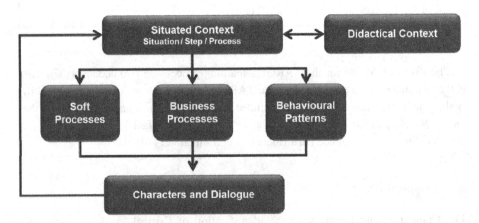

Fig. 4. Relationship between the Scenario Descriptive Tables of a game scenario

For each Critical Incident, a set of one or more Situated Contexts are considered in detail, which corresponds to a situation, step or process, identifying the triggers, the types of decisions and the outcomes of the situations, the characters that are involved in the Situated Context and the type of environment the situation would take place.

The Didactical Context takes into account the pedagogical content that should be supported in the game scenarios, how difficult or challenging they may be for the learner to learn. It also identifies the common pitfalls that are associated and identifies cues and strategies that may be considered in the design of the game scenarios.

Within a Situated Context, there are a number of Soft Processes, which may not directly lead to a tangible result, but they are very important within the context of the scenario (eg: motivating someone, engaging in small talk). Also in a Situated Context are Business Processes, which have inputs and/or triggers of activities that lead to outputs. Associated to each activity, one may consider influential factors, such as risk.

The Behavioural Patterns describe particular behaviours of a player or a Non-Player Character (NPCs), which may be observable which is one source of embodied Behaviour Indicators from the Competences strand.

The Soft Processes, Business Process and Behavioural Patterns contribute to defining the Game Models that shape the reality captured by the game that encapsulates a particular Situated Context. This model of "alternate reality" also includes the definition of characters and the associated dialogues. The involvement of characters in all the business processes need to be checked. If a character is not involved in at least one business process, there is no need for implementation - or this is a hint of revisiting the story outline.

The definition of the Game Models is the basis for the next step of the Contexts strand, which are defined in terms of formalised concepts and specifications, both of them build the basis for later implementation (programming). The snapshot of Fig.5

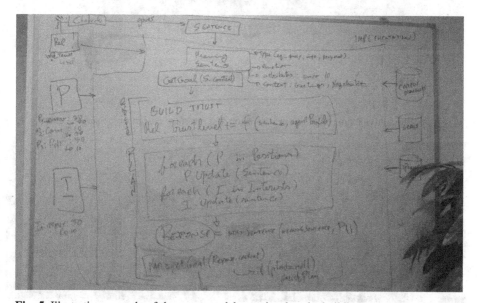

Fig. 5. Illustrative example of the game model associated to the building trust game mechanic associated to non-player characters

shows the specification of the communication game model, which shows the algorithm of how a NPC derives a response (answer) for a given sentence in the dialog system.

The final step of the Contexts strand consists on the definition of the set of Narrative Building Blocks (NBB). Definitions have to be in such a way that the models defined in the previous step can be implemented. This step also includes the visualisation of NBBs related data, or in other words, the user interface part of NBBs. This also contains the interaction options for players, as illustrated by the example photographic snapshot of Fig. 6.

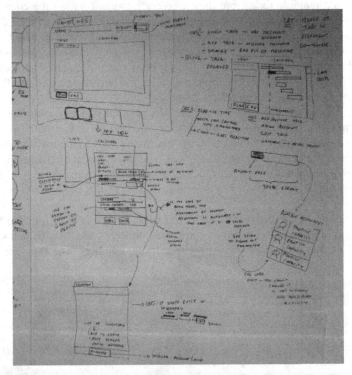

Fig. 6. Illustrative example of the visualization and interface design of the serious game

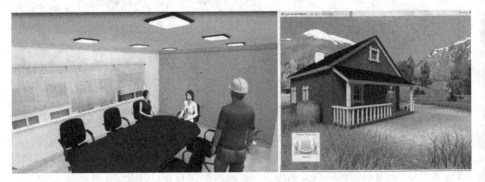

Fig. 7. Screenshots of the stakeholder management game scenario

The sketch presented in the figure above shows a draft of how specific game elements can be presented to the player (user). The combination of both strands results in the Game Scenario, which in the case of the stakeholder management scenario where Fig. 7 captures some illustrative snapshots of the serious game.

3.4   Multidisciplinary Team

The CISD^2 methodology also takes into account the need of a multi-disciplinary team when creating and developing a serious game, thus the methodology also assigns the roles of particular stakeholders (eg: pedagogics, game designers, game developers, domain experts) to certain steps of the methodology:

- Domain Experts are necessary to identify typical critical incidents for a given domain. This is important to provide realism in terms of approximating real life situations in that domain as good as possible.
- Pedagogical Experts need to be involved to model and interlink the necessary competences in the considered domain. They break down the competences into sub-competences and identify all relevant factors influencing a competence when applied in a situated context.
- Developers (system architects, programmers, media designers) are involved in implementing the story elements as Narrative Building Blocks (NBB) for a given game engine and to assure proper measurement of Performance Indicators (PI) during game play.
- Finally, a Facilitator who is able to bridge the other three stakeholders (i.e. by translating the different "languages" spoken by the experts from different fields) and who organises the common work is necessary.

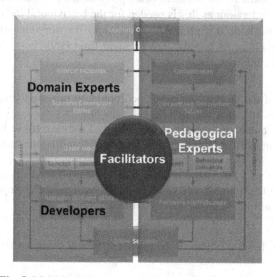

Fig. 8. Multidisciplinary team of four types of stakeholders

4   Development Costs

Estimating time and costs for development of game scenarios is an important issue to support the decision on complexity and uniqueness of the final solution. The question often is whether a learning story is better composed from existing elements or to be developed from scratch. The effort in terms of time needed for the development of a story depends on how much reusable elements are available in the story repository and how much has to be developed from scratch and the complexity of the story. A typical story development project is shown as a Gantt chart in Fig. 9 (which tends to be very optimistic in terms of timing).

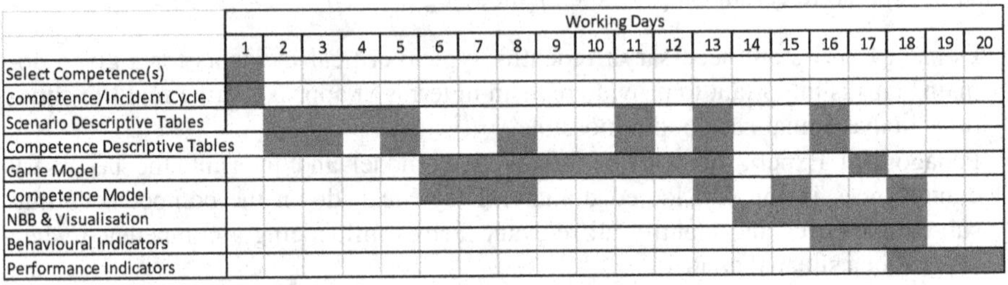

	Working Days																			
	1	2	3	4	5	6	7	8	9	10	11	12	13	14	15	16	17	18	19	20
Select Competence(s)																				
Competence/Incident Cycle																				
Scenario Descriptive Tables																				
Competence Descriptive Tables																				
Game Model																				
Competence Model																				
NBB & Visualisation																				
Behavioural Indicators																				
Performance Indicators																				

Fig. 9. A typical scenario development project

Each story development project consists of nine tasks which are primarily executed in a waterfall model approach, but including some back loops for further refinement of elements. This makes it necessary to revisit some tasks which have been temporarily completed before. E.g. while working on the behavioral indicators it might be necessary to re-visit some of the scenario descriptive tables to adjust e.g. a soft process to include specific behaviour as this is needed for the behavioural indicator.

The presented methodology proposes a repository for story elements allowing the re-usage of single elements to save development time (and costs). Therefore, three basically different situations can occur:

1. All elements of the story to be developed could be retrieved from the repository which results in little time and low costs for the project.
2. None of the elements of the story to be developed can be retrieved from the repository. Everything has to be developed from scratch resulting in lots of time and costs to be spend.
3. Some elements can be retrieved from the repository of which some need to be adapted for another purpose and some elements have to be developed from scratch. An estimation of time and costs needs to be performed.

Fig. 10 shows the basic problem of estimating time and costs for story development projects.

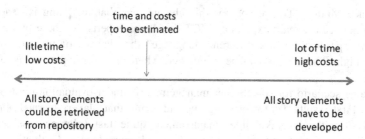

Fig. 10. Estimating time and costs for game scenario development

Other factors which highly influence development time and costs are:

- **Complexity**. The complexity of a story is given its total number of elements, i.e. the number of scenario descriptive tables, game models, narrative building blocks, competences and their contextual factors, etc. Development time (and costs) is expected to grow non-linear with growing complexity because by adding story elements on either side (contextual or competence) results in a quadratic expansion of the inter-relationship space.
- **Similarity**. Whenever an element retrieved from the repository needs to be adapted the similarity of the element to its final shape determines the efforts needed for adaptation.
- **Refinement/Iteration**. Whenever there is a need to revisit one of the earlier steps to do refinement and/or adjustment all successive steps have also to be revisited and consistency checked and might be subject to refinement and/or adaptation.
- **Development Team**. The number of persons involved in the story development determines the time (when working in parallel) and the costs. At least, a multidisciplinary team requires four persons: domain expert, pedagogical expert, software/game developer, and facilitator.

5   Conclusions

The Contextualized Interactive Story Driven Development (CISD^2)methodology has been applied to develop three game scenarios dealing with stakeholder management in complex projects, performing a Lifecycle Analysis in the context of sustainable manufacturing strategies, and the construction of socially effective development teams.

During the application of the CISD^2 methodology some draw backs and inconsistencies have been discovered and eliminated. Therefore, the methodology as presented in this paper can be called "version 2.0". For example, in earlier versions of this methodology model development was distributed between two steps (2 and 3). This has been changed to have all models just in one layer (steps Game Model and

Competence Model). The reason for this change was that modeling is exactly the boundary between domain experts and ICT developer experts. As these two different groups of experts often talk different "language" the chances of misunderstanding are quite high. These risks can be minimized when the overlapping is as small as possible.

The game scenario for stakeholder management is under evaluation until September 2012. First results were promising and indicating that players learned about pitfalls and strengths in stakeholder management quite fast (playing sessions were around 10-15 minutes) and related to the selected competences. Evaluations of the sustainable manufacturing and the social architect scenario are currently under preparation. After analyzing all evaluation results in detail, it is expected have more detailed conclusions on the quality of the $CISD^2$ methodology

References

1. McKinsey & Company (1997), http://autoassembly.mckinsey.com/html/downloads/articles/War_For_Talent.pdf (accessed July 1, 2012)
2. Sullivan, J.: The War on Talent is Returning; Don't Get Caught Unprepared, ere.net (March 2012), http://www.ere.net/2012/03/19/the-war-for-talent-is-returning-dont-get-caught-unprepared/
3. O'Leonard, K.: The Corporate Learning Factbook 2012. Bersin & Associates (January 2011)
4. Economist Global Talent Report (2011)
5. http://www.simulearn.net (accessed July 1, 2012)
6. Gunter, G., Kenny, R., Vick, E.: Taking Educational Games Seriously: Using the RETAIN model to design endogenous fantasy into standalone educational games. Educational Technology Research and Development 56(5), 511–537
7. Aldrich, C.: The Complete Guide to Simulations and Serious Games: How the Most Valuable Content Will be Created in the Age Beyond Gutenberg to Google. Jossey Bass (2009)
8. Vidani, A., Chittaro, L.: Conference in Games and Virtual Worlds for Serious Applications. In: VS-Games. IEEE Computer Society, Coventry (2009), http://www.computer.org/portal/web/csdl/doi/10.1109/VS-GAMES.2009.24 (accessed July 1, 2012)
9. Paterno, F., Mancini, C., Meniconi, S.: ConcurTaskTrees: a Diagrammatic Notation for Specifying Task Models. IFIP, pp. 362–369. Chapman & Hall Ltd., London (1997), http://portal.acm.org/citation.cfm?id=723688 (accessed July 1, 2012)
10. Fradinho, M., Andersen, B., Lefrere, P., Oliveira, A.: The New Path to Compe-tence Development. In: Cunningham, P., Cunningham, M. (eds.) eChallenges e-2009 Conference Proceedings (2009)
11. Barrows, H., Tamblyn, R.: Problem-Based Learning: An Approach to Medical Education. Springer Publishing Company, New York (1990)
12. Gabrielsson, J., Tell, J., Politis, D.: Business simulation exercises in small business management education: using principles and ideas from action learning, pp. 3–16. Routledge, Taylor & Francis Group (2010)
13. Petersen, S.A., Heikura, T.: Modelling Project Management and Innovation Competences for Technology-Enhanced Learning. In: eChallenges 2010, Warsaw, Poland (2010)

14. IPMA, ICB - IPMA Competence Baseline, v 3.0., http://www.ipma.ch/publication/Pages/ICB-IPMACompetenceBaseline.aspx (retrieved May 2010)
15. Smyth, H., Gustafsson, M., Ganskau, E.: The Value of Trust in Project Business. International Journal of Project Management 28(2), 117–129 (2010)
16. Hubbard, D.: The Failure of Risk Management: Why its Broken and How to Fix it?. John Wiley & Sons (2009)
17. Bedek, M., Seitlinger, P.: PIs and BIs for Communication, Negotiation & Trust Building. TARGET Internal Document (November 22, 2011)

Value Propositions for Serious Games in Health and Well-Being

Rosa García Sánchez[1], Alasdair G. Thin[2], Jannicke Baalsrud Hauge[1], Giusy Fiucci[3], Thierry Nabeth[4], Michel Rudnianski[3], Angelo Marco Luccini[5], and Kam Star[6]

[1] Bremer Institut fuer Produktion und Logistik GmbH-BIBA, Bremen, Germany
{gar,baa}@biba.uni-bremen.de
[2] Heriot-Watt University, Edinburgh, United Kingdom
a.g.thin@hw.ac.uk
[3] ORT France, Paris, France
{giusy.fiucci,michel.rudnianski}@ort.asso.fr
[4] ATOS, Spain
nabeth.thierry@gmail.com
[5] CEDEP, France
marco.luccini@cedep.fr
[6] PlayGen, London, United Kingdom
kam@playgen.com

Abstract. There are many different potential applications for Serious Games (SGs) in the field of Health and Well-being. While a significant number of SGs have already been produced, there is often a lack of consideration of the business aspects of the development including the market realities for a particular SG application. The development of a value dimensions framework and the analysis of a representative sample of SGs across a range of different Health and Well-being functional (market) sectors revealed significant diversity between functional sectors. Furthermore, an additional level of complexity may be added when the end-users of a SG are separate and distinct entities from the stakeholder(s) commissioning (and paying) for the development of a SG and as a result may differ in their perceptions of value. It is recommended that value propositions need to be carefully considered when planning the development of SGs in the field of Health and Well-being.

Keywords: Serious Games, Value Dimension, Value Proposition, Health, Well-being.

1 Introduction

Health and Well-being are important aspects of every citizens' daily life, yet are often taken for granted until there is a problem. In the developed world, the major infectious causes of diseases have by and large eliminated. However, there has not been a corresponding reduction in spending on healthcare and it remains a significant proportion of

M. Ma et al. (Eds.): SGDA 2012, LNCS 7528, pp. 150–157, 2012.

developed countries' gross domestic product (GDP, considered to be an indicator of a country's standard of living). Physical inactivity and over-consumption of food along with other lifestyle factors have replaced infectious agents as the major determinants of ill-health. The cost of healthcare treatments including drugs tends to increase by around 15 % per year (so called "Medical Inflation") and hence is a major financial pressure.

There have been many attempts to define Health, but the aspirational nature of the World Health Organization's definition "Health is a state of complete physical, mental and social well-being and not merely the absence of disease or infirmity."[1] This a good starting point for potential applications of Serious Games (SGs) in the field of Health and Well-being the nature of which is very diverse and includes variation along timelines of disease processes from prevention all the way through to treatment and scales of magnitude from an individual's health choices and actions all the way up to the operation of an entire healthcare system. The Robert Wood Johnson Foundation in USA has been a pioneer in application of SGs on the field of Health and Well-being with their "Games for Health" project initiated in 2004. Their working definition is "use cutting-edge games and game technologies to improve health and health care" [2].

Estimates for the size of the health and well-being SGs market are difficult to come by but in 2008 it was estimated at the time to be worth US$ 7 billion, with consumer exercise SGs being by far the largest segment [3]. More recently, an established video games company (Electronic Arts) published "EA Sport Active" in 2009 and in the first two week sold over 600,000 units world wide [4].

While there are many different potential applications for SGs in the field of Health and Well-being and already a significant number have been produced [5], there is often a lack of consideration of the business aspects of the development process including market realities [6]. In order to be commercially successful, SGs need to have clear and unambiguous value propositions in order to generate demand. As a first step, this article will discuss potential value propositions for the various different stakeholders in the Health and Well-being field.

2   Health and Well-Being Functional Sectors

In order to consider types of value propositions that would be relevant to SGs health and well-being applications, it is necessary to divide the field into various different market (functional) sectors. The first and most obvious distinction is between treatment (of ill-health) and prevention. There are entire ecosystems built up around the treatment of ill-health (e.g. hospitals, community facilities, health profession administrators, insurers, and researchers). The associated activities can be grouped into a number of distinct functions:

- Treatment of Ill-Health (i.e. practical application of clinical knowledge and skills in clinical practice)
- Patient Education (i.e. knowledge, skills and behavioural education of patients undergoing treatment/chronic conditions)
- Medical Education (i.e. training of health professionals)
- Medical Research (i.e. knowledge generation)
- Operations Management (i.e. management of healthcare systems)

In response to the need to enable people to have greater control over, and to improve their own health, the World Health Organization developed a charter [7] in order to focus action on promoting health in a number of different areas:

- Health Policy (i.e. strategic planning of healthcare system)
- Health Promotion (i.e. knowledge, skills and behavioural education of the public)
- Health Advocacy (i.e. building healthy public policy)
- Creating Supportive Environments (i.e. improving social and environmental context)

Finally, growing consumer interest in their own health and well-being has resulted in a growing sector where products and services are marketed and sold direct to the public:

- Consumer Wellness (i.e. products and services aimed at consumers who want to live healthier lives)

3   Value Dimensions Framework for Health and Well-Being

In order to develop a framework for analysing potential value propositions for SGs in the field of Health and Well-being, there was first a need to identify value dimensions that are already established in the field. A review of the existing, although rather limited, literature on innovation in health products and service development was undertaken. A recent evaluation of the way in which value propositions for medical devices were framed by manufacturers [8] found that they could be grouped under a number of different headings: *technologically superior; new technological response to an unmet need; enhancement of existing treatment; add-on to address shortcomings of existing technology;* and *shift upstream to prevention rather than treatment.* In addition to this list, there are a variety of different value dimensions that are already recognised and established in the health field. In seeking to provide "independent, authoritative and evidence-based guidance on the most effective ways to prevent, diagnose and treat disease and ill health, reducing inequalities and variation" the National Institute for Health and Clinical Excellence in the UK [9] includes *cost effectiveness* of interventions and *social value* judgements. With regard to public health interventions intended to promote health, the RE-AIM framework [10] has five dimensions on which to evaluate the overall impact of interventions: *reach*; *efficacy*; *adoption*; *implementation*; and *maintenance*.

The advent of the networked society has resulted in the emergence of several new value dimensions in the health field and these include *data-mining* virtual interactions (both patient-2-professional and patient-2-patient) [11] with the aim of "providing a better, more effective way for you to share your real-world health experiences in order to help yourself, other patients like you and organizations that focus on your conditions." [12] There is also growing interest in the use of the internet to use *crowd-sourcing* effort into solving computationally complex research problems [13-15].

Finally, with regard to consumer value propositions, a framework developed based one of the most successful start-up companies in the digital economy [16] includes the value dimensions: *performance*; *ease of use*; *reliability*; *flexibility*; and *affectivity*.

4   Value Proposition Analysis of Existing SGs in Health and Well-Being

A representative cross-sectional list of SGs across the various listed Health and Well-being market (functional) sectors was compiled from a literature research supplemented by internet searches. Details collated included: the name of the developer; the funder; the intended end-user(s); the licensing arrangements; and the game platform. Information on 30 SGs across the various health and well-being functional sectors was compiled and basic details are shown in Table 1 with each SG being allocated a code letter.

Each of the SGs were then examined in turn against the list of potential value dimensions. The results of this analysis are shown in Table 2 where the value dimensions of each SG (referenced using its designated letter code from Table 1) are cross-tabulated against its functional (market) sector. Taken as a whole, the results of this analysis reveals that *within* a given functional sector the value dimensions appear broadly similar, whereas in contrast there are distinct differences in the exhibited value dimensions *between* functional sectors.

It was not possible to obtain licensing information for eight of the SGs. Out of the 22 where licensing information was available, just over half of them (12) were available for free to the end-user. A further two had a limited free-to-play version, with payment required to unlock the full game.

Table 1. SGs in Health and Well-being used in the Value Proposition Analysis. Each SG has been designated a code letter for cross-referencing in Table 2

Code	Game	Description	Reference
A	Snow World	Pain distraction during treatment.	http://www.hitl.washington.edu/projects/vrpain/
B	SpiroGame	Improve diagnostic value of lung spirometery in children.	Vilozni. Am. J. Respir. Crit. Care. Med. 164, 2200 (2001).
C	Bronkie the Bronciasaurus	Asthma self-management	http://www.mobygames.com/game/bronkie-the-bronchiasaurus
D	Glucoboy	Diabetes self-management.	http:// www.glucoboy.com
E	Packy and Marlon	Diabetes self-management.	http://www.mobygames.com/game/snes/packy-marlon
F	Remission	Improve adherence to drug treatment for cancer.	http://www.re-mission.net
G	Air Medic Sky One	Performance management and patient safety.	http://www.airmedicsky1.org/
H	Coronary Artery Bypass Surgery	Training surgeons.	http://playgen.com/CABS
I	Pulse!!	Practice clinical skills.	http://www.breakawaygames.com/serious-games/solutions/healthcare/
J	Triage Trainer	Practice emergency triage.	http://www.trusim.com/
K	Foldit	Crowd-sourcing discovery of protein structure.	http://fold.it/portal/info/science
L	The Oncology Game	Selection of treatment options and resource management.	Fukuchi. Am. J. Surg. 179, 337 (2000).
M	Climate Health Impact	Health impact of climate change.	http://playgen.com/portfolio/climate-health-impact/
N	Dumptown	Reduce environmental pollution.	http://www.epa.gov/recyclecity/gameint.htm
O	International Health Challenge	Physical activity and diet education.	http://hhp.uh.edu/obesity/research/ihc.php
P	Sid the Slug	Reducing salt intake.	n/a
Q	What Should We Tell the Children	Sexual health communication tool.	http://playgen.com/sexualhealth
R	Emergency Birth	Awareness of issues relating to giving birth in rural setting in developing world.	http://www.ardeaarts.org/birthBeta/
S	Fatworld	Food policy.	http://www.persuasivegames.com
T	Food Force	Raise awareness about global hunger.	http://www.wfp.org/how-to-help/individuals/food-force
U	Fizzees	Active lifestyle game using wearable motion sensor.	http://archive.futurelab.org.uk/projects/fizzees
V	Get Fit	Lifestyle and social media-based health game.	http://newsroom.gehealthcare.com/articles/get-fit-with-ge-healthcare-2011/
W	GPS Mission	Outdoor location-based game.	http://gpsmission.com/
X	Tourality	Outdoor location-based game.	http://www.tourality.com/
Y	Web Racing	Interactive virtual cycle racing over the internet.	http://www.webracing.co.uk/
Z	Dance Central	Interactive exercise games.	http://www.dancecentral.com/
a	iDance	Interactive exercise games.	http://www.idancegame.com/
b	Lightspace	Interactive exercise games.	http://www.lightspace-fitness.com/
c	Makoto II	Interactive exercise games.	http://www.exergamefitness.com/products/item.php?show=makoto_ii_exergame_arena
d	Sports Active 2	Interactive exercise games.	http://www.easportsactiveonline.com/

Table 2. SGs Value Dimensions cross-tabulated by Functional (Market) sector. Each SG is referenced by its designated code letter. See Table 1 for details.

Functional Sector	technologically superior	new technological response to an unmet need	enhancement of existing treatment	add-on to address short-comings of existing technology	shift upstream to prevention rather than treatment	cost effectiveness	social value	reach	efficacy	adoption	implementation	maintenance	data-mining	crowd-sourcing	performance	ease of use	reliability	flexibility	affectivity
Treatment of Ill-Health	AB	B	A						AB										
Patient Education			CDEF			CDEF		F	CDEF		F								CDEF
Medical Education		GJ		H		GHIJ			GHIJ		GHIJ						GHIJ		
Medical Research						K	K						K	K	K				
Operations Management		L				L		L	L										
Health Policy							MN	MN		MN	MN				MN				
Health Promotion					OPQ		OPQ	OPQ			OPQ				PQ				
Health Advocacy							RST	RST			RST				RST				RST
Supportive Environments		UY			UVWXY	Y	VY	VWX	UY					W			UVWXY		U
Consumer Wellness		Zabcd			Zabcd	Zd		Zd	Zd						Zabcd	Zabcd	Zabcd	Zabcd	Zad

5   Discussion

As a first attempt at developing a framework for value propositions for SGs in the field of Health and Well-being, it suggests that there is considerable diversity in the value dimensions exhibited by the sample of SGs across the various different functional (market) sectors. This therefore means that the nature of the value proposition for a SG in the field of Health and Well-being is going to be sector specific.

The readily distributable nature of digital media (at potentially low- or no-cost to the end-user) means that SGs have the potential for significantly enhanced *reach* to patients and members of the public compared to traditional media and that this is a value dimension that was evident across the majority of functional sectors. Similarly: *efficacy, affectivity* and *social value* are particularly prominent in this regard. However, it is a significant undertaking to demonstrate these types of value, given the complex nature of human behavior that underlies and influences many aspects of health and well-being [17].

The results of the analyses of the licensing arrangements indicate that an additional level of complexity in the value dimensions of a SG is may arise when the stakeholder commissioning (and paying) for a SG to be developed for a particular application is not the same as the intended end-user(s). In such a scenario, each of the stakeholders (including the intended end-user(s)) are likely to have their own set of priorities with regard to the particular value dimensions that they perceive as important. There is therefore significant potential for conflict in this regard which warrants careful and considered attention in the SG development process.

6   Conclusion

The results of the analysis presented in this paper are a first step towards developing a framework for value propositions for SGs in the field of Health and Well-being. The findings emphasise the wide range of diversity in value dimensions between the various different functional (market) sectors in this field. This means that when planning the development of a SG for a Health and Well-being application, the intended value proposition will need to be sector-specific.

Acknowledgements. This work has been co-funded by the EU under the FP7, in the Games and Learning Alliance (GALA) Network of Excellence, Grant Agreement nr. 258169.

References

1. World Health Organization.: Preamble to the Constitution of the World Health Organization as adopted by the International Health Conference, New York, 19 June-22 July 1946; signed on 22 July 1946 by the representatives of 61 States (Official Records of the World Health Organization, no. 2, p. 100) and entered into force on 7 April 1948
2. Games for Health Project, http://www.gamesforhealth.org/aboutus.html
3. Goldstein, D., Loughran, J., Donner, A.: Health eGames Market Report (2008), http://gaming4health.com/hgmr2008
4. Investor EA Sport, http://investor.ea.com/releasedetail.cfm?ReleaseID=387220
5. Kato, P.M.: Video games in health care: Closing the gap. Rev. Gen. Psych. 14, 113–121 (2010)
6. Gershenfeld, A.: Response to Merrilea Mayo's paper Bringing Game Based Learning To Scale: The Business Challenges of Serious Games, http://www7.nationalacademies.org/bose/Gershenfeld_Gaming_CommissionedPaper.pdf

7. World Health Organization.: Ottawa Charter for Health Promotion. First International Conference on Health Promotion Ottawa (November 21, 1986), http://www.who.int/hpr/NPH/docs/ottawa_charter_hp.pdf

8. Lehoux, P., Hivon, M., Williams-Jones, B., Miller, F., Urbach, D.: How do medical device manufacturers' websites frame the value of health innovation? An empirical ethics analysis of five Canadian innovations. Med. Health Care & Phil. 15, 61 (2012)

9. National Institute for Health and Clinical Excellence, http://www.nice.org.uk/aboutnice/about_nice.jsp

10. Glasgow, R.E., Vogt, T.M., Boles, S.M.: Evaluating the public health impact of health promotion interventions: the RE-AIM framework. Am. J. Pub. Health 89, 1322–1327 (1999)

11. Laing, A., Keeling, D., Newholm, T.: Virtual communities come of age: Parallel service, value, and propositions offered in communal online space. J. Mark. Man. 27, 291–315 (2011)

12. PatientsLikeMe, http://www.patientslikeme.com/about

13. foldit Solve Puzzles for Science, http://fold.it/portal/

14. Gamers outdo computers at matching up disease genes, http://www.nature.com/news/gamers-outdo-computers-at-matching-up-disease-genes-1.10203

15. Kawrykow, A., Roumanis, G., Kam, A., Kwak, D., Leung, C., Wu, C., Zarour, E., Sarmenta, L., Blanchette, M., Waldispühl, J.: A Citizen Science Approach for Improving Multiple Sequence Alignment. PLoS ONE 7, e31362 (2012)

16. Lindič, J., Marques da Silva, C.: Value proposition as a catalyst for a customer focused innovation. Man. Dec. 49, 1694–1708 (2011)

17. Glanz, K., Rimer, B., Viswanath, K.: Health Behavior and Health Education: Theory, Research, and Practice. Jossey-Bass, San Francisco (2008)

Dealing with Threshold Concepts in Serious Games for Competence Development

Stefano Bocconi[1,2], Yulia Bachvarova[1], Martin Ruskov[3],
and Manuel Fradinho Oliveira[4]

[1] Cyntelix, Barneveld, the Netherlands
[2] Vrije Universiteit, Amsterdam, the Netherlands
[3] University College London, London, UK
[4] SINTEF, Trondheim, Norway
{sbocconi,ybachvarova}@cyntelix.com,
m.ruskov@cs.ucl.ac.uk,
Manuel.Oliveira@sintef.no

Abstract. This paper presents an approach to integrate Threshold Concepts into a Serious Game based learning platform aimed at learning soft skills such as leadership, stakeholder involvement and negotiation. Threshold Concepts are concepts that once grasped, transform the way a learner sees a discipline, marking the difference between a novice and an expert. However, learners have difficulties when dealing with Threshold Concepts as they are counter intuitive. Therefore the design of a Serious Game needs to take into account the existence of Threshold Concept that may affect the overall learning experience of the learner, and subsequently design recovery actions when the hoped learning effect does not take place. In this paper we describe what Threshold Concepts are and how they were taken into consideration in the scope of the TARGET project when doing the design of the Game-Based learning platform.

Keywords: Threshold Concepts, Serious Games, Game-Based Learning, Competence Development.

1 Introduction

The European project TARGET[1] aims at creating a game-based learning environment in the domains of project management, innovation and sustainable manufacturing. One of the foundational concepts of the project is the use of Threshold Concepts, i.e. those aspects of a discipline that are essential to a grasp of the discipline, that are troublesome when encountered but once grasped will lead to the deep transformation of the learner's view of that discipline. When this happens, one might say that the learner will begin to think as a practitioner of their discipline does, e.g. think as a manager, think as an engineer.

In this paper we describe our approach to incorporate Threshold Concepts in the learning process. Three phases can be outlined in this process:

---

[1] www.reachyourtarget.org

M. Ma et al. (Eds.): SGDA 2012, LNCS 7528, pp. 158–169, 2012.
© Springer-Verlag Berlin Heidelberg 2012

- **Identification** of Threshold Concepts within the domain, being for TAR-GET project management, innovation and sustainable manufacturing
- **Usage** of Threshold Concepts in facilitating the learning of individuals.
- **Evaluation** of the impact caused by the use of Threshold Concepts within the learning process.

At the current stage TARGET has carried out the first two phases, while the third is in progress. This paper will therefore focus on the first two phases, and in particular on the usage of Threshold Concepts in facilitating learning using a serious game, since to the best of our knowledge, there are no other game-based approaches that use Threshold Concepts.

The paper is organized as follows: section 2 provides background information on Threshold Concepts and how they influence the learning process. Section 3 provides general information about the TARGET project, while the core of the paper is in section 4 and 5, where we discuss how Threshold Concepts inspire the scenario of the Serious Game and the interventions to help the learner in case of difficulties in learning. Interventions are based on a pedagogical theory called Variation Theory, also discussed in section 5. Finally we present some conclusions and future work in section 6.

2   Threshold Concepts

Threshold Concepts are a promising and relatively new discipline in pedagogy, and can be briefly described as the key concepts in a particular field that, once mastered, transform the understanding of the learner from a superficial or notionistic knowledge to an operative and expert-like knowledge.

2.1   Definition

The Threshold Concept framework arose from a study of the teaching of economics but has now been taken up by educational researchers and teachers across a wide range of disciplines [1]. Meyer and Land [2] characterize Threshold Concepts as:

- **Transformative**: once a Threshold Concept is understood, a significant shift appears in the student's perception of the subject. This will involve not only a conceptual shift but also an ontological shift. This is a crucial aspect that always occurs.
- **Integrative**: Threshold Concepts, once learned, are likely to bring together different aspects of the subject that previously did not appear, to the learner, to be related.
- **Irreversible**: given their transformative potential, a Threshold Concept is also likely to be irreversible, i.e. they are difficult to unlearn.
- **Bounded**: a Threshold Concept will probably delineate a particular conceptual space, serving a specific and limited purpose.

- **Discursive**: Meyer and Land suggest that the crossing of a threshold will incorporate an enhanced and extended use of language, where the learner begins to express herself as a practitioner.
- **Troublesome**: Threshold Concepts are most likely to be troublesome for the learner, since they are counter intuitive. A Threshold Concept is often in contrast with common sense knowledge [3].
- **Liminality**: Meyer and Land have likened the crossing of the pedagogic threshold to a "rite of passage" (in which a transitional or liminal space has to be traversed); "mastery of a Threshold Concept often involves messy journeys back, forth and across conceptual terrain" [4].

2.2 Mastering Threshold Concepts

The process of mastering a Threshold Concept depends on the personal charac-teristics of a learner and her previous experience and acquired knowledge. Not all learners have difficulties with Threshold Concepts. For the ones who do, the path of transition from a stage of non-mastering or non-understanding to one of mastery may be described as consisting of three different stages: **prelimi-nal**, **liminal** and **postliminal**. A real learning trajectory will be characterized by being non-linear, iterative and moving back and forth between the various modes. First, it is the preliminal or initial mode that the learner starts with, and which brings the learner in contact with a situation or a case that is unknown or alien to her. Typical of this stage is that the learner feels confident as to her own resources when facing a new situation, and do not realize the difference in the situation facing her. In this stage the learner will investigate, first by trying to hone her existing skills and abilities for better performance, thinking she has not tried hard enough. The liminal state is quite problematic and troublesome since the learner here is typically caught between the known approaches, such as short term perspectives, and what has not emerged yet. The resources she has to her disposal are not yet crystallized enough to take the necessary steps ahead. The transition to the third stage, the postliminal stage, involves a transformation in the way of thinking, in the way of looking at the world in an ontological sense and thereby a change in what is perceived as knowledge (i.e. how to negotiate, how to identify the needs of various stakeholders and balance them).

According to Perkins [5] there are three phases in acquiring a Threshold Con-cept: the **object**, the **tool** and the **frame** phase. In the first phase, when the learner is presented with a Threshold Concept, she just observes it and studies it as an 'object'. All the attention of the learner is focused on the new concept; she gains an understanding of it by contrasting it to other concepts, analyzing it or in other words approaching it from a more academic perspective. In the subsequent stage the learner starts using the Threshold Concept as a 'tool'. This is when she starts applying it, which involves the process of thinking in terms of the new concept. Gradually, the acquired concept becomes like a second nature; it loses its conceptual framework and becomes a frame. The last phase, in which the learner starts thinking from the sense of the Threshold Concept, is the final destination of the Threshold Concept experience. This is when the concept has been acquired.

The liminal state, when the learner is trying to apply the Threshold Concept as a tool, is a period of potential failure and frustration. The potential of serious games represents one possible way of providing opportunities for iteration of the learning processes, of providing different scenarios, of moving back and forth in one's own learning trajectory for reflection. For the purpose of this paper, this is the learning phase on which the serious game developed by TARGET focuses. This means that in the following we discuss how to game requires the learner to apply Threshold Concepts she has already been presented with.

2.3 Threshold Concepts Identification

The approach taken to operationalize Threshold Concepts in TARGET is to capture the process employed by educators that use Threshold Concepts in their pedagogical teaching framework. This means that when an educator is aware of the Threshold Concepts within a certain domain, they can adopt more effective strategies that will facilitate the learner in overcoming the threshold. Within TARGET educators from industry as well as academia are present. In the domains of project management and innovation, TARGET has used sources such as:

- Best practices in project management from industry, resulting from more than 15 years of project retrospective analysis and interviews with key stakeholders in real projects.
- Studies towards the identification of Threshold Concepts within University courses addressing project management.
- In-company interviews with key individuals concerning their understanding of the innovation process, based on their experience.

The Threshold Concept that is best documented within TARGET is the concept of Position/Interest, associated to the competence of Negotiation in the domain of project management [6]. In this paper this is the Threshold Concept we will focus on.

Position/Interest indicates the distinction between an individual's position and that individual's interest in a negotiation situation. For example, an individual's position may be "I want an increase in my salary" whilst that same individual's interest may be "I wish to protect my status within the company", or "I want to enhance my feeling of security". A manager coming to terms with this distinction would certainly have a transformed view of negotiations. Such a concept would underlie many aspects of decision making but also the successful managing of individuals within interdisciplinary or intercultural teams.

3   TARGET

With rare exceptions, serious games are seldom very concrete about the pedagogical principles they employ [7]. Furthermore, because of the relative complexity of developing games in comparison to other learning materials, it is important that the serious game addresses carefully selected learning objectives for a better impact.

TARGET is an EU project in the area of Technology Enhanced Learning and it aims at competence acquisition in the soft skill domains, such as project management. A serious game in the form of an interactive story is used to provide a situated context for the learner to engage and develop the competences. Three scenarios are developed, of which the first one will be the focus of this paper.

The **Stakeholder Management** [8] scenario is based on an oil company, the Energy Future company, that is looking for new business opportunities in renewable energy. The management has decided to enter the market of renewable energy, and has initially focused its interest in onshore windmill farms. They are about to launch their first windmill project, which requires negotiations with several stakeholders including the Mayor of the town, a local farmer that owns the land through which a new road is planned and a local environmental activist; each with their own interests. The project manager has the task of pursuing the project according to the plan and budget, while meeting the expectations of all the stakeholders

The **Sustainable Global Manufacturing** [9] scenario is about performing a Lifecycle Assessment (LCA) in a globally acting manufacturing enterprise which is producing household machinery like coffee machines. The player encounters a series of critical incidents with the task to define objectives, goals and boundaries of the LCA, to acquire production related knowledge to define a materials and energy flowchart, to collect relevant data, to calculate environmental (and other) impacts and to interpret the results. To be successful in this mission, the player needs to know about the pitfalls of the LCA process as well as maintaining good social relationships with managers on the executive layer of the company. Otherwise, the quality of the LCA will be so poor that no useful recommendations can be drawn from it.

The **Social Architect** [10] scenario is about how a project manager establishes a project team as a self-governed social system where all the team members have clear understanding of their responsibilities and are committed to the project. Once established, the Project Manager monitors and facilitates the social system through their challenges and ensures they reach their full potential through self-governance. The scenario also captures the need for the Project Manager to be the interface between the upper management and the team, defending the interests of the latter and ensuring that the social system has their needs met to have a supportive work environment.

In TARGET, Threshold concepts are taken into account in the design of:

- The *game scenario*, based on situated contexts that provide the problem-based learning experience.
- The recovery actions (*interventions*) that need to be taken when the platform assesses that the learner has not acquired the competence.

In the following we explain both phases, limiting the scope to the Stakeholder Management scenario.

4   A Game Scenario Based on Threshold Concepts

The design of the situated context has been based on extensive research about potential Threshold Concepts in the domain of soft skills, as discussed in section 2.3. Particularly, the Stakeholder Management scenario has been developed based on a face to face role-play exercise that features negotiation (among other competences). As discussed in section 2.3, the Position/Interest Threshold Concept is associated to the competence of negotiation.

Fig. 1. A screenshot of the dialogue between the farmer (*on the left*) and the project manager (*on the right*)

As explained in section 3, in this scenario a project manager needs to negotiate with a local farmer and the mayor of the area in order to acquire land for the construction. In this negotiation process the player is expected to explore what the monetary and non-monetary drives of stakeholders are and how to address them in order to accomplish the project. The negotiation is carried out as a dialogue between the learner and the Non Player Characters (NPCs) of the scenario, such as the farmer and the major (see also Fig. 1). The learner can select from an extensive set of already-made sentences, which address the different phases of a negotiation discussion, such as informal chatting (greetings, smalltalk, gossips), personal matters, and business talks (the project benefits, the access road, land negotiation).

The details of how the dialogue is designed are out of the scope of this paper, here it suffices to say that each possible sentence that the learner can choose is categorized according to topic discussed and modality (i.e. kind or rude). The dialogue is then modeled as a state-machine and the sentences determine the transitions among states.

Since Position/Interest has been identified as a Threshold Concept of interest to address negotiation, the interactive dialogue that each NPC is capable of is driven by the positions and interests assigned to that character, as explained in the following.

4.1   Modeling Position/Interest

In TARGET the interplay between interest and position is represented through the agent model of the NPCs. Each NPC has a representation of their interests and positions, which are modeled on top of the agent framework for Belief, Desire and Intentions (BDI) parameters.

In particular, in the Stakeholder Management scenario the NPCs can have the following interests and positions:

- **Community**: the NPC seeks the well-being of the community she belongs to, e.g. the local inhabitants of the area where the road should be built.
- **Money**: the NPC seeks her personal monetary gain in the negotiation
- **Environment**: the NPC seeks to minimize the impact on the environment
- **Popularity**: the NPC seeks to maximize her standing in the community

Each of these factors can be present either as a position or an interest of the NPC. The difference is that NPCs "spontaneously" only talk about positions, while their interests are hidden, but represent what really matters for the negotiation. In other words, the NPCs are initially modeled as hypocritical agents that have a facade (their positions) different from what they want to achieve.

This situation represents the initial condition when the negotiation dialogue starts. In order to conclude successfully the negotiation, the learner needs to engage in a discussion about the real interests of the NPC. This is only possible when an NPC agrees to transform her interests (hidden) in positions (open) that can be brought on the negotiation table. A simplified model of how this can happen is depicted in Fig. 2.

When the learner tries to negotiate using one of the factors (X in the figure) described above, the NPC reacts depending whether that factor is in her interests. In case it is not, she just does not engage in the negotiation or, if this happens repeatedly, shows negative feedback as getting annoyed. If X is in her interests, the reaction depends on whether the learner has gained the *trust* of the NPC. If this is not the case, the reaction is the same as in the previous case. Trust is gained when the learner's dialogue is not too rude or direct (the concept of modality introduced in section 4), such as when the learner brings bluntly an interest in the negotiation. If the learner has gained the trust of the NPC, the NPC might reveal her interest and engage in negotiation if the learner has brought up the topic a sufficient number of times, otherwise she will not.

As mentioned above, a successful negotiation will only be possible when the interests of the NPC have been made explicit. This scenario enforces therefore

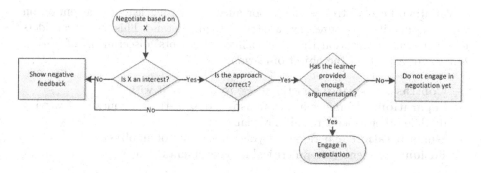

Fig. 2. A simplified diagram of the agent dialogue (*X is either a position or an interest*)

the importance of understanding what motivates people, regardless of what they explicitly say, a fundamental concept in negotiation. The next section deals with the case when the learner fails to grasp this concept.

5   TC-Inspired Interventions

At the end of each game[2], the platform evaluates the learner's performances using two factors:

- A *probabilistic assessment* based on behavioral indicators, i.e. by measuring how the learner behaves during the game [11].
- The learner's *feedback* about how difficult the scenario was.

If the learner's performances are assessed as poor and the learner's feedback is that the game was difficult, we assume that the learner encountered troublesome knowledge related to the Position/Interest Threshold Concept. We need therefore to design interventions that will help the learner overcome these difficulties.

5.1   Variation Theory

Although the approach towards a Threshold Concept might be different and possibly individual, there is one pedagogical principle that has been repeatedly brought up by researchers, namely the one of learning variation [12]. Variation has been used in learning for many years, e.g. by [13], but Marton and Pang [14] have developed a systematic framework to apply it, called Variation Theory. Researchers in the domain of Threshold Concepts have argued that exactly variation would enable learners to grasp the complexity of a particular Threshold Concept and have initiated collaborations intended to explore the connections [3].

---

[2] Each game the learner plays is also called a **story**.

Variation Theory stresses the importance of focusing learners' attention on variations in critical features they are trying to understand. This theory considers four patterns of variation that can facilitate students' discernment of critical features or aspects of the object of learning [15]:

- **Contrast**: experience something else to compare it with
- **Separation**: experience a certain aspect of something by means of varying it while other aspects remain invariant
- **Generalization**: experience varying appearance of an object
- **Fusion**: experience several critical aspects simultaneously

According to Perkins [5], the two critical places where the learning process related to the acquisition of a Threshold Concept can get stuck are:

- in the transition between the *object* and the *tool* phase
- in the transition between the *tool* and the *frame* phase where the concept is still difficult and 'unwieldy'

These critical places need specific support for the learner. Although Variation Theory is not specific to learning in the presence of Threshold Concepts, in TARGET we adopt it as a strategy to help the learner acquire the competences that are possibly related to Threshold Concepts. Therefore, in the case the learner has encountered "troublesome" knowledge, we assume that simplifying the scenario might just remove its pedagogical value, since Threshold Concepts are intrinsically difficult to master. Instead, the TARGET project makes the assumption that Variation Theory can provide an adequate support for the above mentioned transitions, especially for the second bullet point, since the game forces the learner to engage in the negotiation and make use of her skills.

In the scope of TARGET interventions are actions that define a set of new stories the user has to play after the story that led to poor performances. The goal is that the user will experience a different situated context that will help her better understand and master the competences (and related Threshold Concepts) she is trying to acquire. Each of the stories in this set is "varied" according to the principles of variation theory.

Two important factors come into play when determining how to define the set:

- What are the relevant story parameters to vary?
- What is the dimension of the set, i.e. how many stories should it contain?

The first factor is naturally related to the fact that the variation needs to be meaningful to the competences being learned. The second factor has a more practical nature since ideally the relevant parameters can be many, and producing a story for each possible parameter variation can lead to an explosion of the number of stories.

As an example, if we assume we can vary three linear parameters, a possible set of stories generated by an intervention can be represented as points in a three-dimensional space (see Fig. 3).

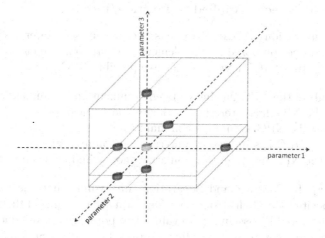

Fig. 3. Three-dimensional parameter space with "variation" points (*the yellow dot is the original story, green dots are varied storied, according to Variation Theory principle. The hyper-rectangle in blue defines the space of allowed parameter values*).

Each of the four principles from variation theory can be mapped to a new point in the multidimensional parameter space. The last story the learner played, when she encountered problems, can also be represented by a point in the parameter hyperspace. This story can be mapped to the origin of the hyperspace (i.e. the point $(0,...,0)$), since variations are always with respect to what the learner has previously experienced.

As already said above, in case of several parameters the number of possible stories increases rapidly. In our approach, we have initially limited this number using two working assumptions that will be evaluated subsequently:

- varying a single parameter at a time. Only in case of a negative assessment, we choose another parameter to vary.
- limit the variation principles to Contrast and Separation.

To perform the single-parameter variation we use Contrast and Separation as follows: **Contrast** causes a parameter to vary between the limits of its range of values, while **Separation** causes one parameter to vary gradually while all the others are constant. As an example, if parameter p_1 has range of values $Low, Medium, High$, Separation generates 3 points in the parameter space, having respectively $p_1 = Low$, $p_1 = Medium$ and $p_1 = High$ while the rest of the parameters is constant. Contrast generates 2 stories corresponding to the point $p_1 = Low$ and $p_1 = High$. We make therefore the working assumption that Contrast can be considered as generating the endpoints of Separation. This assumption allows us to reduce the number of stories generated as a result of interventions. In the following we discuss how to apply variations to Position/Interest.

5.2 Variation Theory Applied to Position/Interest

As explained in section 4.1, each NPC has two disjoint sets, interests and positions, which can be composed by the elements *community, money, environment* and *popularity*. In TARGET we consider five possible NPC profiles:

- **Sustainable**: the NPC has interests environment and community
- **Selfish**: the NPC has interests popularity and money
- **Optimist**: the NPC as interest community
- **Social**: the NPC has interest popularity and community
- **Active**: the NPC has interest popularity, money and environment

In order to apply Contrast and Separation, we assume that the Sustainable profile is opposite to the Selfish one, i.e. they form the two ends of the spectrum. This can be achieved by assigning the value -1 to popularity and money and +1 to environment and community, yielding a total value of -2 for Selfish and +2 for Sustainable. The profiles can be therefore ordered linearly, allowing to apply the technique described in the previous section. The learner will be presented first with the two opposite profiles (Contrast) and subsequently with the intermediate ones (Separation) until the performance assessment is positive.

If no intervention is able to help the learner achieve satisfactory performances, the recovery action fails and the learner needs to be supported in other ways (such as with a tutor).

6 Conclusions and Future Work

In this paper we present an approach to include Threshold Concepts in the design of a Serious Game based learning platform. Threshold Concepts inspire the design of the game scenarios as well as of the corrective actions (interventions) needed to support the learner in case of problems with mastering the Threshold Concepts. These interventions are based on a pedagogical theory called Variation Theory.

As mentioned in the introduction, the TARGET project is carrying out evaluation studies to measure the effectiveness of the approach presented in this paper. Validation therefore constitutes the major part of the future work that we envision. Nonetheless, from a theoretical point of view there are two interesting directions that we would like to explore further.

The first one is to use Variation Theory not only in the transition between the *tool* and the *frame* phases, as discussed in section 5.1, but also for the transition between the *object* and the *tool* phase. According to [5], one of the actions that can support this transition is to bring forward the tacit concepts and the commonsense knowledge that prevent a learner to master a Threshold Concept. Pang [3] claims that Variation theory can be used to determine the extent to which each critical aspect of a Threshold Concept is mastered by learners presented with it. This also determines where and why in their learning trajectory students might get stuck.

The second research direction we want to pursue is to study an architecture that allows interchangeability of different pedagogical strategies (or different actions inspired by the same pedagogical strategy) without modifying the game engine. In this way different pedagogical theories could be experimented with the same game engine. This would require decoupling the pedagogical strategy from the game engine that implements the game mechanics.

References

1. Meyer, E., Flanagan, M.: Exploring transformative dimensions of threshold concepts (2010)
2. Meyer, J., Land, R.: Threshold Concepts and Troublesome Knowledge: Linkages to Ways of Thinking and Practising within the Disciplines. Technical report, Enhancing Teaching-Learning Environments in Undergraduate Courses Project, Higher and Community Education, School of Education, University of Edinburgh, Edinburgh (2003)
3. Pang, M.F., Meyer, J.H.F.: 22. In: Modes of Variation in Pupils' Apprehension of a Threshold Concept in Economics, pp. 365–381. Sense Publishers, Rotterdam (2010)
4. Cousin, G.: Transactional curriculum inquiry: researching threshold concepts. In: Researching Learning in Higher Education: an Introduction to Contemporary Methods and Approaches. Routledge, New York (2009)
5. Perkins, D.: Threshold Experiences: Moving Concepts from Object to Instrument to Action (2010)
6. Flanagan, M., Hokstad, L.M., Zimmermann, M., Ackermann, G., Andersen, B.R., Fradinho, M.: Transformational Learning and Serious Game Design (2010)
7. Kebritchi, M., Hirumi, A.C.: Examining the pedagogical foundations of modern educational computer games. Comput. Educ. 51(4), 1729–1743 (2008)
8. Petersen, S.A., Fradinho, M., Bedek, M., Seitlinger, P., Santos, G., Campelo, F., Ekambaram, S.: D11.2 - Stakeholder Management. Technical report, TARGET project, Seventh Framework Programme (Grant Agreement N 231717) (2012)
9. Duin, H., Cerinsek, G.: D11.4 - Sustainable Global Manufacturing. Technical report, TARGET project, Seventh Framework Programme (Grant Agreement N 231717) (2012)
10. Petersen, S.A., Fradinho, M., Ekambaram, S., Zimmermann, M.: D11.3 - Social Architect. Technical report, TARGET project, Seventh Framework Programme (Grant Agreement N 231717) (2012)
11. Bedek, M., Petersen, S.: From Behavioral Indicators to Contextualized Competence Assessment. In: Proceedings of the 2011 IEEE 11th International Conference on Advanced Learning Technologies (2011)
12. Meyer, J.H.F., Land, R., Davies, P.I.: Threshold concepts and troublesome knowledge (4): issues of variation and variability, pp. 59–74. Sense Publishers (2008)
13. Dienes, Z.P.: A theory of Mathematics Learning. C. A. Jones Pub. Co. (1973)
14. Marton, F., Pang, M.F.: On Some Necessary Conditions of Learning. Journal of the Learning Sciences 15(2), 193–220 (2006)
15. Marton, F., Runesson, U., Tsui, A.B.M.: The space of learning. In: Marton, F., Tsui, A.B.M. (eds.) Classroom Discourse and the Space of Learning, pp. 3–42. Lawrence Erlbaum Associates, New Jersey (2004)

Betaville – A Massively Participatory Mirror World Game

Martin Koplin[1] and Carl Skelton[2]

[1] M2C Institut für angewandte Medienforschung, Bremen, Germany
mkoplin@m2c-bremen.de
[2] Brooklyn Experimental Media Center (BxmC), New York, U.S.A.
cskelton@poly.edu

Abstract. Changes to the urban fabric share some of the same characteristics as new software applications, whether at the relatively small scale of a new public sculpture or the very large scale of new buildings, parks, roads, or entirely new districts. In particular, they present overlapping issues with special regard to the question of participation. This paper addresses some of those issues by discussing the Betaville project in particular.

Keywords: Participatory design, 3D-modelling, real-world games, urban development, user-generated culture.

1   Introduction

There are two sections of literature about "participatory design" which show considerably overlapping: participatory software design, with open-source software being one example, and participatory urban design/planning. In many cases, public participation appears only as a kind of formal requirement of the planning approval process, at the very tail end of an arduous and expensive enterprise in the commercial or public-sector [1]. Even if full community engagement is formally desired, technical requirements and the financial burden of current practices may prune expectations on both sides [6]. However, it is also true that the technical capabilities of software and of the expanding network of personal computers have evolved rapidly since the first recorded participatory software design project was undertaken [3]. Concurrently, the tremendous commercial success of computer games for entertainment has stimulated not only the spread of powerful networked graphics computing to the mass consumer level, but also created a pool of young people skilled in the navigation and manipulation of complex virtual environments. It also motivated young professionals with creative and programming talent to develop ambitions as game designers and developers.

Have conditions changed to the point where fuller creative, critical, and technical participation in the means of development of new plans is practicable, and potentially effective? How can we find out about future needs? Which approach offers the best likelihood of long-term success? How can governments contribute most effectively to broader participation through online "public development environments", while helping to ensure that the integrity of the public process is safeguarded and cultivated?

M. Ma et al. (Eds.): SGDA 2012, LNCS 7528, pp. 170–173, 2012.

A recent white paper published by the MacArthur Foundation [5] points out the potential for development of awareness and practice of civic values through, ironically, "God games" like Sim City and Civilization, where a player is called upon to design and govern a city or state. The Neighborhood Networks Project developed by Carl DiSalvo and others at Carnegie Mellon [2] provides a great demonstration of the local cultural and civic value of access to the kinds of visualization and data tools conventionally used by planners and policy-makers, if only those communities can get "access", meaning awareness, software and hardware, skills, and legitimacy. The target user communities are already competent, and getting better fast: through the popularity of computer games, young people in particular have informally developed a range of 3D navigation and manipulation skills that were traditionally exclusive to trained experts in architecture, engineering, and certain fine arts.

Designing back from the real-world stakes via a thorough assessment of current formal and informal capabilities to a feasible design problem, we may arrive at a design strategy in which the platform development, as well as its use, might be characterized best as "constructive play" as formulated by E.S. Raymond [7]: "It may well turn out that one of the most important effects of open source's success will be to teach us that play is the most economically efficient mode of creative work."

2   The Betaville Game

Betaville is an editable online mirror world designed to develop broader positive participation in development of new ideas for urban environments, particularly for new initiatives in public art, urban design, and both development and redevelopment. A "mirror world" of any city, based on public terrain and GIS data supplemented by embedded links to background information, can be further developed by user-created proposals for additions and modifications to the environment. Betaville is a research and development collaboration between the Brooklyn Experimental Media Center of the Polytechnic Institute of New York University and the M2C Institute for Applied Media Technology and Culture at the University of Applied Sciences of Bremen, supported by a Cultural Innovation Fund grant by the Rockefeller foundation and the ThinkBETA think tank funded by the BMBF (German Federal Ministry of Education and Research), with many partners worldwide. In the case presented here, the Brooklyn group, initially working with researchers at the New York City College of Technology, had developed a prototype graphical interface for a mirror world of Brooklyn, in which users could "fly through" an online 3D map as the primary interface for rich media resources. The Bremen group had been developing NewsFlush (Helmut Eirund), a mobile technology for informal tagging using GPS, a sort of "virtual graffiti" system, and mobile city-guide systems and participative virtual exhibition systems for European museums through R&D projects. Since having discussed their ideas and schemes in Brooklyn, the proponents came to believe that a unique and enormous opportunity exists at the intersection of computer games and modeling tools traditionally reserved for creative and engineering professionals: full-scale visualizations of specific communities, that can be used as "base models" for speculative, and ultimately practical, changes to the built environment of local communities in their regional context over the long term.

Fig. 1. Table 1. Betaville interface, showing several versions of an ambitious concept for extending the tip of Manhattan with an expanded park including new kinds of sustainable mixed-use developments

Participatory design understood as the extension of the concept of participatory democracy, actually originated as a software development project initiated by a Norwegian metal workers' union in 1970 [3]. In fact, this developed further into a synthesis of participatory democracy in design and in the workplace. Two decades later, computer scientist David Gelernter was imagining Mirror Worlds as an infrastructure for public information and participation [4], 3D graphic representations in which citizens would eventually find public information resources and a vehicle for participation in debate. He did not, however, predict the possibility of using those graphical environments as a vehicle for proposing or developing ideas for alterations to the world being mirrored. However, adapting games like Sim City and Spore to social and constructive outcomes seems like an idea worth investing in.

M2C and BxmC share some unusual features: they deal with cultural programs embedded in engineering schools. As consumers of entertainment games, students in the academic programs arrive with skills in navigation and interaction with complex virtual environments. As a result, our respective research groups, working with teaching faculty on well-coordinated project courses, are in a position to modify the game software itself, to support innovative design and/or new functionalities. In the Betaville online 3D environment, anybody with time, volition, and skills can serve up a "mirror world" of their own building, district, or city (e.g. of Manhattan with sustainable mixed-use developments, Fig. 1 shows example). Proposals for physical changes can be modeled directly in an alternate version of the world. Alternate versions can be "forked", new processes initiated; anyone dissatisfied with the environment itself is free to engage Betaville's development community on similar terms.

3   Outlook

Betaville is designed to bring capabilities already at the disposal of professional engineers, planners, and architects within reach of artists and communities.

We anticipate that one of the most fundamental contributions Betaville can make to day-to-day urban life is by providing a virtual world platform for the kinds of consultation and due diligence that have been so hard to make productive up to now: RFC's for new development initiatives, full deliberation about alternative proposals, and the general broadening of participation in the physical culture of cities. If Betaville succeeds, the fundamental plasticity of cities may yet become an opportunity for local communities to construct themselves, rather than a threat to their continuity under the constant pressure of endlessly primitive commercial and government re-inventions. At the very least, it can provide an opportunity to test and develop those ideas in a public space before it's too late to grow them up.

References

1. Al-Kodmany, K.: Combining Digital and Traditional Visualization Techniques in Community-Based Planning and Design. Journal of Digital Creativity 10(2), 91–103 (1999)
2. DiSalvo, C., Nourbakhsh, I., Holstius, D., Akin, A., Louw, M.: The Neighborhood Networks Project: A Case Study of Critical Engagement and Creative Expression Through Participatory Design. In: Proceedings, PDC 2008. Indiana University, Bloomington (2008)
3. Ehn, P.: On Participation and Skill: Scandinavian Design. In: Schuler, D., Namioka, A. (eds.) Participatory Design, pp. 50–52. Taylor & Francis/ CRC, Boca Raton (1993)
4. Gelernter, D.: Mirror Worlds: or The Day Software Puts the Universe in a Shoebox...How It Will Happen And What It Will Mean. Oxford U.P., New York (1992)
5. Kahne, J., Middaugh, E., Evans, C.: The Civic Potential of Video Games. An occasional paper of the John D. and Catherine T. MacArthur Foundation Digital Media and Learning Program (2008)
6. O'Coill, C., Doughty, M.: Computer game technology as a tool for participatory design. In: eCAADe 2004: Architecture in the Network Society, Copenhagen, Denmark, September 15-18 (2004)
7. Raymond, E.S.: The Cathedral and the Bazaar: Musings on Linux and Open Source by an Accidental Revolutionary. O'Reilly, Sebastopol

Logical Thinking by Play
Using the Example of the Game "Space Goats"

Thorsten Wahner, Moritz Kartheuser, Stefan Sigl, Jördis Nolte,
and Axel Hoppe

Mediadesign University of Applied Sciences,
Department of Gamedesign,
Claudius-Keller-Straße 7, 81669 Munich, Germany
http://www.mediadesign.de/

Abstract. The idea of "Serious Games" mainly describes games that generate overvalue.

According to James P. Gee's learning theories, game worlds are some of the best learning environments imaginable as they encourage the utilization of the actively learned skills in other domains.

The game "Space Goats" is designed according to these principles. The graphical scripting interface it uses encourages logical thinking, while the "game characteristic" is retained. Thus, the player does not realize he is being taught.

1 Introduction

"Typical eLearning content involves heaping reams of mainly text-based information upon learners, dropping in some small multimedia elements and/or simplistic Flash Movies and then bolting on a simplistic drag 'n' drop quiz or MCQ assessement..."
—Kevin Corti in [1, p.10]

So called "Serious Games" have been heavily discussed over the last years and seem to be the successors of the mentioned "eLearning"-systems. These systems failed because of a poor game design and "drill-and-kill learning" as Susi et al. pointed out in [2, p.2].

But there seems to be no consistent definition of what these "Serious Games" are nor of their specific characteristics. One of the more important questions is: "Is fun a required attribute of 'Serious Games'?" Susi et al. summarize the different opinions in [2, p.2–8] which range from

- fun is not required and could even be counterproductive, to
- the entertainment and fun component of serious games is most important.

So the conclusion and minimal consensus of what "Serious Games" are is:

"...serious games are (digital) games used for purposes other than mere entertainment."
– Susi et al. in [2, p.1]

M. Ma et al. (Eds.): SGDA 2012, LNCS 7528, pp. 174–182, 2012.

As a game designer it is hard to consider games without fun even to be games. Still, the goal should be to get game designers on board with interactive learning software as they have the necessary knowledge to create intense and immersive virtual worlds which seem to be one of the best learning environments possible, as it will be motivated in Section 2.

So, the ambition of "Space Goats[1]" is to be a game in the first place, but to use the game mechanics and interactivity to "teach" logical reasoning without letting the player know he has been taught. This awareness of "being coerced into learning" is, according to Kirriemuir and McFarlane in [3, p.4], one of the reasons why classical edutainment software meets so much resistance with the target users.

Therefore, the educational approach of "Semiotic Domains", described by Gee in [4], is adapted to link the experience made in the game to problems in the real world.

2 Theoretical Foundations of "Space Goats"

According to Gee in [4] video games seem to incorporate learning theories in such an exceptional manner that they belong to the best learning environments. He further describes video games as a language the player has to learn and the more he does, the more he can do in the context of the game world und the game mechanics. But in video games this learning progress has to be achieved by active and critical learning. This means the player needs to understand the game mechanics and rules in such a manner that he is able to actively use his knowledge to solve the problems inside the game world.

Further, there is an effect that Gee in [5, p.4–6] calls "Embodied Empathy for a Complex System". It describes what game designers call "Immersion": The player identifies himself with his virtual avatar and experiences the virtual world from his avatar's point of view.

According to Gee, this effect also exists in complex scientific systems where scientists sometimes talk about, for example graphs, as if they were inside the system. The nature of video games encourages this way of thinking and helps adapting it to other semiotic domains.

The target of "Space Goats" is to design the game in a way that allows the player to adapt the knowledge he acquired in the virtual world to the semiotic domain "Logical Thinking", especially scripting languages.

As described in [6, p.15]: "There are numerous other research-based indications that digital games have some potential in teaching, learning, and education." It is specifically outlined that games are effective when they are designed and developed around a concrete field of skills, which is in the case of "Space Goats" the usage of a simple scripting language as the main gameplay element.

---

[1] The game "Space Goats" is beeing developed by the Gamedesign Master of Arts students at the Mediadesign University of Applied Sciences in Munich. The project will be finished end of August 2012.

3   The Design of "Space Goats"

The game will be developed for smartphones and tablets and will be available for both major operating systems iOS and Android. Thus, it will be widely available and easy to install and it will use the respective AppStores for distribution.

"Space Goats" borrows elements from the widely known games "Space Invaders[2]", "Missile Command[3]" and "Tower Defense[4]". The player has to place defensive—automatically shooting—towers in order to defend his main base from invading aliens. Figure 1 shows an early mockup of the main game screen. At the bottom of the screen one can see the already placed defensive towers while the aliens are located at the top of the screen.

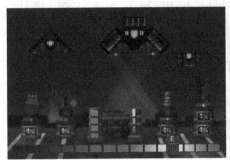
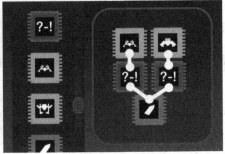

Fig. 1. Early mockup of the main interface of "Space Goats"

Fig. 2. Early mockup of the scripting interface

But the main aspects covering the learning theories are elucidated in Section 2; the differences between "Space Goats" and the previously mentioned games are:

1. The player has to choose the right composition of towers in order to defend against different compositions of alien ships and
2. Prior to entering the battle the player has to script his individual towers using a graphical scripting language as illustrated in figure 2 so that the towers "know" which alien they should attack under which circumstances.

Different towers with different hardware characteristics combined with individually scripted behavior allows great variation in the level design. Furthermore, it allows a smooth learning curve, which ends in a high complexity as shown in section 4.2.

So, in order to beat the game the player has to get familiar with the basic principles of scripting languages and use his newly aquired skills actively in different situations. The implementation of the scripting system is inspired by the

---

[2] For further information see http://en.wikipedia.org/wiki/Space_invaders

[3] For further information see http://en.wikipedia.org/wiki/Missile_command

[4] For further information see http://en.wikipedia.org/wiki/Tower_defense

graphical scripting interface of "Lego Mindstorms[5]" which has been sucessfully used in teaching children robotics as one can see in the "RoboCupJunior[6]", the youth division of the "RoboCup[7]".

That the scripting language is the core element of the game is important, because "computergames foster what they demand" as argued by Wagner in [7]. According to him, a player only learns skills he need to beat the game.

The following section explains the scripting language and is followed up by an example to showcase the possibilities of the system.

4 The Scripting-Language

The graphical scripting interface consists of different block types, which the player can use to define the behavior of the turrets. Figure 3 explains the different

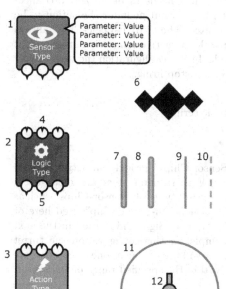

1. Sensor-Chip with parameters
2. Logic-Chip (for example "AND", "OR" and "NOT")
3. Action-Chip (for example "FIRE weapon")
4. Input node
5. Output node
6. Enemy
7. Active connection
8. Inactive connection
9. Representation of "Line of Sight-Sensor"
10. Trail of bullets
11. Representation of "Range-Sensor"
12. Representation of the tower

Fig. 3. Legend of scripting symbols

---

[5] see http://mindstorms.lego.com/en-us/Default.aspx
[6] see http://rcj.robocup.org/
[7] see http://www.robocup.org/

symbols that are used for the following example case. Yet they do not represent the final art style of the game.

4.1 Basic Functionality

The following figures showcase the basic usage of the different types of chips:

1. Figure 4 explains how the connections work and the usage of the "TRUE-Logic-Chip",
2. Figure 5 expands the example and intruduces the usage of the "Sensor-Chips" and finally
3. Figure 6 utilizes "Logic-Chips" to further improve the functionality of the script.

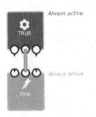 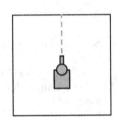 "Action-Chips" need an activator. Therefore, there needs to be an active connection in its input node for the action to be executed. The "TRUE-Logic-Chip" always provides an active connection at its output node. In this configuration the turret tower will not stop firing.

Fig. 4. Most basic script

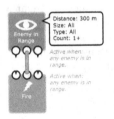  "Sensor-Chips" provide an active connection if their parameters are met. There are several types of "Sensor-Chips" such as the "Enemy-in-Range-Chip" used here or the "Line-of-Sight-Chip" used in the next example. In this configuration the turret tower will fire as long as one enemy or more is within the specified range of the sensor.

Fig. 5. Sensor-Chips

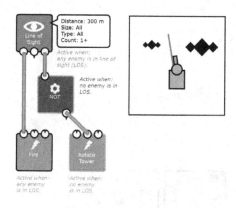

Fig. 6. Logic-Chips

"Logic-Chips" compute signals routed to their input nodes.

"AND-Logic-Chips" will only emit an active output when two of their inputs receive an active signal.

"OR-Logic-Chips" emit an active signal if one of their inputs is provided an active signal.

In this configuration the "NOT-Logic-Chip" will provide the opposite of its input signal thereby powering the "ROTATE-TOWER-Action-Chip". The tower will rotate until an enemy is detected by the "Line-of-Sight-Sensor" mounted on the turret's gun. Then, the sensor will provide an active signal, which will be negated by the "NOT-Logic-Chip". The "FIRE-Action-Chip" will recieve an active signal and the "ROTATE-TOWER-Action-Chip" will not.

4.2   Example

The tower has to make distinctions between two different sizes of alien ships. The goal is to fire primarily at large ships, when there is more than one ship type in sensor-range of the tower. If the tower is firing at a small ship while a large ship enters its radius, it is to cease fire upon the small ship and open fire at the large ship.

Figure 7 showcases this more complex usage of the scripting language and explains the state of the chips, when no enemy is in sight.

The following steps illustrate the changes of the chips in different situations and, accordingly, the behavior of the tower:

1. A small alien ship has entered range: The "Enemy-in-Range-Sensor-Chip" becomes active and the "ROTATE-TOWER-Action-Chip" recieves an active input. The towers turret is rotating.
2. The "Line-of-Sight-Sensor" for small ships has lined up with a small alien ship. Its Sensor chip is emitting an active signal. No more power is provided for the "ROTATE-TOWER-Action-Chip". Now the "FIRE-Action-Chip" receives an active signal. The tower is firing at the small alien ship.
3. Now, a large alien ship enters the towers range. The "Enemy-in-Range-Sensor-Chip" with the parameter for large ships becomes active. The "FIRE-Action-Chip" does not get an active signal anymore. The "ROTATE-TOWER-Action-Chip" is activated again and the tower begins rotating although the small ship is still within its line of sight.
4. The tower's line of sight is now lining up with the large alien ship, activating the corresponding "Line-of-Sight-Sensor-Chip" with the size parameter

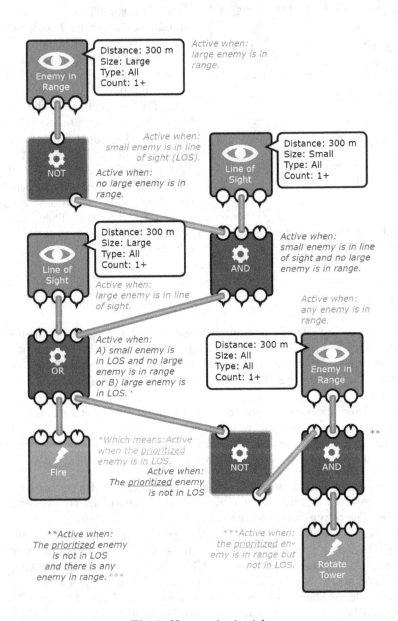

Fig. 7. No enemies in sight

"LARGE". The "ROTATE-TOWER-Action-Chip" is no longer powered and the "FIRE-Action-Chip" is provided an active connection again. The tower is now firing at the large ship.

5   Thesis

The graphical scripting interface of "Space Goats" gives the player an easy introduction to the world of scripting languages and sharpens the ability to think logically. So, according to Gee's learning theories in [4] the player should be able to translate his experiences from the game to real world boolean algebra.

Further, the game's mechanisms are optimized to deliver a fun gaming experience for the player, so that there is an intrinsic motivation for him to play the game.

6   Verification and Evaluation

To verify if "Space Goats" achieves its targets it is necessary to evaluate two main aspects of the game:

1. Is "Space Goats" fun to play?
2. Has the player's ability to think logically improved?

It is not possible to measure the fun of a game in an objective way, as each player has his own preferences when it comes to the games he likes to play. But after the games release, the sales and reviews can give a clue about the game's perception in the gaming community. Additionaly, "Space Goats" will not be released or promoted as a "Serious Game" as this could easily shift the perception of the game in public.

The "learning aspect" of the game can be evaluated by comparative tests. Therefore, the test subjects that take part in the test are divided in three comparison groups. First, all groups have to perform logical exercises in which they solve logic problems. Then, group A uses a normal teaching book for a certain amount of time to study logical operations while group B plays "Space Goats". Group C is presented with exercises that have nothing to do with logical thinking. At the end, all groups have to solve logical exercises again.

Afterwards, the results are compared which allows conclusions about the learning aspects of "Space Goats" in comparison to classical learning methods as well as not learning at all.

Of course, this evaluation and the tests applied need to be carefully designed in every regard to minimize potential sources of mistake.

So, the design and execution of the test, and the analysis of the results afterwards will be the next step after the development of "Space Goats".

7 Conclusion

"Space Goats" is a game designer's approach to serious games, using the learning principles described in section 2. The target is to create a fun and immersive game which uses its emphasis on scripting to animate logical reasoning and encourage the players to engage themselves with scripting languages and their functionality.

The scripting language itself uses a graphical user interface to define the behavior of the linked tower. Simple scripts consist of only two "Scripting-Chips", which basically allows the tower to fire straight upwards. But soon, the player needs more complex scripts to succeed in the advanced levels of the game. Therefore, the player is rewarded with new chips and sensors after each level and has to use his knowledge actively to beat the next level.

This slowly rising learning curve with constant rewards helps to motivate the player and encourages him to engage himself in the scripting system to advance in the game.

So, "Space Goats" allows an easy access to programming without the player knowing that he has been taught.

References

1. Corti, K.: Games-based Learning; a serious business application, PIXELearning Limited—Games-based business & management skills development (February 2006), http://202.119.101.57/upload/2006_09/06091415525749.pdf
2. Susi, T., Johannesson, M., Backlund, P.: Serious Games—An Overview. Technical Report HS-IKI-TR-07-001, School of Humanities and Informatics, University of Skövde, Sweden (2007), http://www.autzones.com/din6000/textes/semaine12/SusiEtAl(2005).pdf
3. Kirriemuir, J., McFarlane, A.: Literature Review in Games and Learning. Futurelab (2004), http://telearn.archives-ouvertes.fr/docs/00/19/04/53/PDF/kirriemuir-j-2004-r8.pdf
4. Gee, J.P.: What video games have to teach us about learning and literacy, 1st edn. Palgrave Macmillan, New York (2007)
5. Gee, J.P.: Why Are Video Games Good For Learning? www.academiccolab.org, http://www.academiccolab.org/resources/documents/MacArthur.pdf
6. ELSPA: Unlimited learning—Computer and video games in the learning landscape. Entertainment and Leisure Software Publishers Association (ELSPA) (2006), http://www.org.id.tue.nl/ifip-tc14/documents/ELSPA-report-2006.pdf
7. Wagner, M.: Ludic constructivism. In: Clash of Realities (May 2012), http://www.youtube.com/watch?v=cTF1cOFwCDw&list=UUJW4OzG2g6HArmf3_xpvPIg&index=12&feature=plcp

Squaring and Scripting the ESP Game: Trimming a GWAP to Deep Semantics

François Bry and Christoph Wieser

Ludwig-Maximilian University of Munich, Germany
{bry,c.wieser}@lmu.de
http://pms.ifi.lmu.de

Abstract. The ESP Game, like other Games With A Purpose (GWAP), tends to generate "surface semantics" tags. This article first discusses why this is the case, then proposes two approaches called "squaring" and "scripting" to collecting "deep semantics" tags that both consist in deploying the ESP Game in unconventional manners. It also reports on a very positive first experimental evaluation of the two approaches. It finally briefly discusses the relevance of squaring and scripting for other GWAPs than the ESP Game.

1 ARTigo: A Semantic Search Engine for Art History

Comparing and interpreting art works is at the core of art history. To this aim, databases of art work photographs are very useful but, unfortunately, in most cases still difficult to fully exploit because they lack metadata. Since art works descriptions useful for similarity or semantic search are still out of the reach of image processing algorithms, art work database curators rely on the tedious, expensive and not always bias-free indexing of art works by students and low paid manpower. As an alternative approach to indexing the art work of a database of more than 30,000 art works, we developed ARTigo (http://artigo.org). ARTigo is a gaming platform offering so far an ESP Game [8] that, so as to collect tags' frequencies useful in our context does not prevent entering tags already assigned and a game with a purpose [7,4] we developed called Karido [6] so as to collect tags more image-specific than those the ESP Game –ejainven in its taboo version– tends to collects [9,3,5]. [5] give a game-theoretic analysis pointing to the fact that players of the ESP Game are successful with "low effort" words.

ARTigo is rather successful. Within 4 years, it collected 4.03 million tags 0.855 million (21%) of which have been validated, that is, suggested by at least two players acting independently from each other. Furthermore, ARTigo succeeded in attracting an active community of 14,169 registered users and additional 26.428 unregistered users of which on every day at least 73 play on the platform during visits lasting in average 5.5 minutes. ARTigo users are both players and users of the art work search engine offered on the platform. The semantic search engine developed using the tags so far collected on ARTigo performs quite well. A

M. Ma et al. (Eds.): SGDA 2012, LNCS 7528, pp. 183–192, 2012.

few clues at what an art work represents suffice to retrieve it as well as other art works to which these clues also apply.[1] The query "`Sex -Liebe`", which means in German "sex without love" for example returns –rather appropriately– pornographic photographs from the beginning of photography. Though already quite satisfying, the search engine build from ARTigo would perform even better if a larger number of semantically richer tags would be collected by ARTigo.

This article is structured as follows. The distinction between surface and deep semantics tags is motivated and the concepts are defined in Section 2. The approach "squaring the ESP Game" is presented in Section 3. Section 4 is devoted to the approach "scripting the ESP Game". An experimental evaluation is reported about in Section 5 that points to the effectiveness of squaring and scripting the ESP Game. Combined squaring and scripting is discussed in Section 6. The perspectives offered by the two approaches for other GWAPs than the ESP Game are briefly discussed in Section 7.

Fig. 1.   Heinrich   Wilhelm Trübner, Self-Portrait, 1882

2   Surface vs. Deep Semantics Tags

Consider the art work displayed by Figure 1. The most frequent annotations proposed so far for it are as follows:[2] *black, bow tie, brow, button, dark, dress coat, eye, green, hand, leaned, look, man, moustache, portrait, shadow, shirt, suit, white.* They are all perfectly suitable and, in their set, more informative than it might at first seem. But even though the noticeable look of the man is mentioned among the tags frequently given for this portrait, this look has so far not been characterised as, say, melancholic. For art work search, the melancholy conveyed by this portrait is more than worth noticing. It is of primary importance.

There are no reasons to assume that the ARTigo players have little interest in mentioning, or are not sufficiently capable of recognising, the melancholy of that man's look. We know from exchanges we have had with some of them that they are interested in art works and often do recognise complex feelings conveyed by art works.

Most likely, an ESP Game player confronted with a picture such as that given of Figure 1 will enter "easy tags", that is, tags that his counterparty player is likely to enter as well. Since "suit" and "look" are more likely than "melancholy"

---

[1] The search engine is accessible from the upper right corner at http://artigo.org So far only German queries are well answered. English and French queries still need the platform to generate more tags and/or German tags to be translated in these languages.

[2] Translated from German, listed in alphabetic order and disregarding their relative frequencies.

or "melancholic look" because they are both simpler and more concrete concepts, the former tags are very often entered while the latter are not or very rarely entered.

Let us call "surface semantics tags" tags expressing what an art work, or more generally an image, directly conveys, among other, what it explicitly represents –in the case considered, a man, a bow tie, etc.–, what it is –in our case, a portrait–, or what it consists of –in our case the colours black, green, and white. Surface semantics tags are very likely non-controversial. Let us call "deep semantics tag" any tag expressing what an art work, or more generally an image, might convey as well but does not fall under the notion of "surface semantics tag". Admittedly, there is no clear cut between surface and deep semantics tags. Such a clear cut is not needed, though. Since labelling images with tags using a GWAP is a crowd-sourcing activity, frequencies will at last reveal what a community considers to be surface and deep semantics.

Fig. 2. Olga Rosanowa, Composition Without Subject, 1916

We found is that the ESP Game in its standard realisations, among other on ARTigo collects mostly surface semantics tags and performs particularly poorly at collecting deep semantics tags. This finding is consistent with former observations [9,3,6,5]. Our thesis is that this lies at the very nature of the ESP game: With this game, success is better achieved by focusing at the most likely, therefore at the simplest and most concrete. This thesis is sustained by the following observation: ARTigo players tend to tag abstract art works –such as that of Figure 2– first and mostly with geometric shapes and colours. The composition of Figure 2 has for example been mostly tagged with colours and geometric shapes:[3] *angular, arcs, black, blue, brown, geometry, green, multicolour, orange, rectangles, round, shapes, squares, white, and yellow.* It could have also been tagged with *movement* and *order*, though.

The great ability of the ESP Game to collect simple, concrete and rather immediate descriptions is for two reasons not to be wrongly interpreted as a weakness of that game. First, the simplest and most concrete tags are undoubtedly needed for most applications, among other for the art work search engine we developed. Second, as it is shown below, the ESP Game itself offers all what is needed for collecting not only surface semantics, but also deep semantics tags.

---

[3] Translated from German, in alphabetical order and disregarding the relative frequencies.

3   Squaring the ESP Game

Consider the portrait of Figure 1 which, as already mentioned, has been often tagged with "look", the precise nature of the man's look, however, so far has not been characterised in any manner by players. A variation of the ESP Game we call TagATag[4] asks players to tag the pair consisting of the art work of Figure 1 and of the tag "look". More generally, TagATag is an ESP Game that asks players to tag a pair consisting of an image and a tag that has been formerly collected for this image for this image. We call this variation of the ESP Game a "squared the ESP Game", or (ESP Game)^2, because the ESP Game is applied to data collected with the ESP game itself.

Fig. 3. Holbein, Portrait of Hans Schwarz, 1494/1522

Squaring the ESP Game is possible without any selection of the tags selected for the pairs (image, tag) to be presented to players. Squaring the ESP Games does not require for the gaming platform operators to develop a new game and for players to learn how to perform well at a new game. Some pairs (image, tag) turn out to be tricky to play well with. This, however, as shown by first evaluations, contributes to the attractiveness of the gaming platform. Furthermore, we observed that pairs (image, tag) difficult to tag turn out to collect only a few tags but highly interesting ones. The pair consisting of the drawing of Figure 3 associated with the tag "black", in German "schwarz", can well be tagged with "everything" or, referring to the family name of the portrayed Mann with "man". Both tags are highly valuable for our purpose, the development of an art work search engine. We argue that squared ESP Games are likely to be very useful for other applications as well. First experiments point to the pertinence of squaring the ESP Game –it does generate deep semantics tags– and to its attractiveness for players –players do not leave or avoid the game.

The ESP Game can be squared in more sophisticated manners than the one mentioned above. In the following, we discuss a few. First, automatically generated questions can be posed. A pair consisting of a tag W and an image can be presented with one of the following questions, depending whether W is a noun, an adjective or a verb:[5] *How is W in this image? What is W in this image? What is W-ing in this image?* Second, squaring can be realised using a set of

---

[4] TagATag i s available on a beta version of ARTigo accessible at www.artigo.org for selected users only.

[5] Tags that are neither nouns, nor adjectives, nor verbs can be omitted in generating questions. More sophisticated forms of automated question generation capable of coping with more sophisticated tags can be considered, too.

tags instead of a single tag. The approach is especially promising if the set of tags is selected –of course automatically– for semantic reasons. Tags that are semantically related can for example be selected. Third, squaring can be realised with one tag and several images. Consider the images of Figures 4 and 5 that, understandably, have both been tagged with "bridge". They could be presented with one of the following two questions: *What have the bridges in common in these images? What distinguishes the bridges in these images?* Answers to these questions are not as difficult as it might first seem. For example, both bridges are old and located in England, and in Europe, the one is well visible, small and a photograph, the other is hardly recognisable, large and a painting. Tags entered as answers to the aforementioned two questions express semantic relationships –in case of the images of Figures 4 and 5 on their "bridge-ness". The second question is especially interesting because, like the games Polarity [3] and Karido [6] it yields tags differentiating the images presented.

Fig. 4. Anonymous, Oxford Bridge in Stowe Landscape Gardens, Stowe, Buckinghamshire, 1761

Fig. 5. James Abbot McNeill Whistler, Nocturne in Gray and Gold, Westminster Bridge, 1871/1874

Squaring the ESP Game can be repeated. A squared ESP Game can itself be squared once again in whatever manner deemed convenient. In doing so, one has to reflect on how to display the various tags associated with an image and the various images associated with tags. A simple and effective approach is simply to display them as an ordered or unordered list or as a tag cloud which, possibly and if available, could as well convey the relative frequencies of these tags.

4   Scripting the ESP Game

If one wants players of an ESP Game to propose tags that express, say, the sentiments an art work conveys, then the simplest approach is to explicitly ask them to do so! This approach turns out to be very effective. On the aforementioned beta version of an extension of ARTigo, we propose an ESP Game called Sentiment which does that. The tags collected so far by Sentiment are very promising.

Playing Sentiment is, admittedly, at first not always simple. Consider for example Figure 6. It is not at first obvious what sentiment such a plan might convey. A second thought, however, is that this plan clearly conveys order, which, most interestingly, is a characteristic of 17th century palace garden in Europe. Another feeling this plan conveys is that of depth which, once again, is a very appropriate description of what the architects of baroque theatres, as opposed to theatres of former ages, have intended to convey.

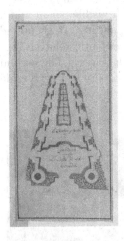

Fig. 6. Anonymous, Plan of the Garden Theatre of Schlackenwerth Palace, 1690

We call the approach outlined above, or more precisely a generalisation of it we discuss in the remaining of this section, "scripting the ESP Game". In pedagogical psychology, scripting denotes techniques to bring learners to perform as desired, for example to tackle the resolution of linear equations in one of the manners that easily and surely lead to success [1,10,2].

Explicitly telling people what to do is a bit crude. It is often not so well received. Setting a context that leads them to do what is desired, that is providing guidance, is more promising an approach. In several fields, among other Human Machine Interaction, researchers have investigated how such contexts can be set for uses. A common observation is that appropriate contexts are more effective at making users act as expected than explicit instructions. We conjecture that this applies to players, too. For this reason we reflected . The remaining of this section is devoted to reflexions on how to "script" the ESP Game so as to lead its players to propose deep semantics tags.

First and foremost, the scoring scheme is a form of scripting. A scoring scheme is a good scripting if it is well understood by the players. Scoring as scripting is, we believe, an important issue deserving more investigations.

Second, deep semantics tags can be displayed on the starting page of a game. We do this on ARTigo. Every day a different art work is presented with its tag cloud. Figure 7 on the previous page shows how ARTigo's starting page might look

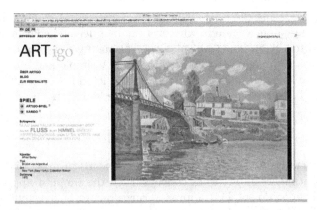

Fig. 7. ARTigo Starting Page – Alfred Sisley, Bridge of Argenteuil, 1872

like. The tag cloud displayed with Sisley's painting of the bridge of Argenteuil reads:[6] *sky, trees, Sisley, landscape, bank, waves, impressionism, bridge, blue, village, boat, boats, tree, multicolour, river, cloud, houses, people, green, house.* We script to deep semantics by extending this tag cloud with: *peace, harmony, repose.*

Third, captions are displayed with the art work on the starting page of ARTigo so as to suggest a critical, or deep semantics, look, at art works. Figures 8, 9, and 10 give examples of such captions.

ARTigo displays every day a different art work with a caption. The cap-

Fig. 8. ARTigo Starting Page – Heinrich Wilhelm Trübner, Self-Portrait, 1882. "The artist as a melancholiac".

tions are informative, sometimes surprising, in some cases even provocative. They always trigger reflexions as in the case displayed by Figures 8, 9, and 10 that respectively point to the mood of the portrayed person, the propagandising of the painting and the social criticism expressed by a rather strange street view. These captions greatly contribute both to the attractiveness of the gaming platform, to its focus on art history, and its collecting deep semantics tag. Some players have reported looking almost every day at the platform starting page for discovering the art work and caption of the day. We conclude that these captions are successful a means for scripting.

ARTigo's captions come, however, at a price: They cannot be automatically generated and require human work. The very quality of the captions that make them good a scripting means also make them more a craft than an –at least partly– automatisable task. This being said, captions are only needed for stetting a context, and only a few captions suffice. A few hundered captions suffice for the scripting thought for: After a couple of months, a same caption is displayed once again.

Fourth, the images selected for a round of the ESP Game can be selected in such a way to induce an atmosphere, for example by selecting only abstract or Impressionist or Gothic art works. Such a notion of "thematic round" can be conveyed to the users, for example by providing the rounds with titles. An essential requirement is that such title do not need being worked out by

---

[6] In German: Himmel, Bäume, Sisley, Landschaft, Ufer, Wellen, Impressionismus, Brücke, blau, Dorf, Boot, Boote, Baum, bunt, Fluss, Wolken, Häuser, Menschen, grün, Haus.

human. Indeed, this would soon, especially if the game becomes even more popular, require more human work than might be provided with. Finally, combinations of the aforementioned forms of scripting can be though of.

Like squaring the ESP Game, scripting it is appealing because it does not require for the gaming platform operators to develop new games and for players to learn how to perform well at new games.

A promising issue for further research is how to automatise scripting.

Fig. 9. ARTigo Starting Page – Jacques Louis David, Napoléon crossing the St. Bernard Pass, 1800. "Napoléon rides a fiery black horse over the Alps. In reality, he rode a donkey."

5 First Experimental Evaluation

In a first experimental evaluation, ten players, that were already registered on ARTigo, have been selected. Between 17 January 2012 and 12 April 2012 they tested beta versions of the aforementioned squared ESP Game "TagATag" and and scripted ESP Game "Sentiment'. The findings are as follows.

First, both games requires players to get used to them. After an adaptation phase, the players have "got the trick" and had no more problems in suggesting deep semantics tags.

Second, TagATag and Sentiments are more difficult to play well with than the plain ESP Game. This is clearly reflected by the fact that, in

Fig. 10. ARTigo Starting Page – Ernst Ludwig Kirchner, Friedrich Street, Berlin, 1914. "This, indeed, is not a realistic view of a street. However, did any other painter ever show prostitution as evidently as the expressionist Kirchner?"

average, less tags are collected with these games than with the plain ESP Game: 195 pairs (image, tag) have been collected in this experiment, 85 (9%) of which were new.

Third, extending the ARTigo platform with additional, more difficult, games has been positively received by the selected players.

These findings let us conclude that TagATag and Sentiment can be offered to all players. We intend to offer in Summer 2012 these two games, as well as an additional version of the ESP Game mixing the three versions plain, TagATag and Sentiment in a round. This will make it possible to start a long term and more thorough analysis of both, the receptions of the new games by non-selected players and of the effectiveness of the squared and scripted ESP Game for collecting deep semantics tags.

In the future, also intend to analyse how the metadata collected with TagATag and Sentiment impact on the result quality of the semantic search engine.

6   Combined Squaring and Scripting of the ESP Game

Squaring and scripting can both be combined, provided that the combination is clearly understandable by the players and is not overloaded with explicit or implicit instructions.

We are investigating squared and scripted versions of the ESP Game that collect semantic relationships either between art works –as described in Section 4 with the two bridges– or between tags given to a same art work. Both approaches promise considerable benefits for the semantic search engine.

We expect to gather more experience with both approaches and their combination. Interesting would be measures of the impact of combining squaring and scripting of the deep semantics quality of the tags collected.

7   Perspectives for Further Research

Long term evaluations of squared and/or ESP Games are necessary. We expect them to suggest new forms of scripting.

Systematic approaches to scripting that would be amenable to automation are desirable because they would make it possible to harness scripting without requiring human work. An interesting issue is thus how scripting could be turned from an art, or craft, into a systematic technique. Obviously, solutions would be interesting not only for scripting GWAPs but also for exploiting scripting in teaching.

Also interesting is how squared and scripted ESP Game are successful depending on the application fields. Art works aficionados might be more easily gained for such meta-reflexive games on the ARTigo platform than players with other interests. Indeed, the more a player is knowledgeable in a filed, the more likely it is she will enjoy thinking of sophisticated tags.

A further interesting issue is whether other games than the ESP Game can successfully be squared or scripted. First investigations convinced us that the games Karido [6] we developed and Polarity [3], both designed for overcoming the tendency of the ESP GAme to collect image-unspecific, or low effort, tags, can as well as the ESP Game be squared and scripted.

Acknowledgements. The authors are thankful to Hubertus Kohle of the Art History department of the Ludwig-Maximilian University of Munich for his many suggestions and explanations. This research has been founded in part by the German Foundation for Research (DFG) within the project Play4Science number 578416.

References

1. Dansereau, D., O'Donnell, A.: Scripted Cooperation in Student Dyads: A Method for Analyzing and Enhancing Academic Learning and Performance. In: Interactions in Cooperative Groups. The Theoretical Anatomy of Group Learning, pp. 120–141. Cambridge University Press (1992)
2. King, A.: Scripting Collaborative Learning Processes: a Cognitive Perspective. In: Fischer, F., Kollar, I., Mandl, H., Haak, J.M. (eds.) Scripting Computer-Supported Collaborative Learning, pp. 13–37. Springer (2007)
3. Law, E., Settles, B., Snook, A., Surana, H., von Ahn, L., Mitchell, T.: Human Computation for Attribute and Attribute Value Acquisition. In: Proceedings of the First Workshop on Fine-Grained Visual Categorization (FGVC) (2011)
4. Law, E., von Ahn, L.: Human Computation. Synthesis Lectures on Artificial Intelligence and Machine Learning. Morgan & Claypool (2011)
5. Jain, S., Parkes, D.: A Game-Theoretic Analysis of Games with a Purpose. In: ACM Transactions on Economics and Computation (TEAC) (to appear, 2012)
6. Steinmayr, B., Wieser, C., Kneißl, F., Karido, F.B.: A GWAP for Telling Artworks Apart. In: Proceedings of the 16th International Conference on Computer Games (July 2011)
7. von Ahn, L.: Games With a Purpose. Computer 29(6), 92–94 (2006)
8. von Ahn, L., Dabbish, L.: Labeling Images with a Computer Game. In: Proceedings of the ACM SIGCHI Conference on Human Factors in Computing Systems, CHI (2004)
9. Weber, I., Robertson, S., Vojnović, M.: Rethinking the ESP Game. In: Proceedings of the 27th International Conference on Human Factors in Computing Systems (CHI). ACM (2009)
10. Weinberger, A., Fische, F., Stegmann, K.: Computer-Supported Collaborative Learning in Higher Education: Scripts for Argumentative Knowledge Construction in Distributed Groups. In: Proceedings of International Conference on Computer-Supported Collaborative Larning (CSCL). International Society of the Learning Sciences, pp. 717–726 (2005)

The Application of the CISD² Methodology
for the Definition of a Serious Game
Competence-Based Learning Scenario in the Domain
of Sustainable Manufacturing

Gregor Cerinsek[1], Heiko Duin[2], Fiorella Colombo[3], Borzoo Pourabdollahian[3],
and Stanislaw Plebanek[4]

[1] Institute for Innovation and Development of University of Ljubljana
Kongresni trg 12, 1000 Ljubljana, Slovenia
gregor.cerinsek@guest.arnes.si
[2] BIBA – Bremer Institut für Produktion und Logistik GmbH,
Hochschulring 20, D-28359 Bremen, Germany
du@biba.uni-bremen.de
[3] Politecnico di Milano, Department of Management, Economics and Industrial Engineering
Via Lambruschini 4/b, Milan, Italy
{fiorella.colombo,borzoo.pourabdollahian}@polimi.it
[4] Lean Enterprise Institute Polska, ul. Muchoborska 18, 54-424 Wrocław
stanislaw.plebanek@lean.org.pl

Abstract. The main aim of this paper is to follow the Contextualized Interactive Story Driven Development (CISD²) Methodology to support the definition of a serious game competence-based learning scenario in the domain of sustainable manufacturing. The core competence to be addressed by the scenario is the "Ability to perform a Life Cycle Assessment (LCA)" in a globally acting manufacturing enterprise. The resulting content can be used as input by the serious game developers in specifying the stories to be implemented. Finally, some first evaluation results on learning outcomes are provided.

Keywords: serious game, sustainable manufacturing, life cycle assessment, content development, competence-based learning.

1 Introduction

The manufacturing industries have the potential to become a driving force for the creation of a sustainable society [1,2]. They can design and implement integrated sustainable practices and develop products and services that contribute to better environmental performance. This requires a shift in the perception and understanding of industrial production and the adoption of a more holistic approach to conducting business [3]. Sustainable manufacturing uses a more holistic approach that considers all life-cycle stages, from pre-manufacturing, manufacturing and use through post-use. This holistic view of sustainable manufacturing takes the aim of adopting

M. Ma et al. (Eds.): SGDA 2012, LNCS 7528, pp. 193–207, 2012.

sustainable principles across the whole manufacturing life-cycle, and identifying all inputs and outputs for continuous improvement action [4].

Becoming a sustainable manufacturing enterprise is a challenge for almost every manufacturing organization in the world because of its multidimensional nature. In this situation having multi-skilled and flexible managers and engineers who can adapt to frequent changes is a competitive advantage for manufacturing companies. The training needs to achieve two criteria: the learners need to be able to apply the learning into complex, life-like situations and the learning outcomes need to be achieved rapidly. Competence-based and technology-enhanced learning (TEL) in general and serious games and simulations in particular have recently attracted a great deal of attention as they have the potential to deliver on both accounts. Serious Gaming has proven to support learners in acquiring new and complex knowledge and is ideally suited to support problem based learning by creating engaging experiences around a contextual problem where users must apply competences to solve these presented challenges [5,6,7].

In the mid 90s of the 20th century, unaware of the term Serious Gaming, several research institutes started to develop games to be applied in the domain of manufacturing [7]. Providing a unique environment where instructional contents and entertainment are combined, serious games have been welcomed by different sections of manufacturing systems in order to improve the knowledge of employees. As an example, the evaluation of the "Shortfall" serious game, which is simulating car manufacturing company to become more sustainable, indicated that students achieved new knowledge and also there was a general consensus among students about enjoying while playing the game. Moreover, as an important point, enhancing the communication skill was highlighted as the most effective outcome in this game [8].

Although important, a serious game alone does not suffice to ensure learning and it is necessary to have a set of methodologies and tools to provide a learning environment that enable the tailoring of personalized learning plans tailored to the needs of the learner and supporting the individual (and the teacher) in assessing the progress made. A key challenge of building a serious game as an effective learning and competence development tool is the need to tailor the game design to address the competence domain [9, 10].

2   The TARGET Learning Process Supporting Rapid Competence Development

The presented challenge of reducing the lead-time for a leaner to achieve target productivity has been addressed by the European FP7 Integrated Project "TARGET". The main objective of the TARGET project is to develop a new genre of TEL environments that support rapid competence development within the learning domains of innovation, project management and sustainable manufacturing. The TARGET Integrative Framework consists of five key developments: Threshold Concepts, Experience Management, Social Communities, Cognitive Management and Knowledge Ecology (further information can be found in [9]). As a result of the project an interactive learning platform is being created. TARGET platform is the main outcome of the project and it integrates its results. It consists of a few elements out of which a serious game is the one directly connected with the process of competence development [11].

2.1   Description of the Learning Process

In TARGET, the learning process draws heavily from Problem Based Learning (PBL) [12] and Action Learning (AL) [13], resulting in the use of digital interactive stories that provide situated rich contexts where a learner is required to apply and develop competences to achieve successful outcomes [9]. Users are confronted with challenges within the game in a form of a digital interactive story. Scenarios, covering the three learning domains, include several stories, which were developed based on cues provided from domain experts.

The learning process begins with curricula design. It consists of creating the learning plans that may be goal-oriented or self-directed. For goal-oriented plan the Competence Analyzer is being used to define the gap between the current and desired competence profile and then the Learning Strategy defines the appropriate set of stories addressing the emerged gap. For the self-directed plan the users themselves choose which stories they want to play, including the competences that are being addressed by certain stories.

Before playing the TARGET serious game the users are presented with a briefing of the story they are going to tackle. It provides the information needed to understand the context (goal of the story, character descriptions, work breakdown structure, etc.). The learners proceed to the game after they select the playable character. Players then enter the 3D world, they need to interact with the virtual environment, make decisions, take actions in order to complete the task they have been presented in the briefing. The environment in the game includes facilities, characters and tools that help in completing the story. Interaction can take various forms: from moving around the area, showing your attitude to Non-Playable Characters (NPC) to engaging in dialogues with them. The attitude of NPCs towards the learner differs between different rounds of playing the same scenario – this makes the game non-repeatable.

After experiencing the story the reflection phase takes place. The learners can observe a playback of their experience by using the Competence Performance Analyzer (CPA). It is presented together with a graphical representation of competence performance measure in time. The competences are being measured throughout the game. Each of them is related to different predefined variables. The visualization of the playback of the game experience and competence performance in time enhances the learners' reflection process. Finally, the experience is being stored in the knowledge ecosystem where it can be shared with player's peers. This part of learning process facilitates exchange of experiences amongst different users and enables learning from others' experiences. The TARGET learning process is further described in details in [9, 11].

2.2   Story Outline with the Description of Game Mechanics

The sustainable manufacturing scenario reflects the phases an enterprise has to run through when dealing with sustainability issues. Within the game scenario, the player takes over the role of a Sustainability Manager who was recently hired by the Chief Executive Manager (CEO) of a production company. The company is an internationally acting manufacturing company for household machines. One of their product lines is coffee machines. The model XC 100 G (Xtended Content 100 cl Green) is offered as a green product because it uses less energy than other coffee machines in the market. Now, the CEO of the company decided the production process of the same coffee machine should also become green. The whole life cycle of the coffee machine XC 100 G consists of production (and assembly) and usage. The player needs to perform a Life-cycle Assessment (LCA) for the production process of the coffee machine. The other managers are aware of that but do not have complete information or knowledge about player's mission. The player needs to communicate with the CEO and the Production Manager in order to obtain important information needed for conducting the LCA. The task is completed when the LCA Report is submitted to the CEO by clicking the "Submit" button in the LCA Tool. The CEO and the other managers are non-player characters (NPCs) who are driven by the game engine. The player starts to execute the relevant steps of the LCA, i.e. 1) setting the objectives, 2) setting the boundaries, 3) selecting the flow chart, 4) selecting inputs and outputs, 5) deciding on the data for inputs and outputs, 6) setting the impact categories.

Fig. 1. Screenshot from the Game Scenario

Fig. 1 shows a screen of the game scenario. Within the game scenario information objects concerning the LCA are coded in such a way that they are either being hidden in a game object or a sentence of a NPC. The two game objects which provide information to the player is a big wall screen showing production processes and a couple of PCs (e.g. on the table of the CEO in Fig. 1) which are accessible by the player showing ERP related data. The most important NPCs of the scenario are the CEO, the Production Manger, and the shift manager from the production site. All of them are equipped with a dialogue corpus allowing them to answer player's questions. When the player asks the relevant questions these NPCs reveal important information which is then could be entered by the player into the accompanying LCA Tool.

3   Contextualized Interactive Story Driven Development (CISD^2) Methodology

To ensure that the process of designing a serious game becomes more predictable, and to enhance the educational or instructional effect of games, a systematic approach to guide and organize game design is needed [14]. In particular, there is a need for methodologies that can reliably distil pedagogical content from domain experts and represent it in a way that can be easily interpreted by game designers [10].

The stories for the sustainable manufacturing scenario were created using the Contextualized Interactive Story Driven Development (CISD^2) methodology [10]. The methodology consists of a process with two strands, one dealing with the definition of competences to be addressed by the game scenario and the other dealing with respective scenario artifacts (characters, objects, interaction possibilities, etc.), thus bridging the gap between domain experts and pedagogues on the one side, and game developers on the other. The two strands of the methodology are interlinked to ensure that there is coherence between them. The development of stories begins with a set of competences that someone would like to gain and ends with a set of stories that the learner must play in the TARGET game environment to gain the desired competences. Within the methodology, each step in the process provides input to the next one and feedback to the earlier steps. The methodology proposed is presented in Figure 1 and described in details in [10].

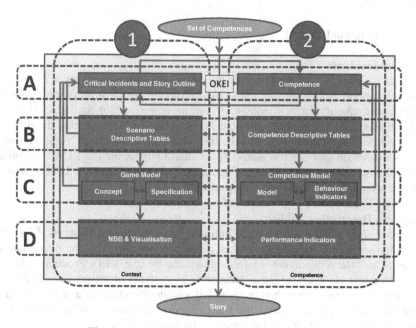

Fig. 2. CISD2 methodology for Story Building

The CISD² provided the necessary details to build the situated learning contexts based on interactive stories where the set of situated contexts, didactical contexts and required models for the scene dynamics were developed. The CISD² was applied to develop a game scenario for the domain of Sustainable Manufacturing based on the LCA method. The work was carried out by a panel of domain experts, competence modellers and ICT specialists who worked collaboratively from: Institute for Innovation and Development of University of Ljubljana (IRI UL), Bremer Institut für Produktion und Logistik GmbH (BIBA), Lean Enterprise Institute Poland (LEIP), Politecnico di Milano (POLIMI) and VirTEch Ltd. The experts forming the panel had extensive experience with the field of sustainable manufacturing and knowledge of the content. There was intentional diversity among experts in perspectives, experience and familiarity with the different areas within the complex field of sustainable manufacturing. Together, the panel ran several face-to-face workshops and many virtual meetings (using the Skype software) applying the framework and discussing and refining results.

4   Serious Game Learning Scenario in the Domain of Sustainable Manufacturing

In this section the paper presents the results of applying the CISD² for the Sustainable Manufacturing scenario. It is structured in two sub-sections; the first sub-section presents the results covering the contextual strand of the methodology, the next sub-section furthermore presents the results covering the competence strand of the methodology.

4.1   Contextual Strand

Critical Incidents
Critical incidents (CIs) identified for the Sustainable Manufacturing scenario are: 1) Getting support before starting the LCA; 2) Making sure that all other involved pay respect and take the LCA seriously; 3) Setting objectives for the LCA; 4) Keep the CEO updated; 5) Setting the right boundaries for the LCA; 6) Getting the right information in sufficient detail to define the flow chart; 7) Definition of "right" (the ones to be used later on and not too many) Inputs and Outputs for the LCA; 8) Collecting accurate and relevant data; 9) Choosing the right impact categories; 10) Preparation of the LCA report based on proper interpretation.

Scenario Descriptive Tables
The analysis of the CIs led to the definition of several **situated contexts (SCs)**, which were furthermore hierarchically broken down into sub-contexts. The three main identified SCs of the scenario are: 1) Talking to someone (e.g. CEO, Production Manager, Line Manager etc.); 2) Taking a decision (e.g. in terms of setting objectives, setting boundaries, defining flow chart etc.); and 3) Visiting the shop floor (e.g. to observe, to take direct measures, to access the ERP system). An example of a Situated context table "Talking to the CEO" is presented in the Table 1.

Table 1. An example of the Situated context table for "Talking to the CEO"

ID: Situated context
Name: Talking to the CEO
Input: Triggers: - *Sustainability Manager:* 1)Decision by himself/herself to visit the CEO; 2) Was reminded by the CEO to visit him - *CEO:* 1) Sustainability Manager shows up; 2) Reminds the Sustainability Manager to visit him
Decision: - *Sustainability Manager:* 1) Just ask the CEO; 2) Make proposals to the CEO - *CEO:* 1) Just say what to do; 2) Agree on the suggestion of the Sustainability Manager; 3) Disagree

Output:
    1.   CEO and Sustainability Manager reach a common understanding
    2.   CEO and Sustainability Manager do not reach a common understanding

Characters:
    1.   CEO
    2.   Sustainability Manager

Environment: Office Space

The didactical context (DC) takes into account the pedagogical content that should be supported in the game scenarios, how difficult or challenging they may be for the learner to learn. It also identifies the common pitfalls that are associated and identifies cues and strategies that may be considered in the design of the game scenarios. Some of the key didactical contexts considered for the scenario are: 1) Conducting the LCA, 2) Decision making, 3) Type of data that can be collected from different departments (e.g. production, marketing, line etc.) and which data is more or less relevant to conducting the LCA, 4) Identification and addressing of the interest of different characters in order to achieve his/her goal of collecting the data etc. An example of a Didactical context table "Decision making" is presented in the Table 2.

Table 2. An example of a Didactical context table for "Decision making"

ID: Didactical context
What to reach: Decision making
Is it difficult? Why? Should take into account all the necessary dimensions, the profile of the characters and the output to be achieved. It has impact on costs, time and quality of the whole process.
Common Pitfalls / Mistakes: - Do not consider all the aspects involved or consider everything in detail. - Waste too much time on a decision - Do not prioritize a decision (something that is extremely important can take time, other things must be decided in a short timeframe)
Cues and Strategies - Focus on the output of the decision and then decide the importance of it within the process considered -Perform a CBA for the most important decisions - Prioritize the decisions -Involve someone that can help

The contextual dynamics are furthermore composed of 1) soft processes, 2) business processes, and 3) behavioral patterns, descriptions of which can be found in [10].

4.2   Competence Strand

The three main competences that Sustainable Manufacturing scenario is designed to address are:

- **Ability to Perform Life Cycle Assessment (LCA):** It is related to conducting and executing the key phases of the LCA concerning a specific product or process.
- **Decision making:** A very important competence for conducting projects such as the LCA as it requires effective and on-time decisions.
- **Data gathering:** The term used for the process of preparing and collecting the data needed for conducting the LCA. The purpose of data gathering is to obtain information to keep on record, to make decisions about important steps, to pass information on to others involved etc.

Other competences addressed are Systems/Holistic Thinking[1]; Interested Parties[2]; Social Networking; Communication; Leadership; Conflict Management; Trust Building; "U-Glasses"[3]; Cost/Benefit Analysis.

Once the CIs had been identified for the scenario (the contextual strand of the methodology process), the following tasks were conducted through discussions with domain experts and pedagogues:

1. The set of competences that were relevant for each CI was identified.
2. The CIs were prioritized, independent of the competences that were related to them. The prioritization was done by considering their meaning and their impact on a possible Story, using a scale of 1 (very important) to 3 (low importance).
3. Once the CIs with priority "1" were identified, the competences were revisited to determine their level of relevance. A competence that is relevant for more than half of the CIs is labeled as "highly relevant"; a competence that is relevant for at least one CI is labeled as "medium relevant"; other competences have low relevance.

Competence Descriptive Tables
The process of describing competences according to the OKEI Competence Modelling Framework [15,16] includes: 1) identifying sub-competences (Individual factors), and 2) identifying the contextual factors (Organization, Knowledge and Environment factors) that may affect the application of the competence and associated sub-competences. Table 3 presents some examples of the competence model for "systems/holistic thinking" structured in accordance with the OKEI competence modeling framework. The full competence model together with the process of identifying and describing competences in the field of Sustainable Manufacturing is described in details in [16].

---

[1] The detailed description of the competence Systems/Holistic thinking can be found in [16].
[2] The identification of all the parties that have an interest in the project, their specific interests and sequencing them in the order of importance to the project [17].
[3] The U-Glasses competence describes the ability to see the world "through the glasses" of someone else, i.e. meaning to understand others positions and interests.

Table 3. Some examples of the competence model for "systems/holistic thinking" structured in accordance with the OKEI competence modeling framework

Competence: Systems/holistic thinking			
Organizational factors (O)	Knowledge factors (K)	Environmental factors (E)	Individual factors (I)
-Accepting environmental responsibilities throughout the value chain -Adoption of more integrated and systematic methods to improve sustainability performance	-Legislation and existing sustainability standards -Best practices and global sustainability trends -Different business models	-Dynamics and ever-changing environment (e.g. climate changes, social inequity) that force organizations to go sustainable -Sustainability as a new way of thinking	-Ability to take a multi-scale perspective -Life-cycle thinking -Ability to perceive environmental challenges and policies (regulations and standards) not as a barrier to growth but as a new opportunity

When analyzing the scenario in terms of specific situated contexts developed, the sub-competences that are relevant for the scenario have been identified and selected using the literature that is central to Sustainable Manufacturing (e.g. [18, 19, 20]) and they have been analysed for the purposes of identifying the specific elements of competences that are particularly relevant for Life Cycle Assessment. The analysis of the sub-competences that are specifically relevant for the Situated Contexts help to further streamline the competences that should be addressed in the game scenario and this leads to more granular learning plans that are adapted as best as possible for learning and to tackle the Situated Context.

Competence Model

Once the OKEI descriptive tables have been developed for all competences that have a high relevance (i.e. Ability to perform LCA, Systems/Holistic thinking, Interested parties, Decision making), the different relationships among the sub-competences (Individual factors) have been furthermore identified: 1) within each single competence of high relevance, and 2) across different competences of high relevance.

Some examples of relationships among the sub-competences of the competence "Ability to perform LCA" are listed below:

- The sub-competences "Analytic skills" and "Ability to collect relevant data" are all prerequisites of the sub-competences "Ability to set objectives", "Ability to set right boundaries", "Flow chart definition skills", and "Ability to define inputs and outputs".
- The sub-competence "Ability to set objectives" impacts the sub-competence "Ability to focus on relevant issues".
- The sub-competence "Cost management skills" is associated to "Ability to focus on relevant issues".

The competence model for the Sustainable Manufacturing scenario is the collection of all the high relevant competences, their sub-competences, contextual factors and all the relationships among them.

Behavioural and Performance Indicators

In order to determine if a person is able to apply a certain competence in practice, it is useful to operationalize them by means of behaviour that can be observed and interpreted while a learner is engaged in the game. The interpretation of such behaviours in terms of competences is mediated by contextual factors. Behavioural Indicators (BIs) are the observable indicators that can be used to determine if a person applies a competence appropriately and effectively in a given situation. Similarly, BIs can be used to determine the lack of a competence of a person. BIs are defined generally for any context, Performance Indicators (PIs) provide the specific measurement of a BI within the game [21, 22].

Table 4. Competences and associated performance indicators

Competence: Ability to Perform LCA **Performance Indicator:** The ability to perform an LCA is measured as the distance between the player's solution and the correct solution. The correct solution is encoded in the information units. Information units always contain correct information. However, some agents also provide thoughts or assumptions with incorrect information, but these are not considered as information units. Whenever the player enters data into the LCA tool, an event with relevant information is sent to the Competence Performance Analyzer (CPA) which updates the calculations. Therefore measuring the Ability to perform the LCA takes into account the time (i.e. when the player enters the data) and the correctness of the data that the player enters in the LCA tool.
Competence: Data Gathering **Performance Indicator:** Gathering data is done by talking to agents and querying game objects. It is directly measured by the quotient of the information units found and the total number of information units.
Competence: Decision Making **Performance Indicator:** A decision is taken whenever the player enters data into the LCA tool. An indicator measures the decision performance, i.e. "how good / competent" the player is in decision making based on: 1) the time he/she needs to take the decision, and 2) the quality (correctness) of the decision. For each decision player needs to take there are information units coded in the game. Only when the player detects information units he/she is able to take decisions (otherwise, they are based on guessing). Each decision has multiple options in the range of [0,1] describing the correctness of the decision. Decision Performance takes into account the time a person needs to take a decision after finding the first connected information unit together with the effective quality of that decision.

Table 4 presents three examples of performance indicators, measuring three main competences addressed by the scenario. Measuring all these competences depends largely on searching and finding relevant and correct data. To support this, the concept of an Information Unit is introduced. An information unit is a piece of information which is coded in the game, e.g. a specific sentence of an agent revealing very specific LCA relevant data.

5   Results from the Evaluation

Evaluation of the Sustainable Manufacturing Scenario has been done from 11th to 13th of July 2012 at a laboratory of the University of Bremen. The sample consisted of 24 master students of Management and Industrial Engineering. Evaluation was divided into three steps:

1. All participants filled the first part of a questionnaire with general and scenario related questions to collect demographic data and to assess present understanding of LCA related issues.
2. An instructor introduces the TARGET software and demonstrated how to play it. The participants played the scenario for 20 minutes. After that all participants reflected on their performance related to the three competences mentioned above. Due to the unavailability of the computerized performance assessment system, the participants have been asked to do a self assessment for the three competences on a scale of 1-9 (where 1 = very poor and 9 = very good) for the phases of beginning, during, and the end of the gaming session. After that, participants were asked how they could improve their performance. All participants played the game for a second time for 20 minutes trying to improve their performance. At the end of the second playing session participants were asked for another self-assessment concerning the three competences during the second round.
3. Finally, all participants filled the second part of a questionnaire to gather in-game experience, updates on the scenario understanding and general post game evaluation

The pre- and post-parts of the questionnaire were all in English language. The native language of most participants was German. Some of the scenario related questions which were asked before and after game play were:

- What is the logical order of steps to perform a LCA?
- What and who are the most valuable sources of data for conducting the LCA?
- What is most important when performing a LCA?

The first question concerning the logical order of steps was answered correctly by 10 participants representing 42% before the game was played. After executing the game scenario 20 participants (83%) were able to give the correct answer. The second question concerning the sources of data were answered correctly by 50% of the participants before the gaming and only 46% afterwards. This not expected change is due to the assumption of the participants that the CEO is a good source of data. However, the CEO just represents the source of information (on boundaries, impact categories etc.); and not the source of data itself. Therefore we consider that this could most probably be due to misunderstanding related to the language barrier (the difference between the concept of information and the concept of data). The last question concerning importance was answered by 46% before and after game play. It can be concluded that learning took place, but there is still potential to enhance the scenario in such a way that the important things are more visible.

The following results are focusing on the question, whether the participants were able to improve performance in competence Ability to Perform LCA through self-assessment during the two rounds of game playing.

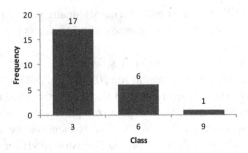

Fig. 3. Distribution of participants self-assessment of competence Ability to Perform LCA in the beginning of the first round of gaming (*n*=24)

In the beginning of the first gaming round more than the half of all participants assessed themselves to have only marginal performance in Ability to Perform LCA (see Fig. 3). 17 of 24 participants (71%) assessed their own competence on a scale of 1-9 as poor (values between 1 and 3), 6 participants (25%) as medium (values between 4 and 6), and only 1 participant (4%) as good (values between 7 and 9). The highest values participants gave was 8 (1 participant).

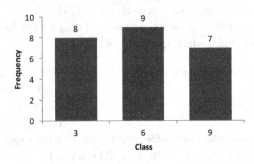

Fig. 4. Distribution of participants self-assessment of competence Ability to Perform LCA at the end of the second round of gaming (*n*=24)

This situation changed by the end of the second gaming round (see Fig. 4). A total of 67% assessed to have medium to good performance in Ability to Perform LCA (38% with values between 4 and 6, 29% with values greater equal 7). Only 33% assessed themselves still with limited performance. The highest values participants gave was 8 (3 participants).

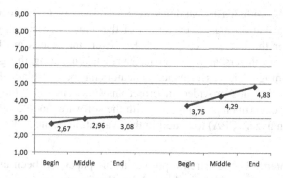

Fig. 5. Development of the average of self-assessment of competence Ability to Perform LCA (left graph represents first round, right graph represents second round of gaming, $n=24$)

The average value of competence Information Gathering grew from the beginning of the first gaming round to the end of the second gaming round from 2.67 to 4.83 (see Fig. 5) with a standard deviation of 1.76 (beginning of first round) to 2.18 (end of second round). 33% of participants said that they learned nothing or only a little (difference of 0 or 1 between beginning and end) while 63% learned medium (difference of 2 to 4) and 4% said to learn a lot (difference of more than 5 points).

6   Conclusion

Traditionally, engineers and managers have been educated to contribute mainly to the production potential of societies focusing on costs, time and quality. However, the ecological imperative and societal changes have caused significant demand for knowledge workers working in a manufacturing company with the competences to address impacts of sustainable development. The sustainable manufacturing has been introduced as a novel area in the face of serious challenges such as global warming and scarcity of natural resources.

The paper has addressed the importance of serious games serving for educational purposes in (sustainable) manufacturing. TARGET project is aiming to develop an innovative TEL tool that could enable tailored competence development, driven by actual needs of users. Applying the CISD^2 methodology in the domain of Sustainable Manufacturing we have developed the specific scenario content. The core competence to be addressed by the scenario is the ability to perform a LCA in a globally acting manufacturing enterprise. This competence is developed by putting the player in a series of critical incidents with the task to define objectives and boundaries of the LCA, to acquire production related knowledge to define a materials and energy flow-chart, to collect relevant data, to calculate environmental (and other) impacts and to interpret the results. To be successful in this mission, the player needs to know about the pitfalls of the LCA process as well as maintaining good social relationships with managers on the executive layer of the company. Otherwise, the quality of the LCA will be so poor that no useful recommendations can be drawn from it.

An evaluation with master students at the University of Bremen has been performed showing that during the execution of the game scenario players learned and performed better the longer they played. However, the results are based on a self-assessment of the players and not on measures taken during the game play. Even though the meaning of the performance indicators has been explained there is still the risk that the participants' provided incorrect answers. Therefore future research will involve another experimental evaluation with the software module called Competence Performance Analyzer (CPA) to underpin the evaluation results.

Acknowledgement. The research reported in this paper has been undertaken within the TARGET project, which is funded by the European Community under the Seventh Framework Programme (Grant Agreement IST 231717). We the authors of the paper wish to acknowledge the Commission for their support. Furthermore, we wish to thank all the other members of the TARGET consortium for their valuable work and contributions to this paper.

References

1. NCS. Standards for Sustainability. Resource manual. National Centre for Sustainability at Swinburne University of Technology (2007), `https://www.skillsonline.net.au/clearhse/Preview.do?no=216&type=O` (accessed September 15, 2010)
2. O'Sullivan, B., Rolstadås, A., Filos, A.: Global education in manufacturing strategy. Intellectual Manufacturing 22, 663–674 (2011)
3. Maxwell, D., Sheate, W., van der Volst, R.: Functional and systems aspects of the sustainable product and service development approach for industry. Journal of Cleaner Production 14(17), 1466–1479 (2006)
4. WCSD. World Centre for Sustainable Development. E-brochure (2010), `http://www.pagegangster.com/p/MwNhJ/` (retrieved October 15, 2010)
5. Wong, W.L., Shen, C., Nocera, L., Carriazo, E., Tang, F., Bugga, S., Narayanan, H., Wang, H., Ritterfeld, U.: Serious video game effectiveness. In: Proceedings of the International Conference on Advances in Computer Entertainment Technology, ACE 2007, Salzburg, Austria, June 13-15, vol. 203, pp. 49–55. ACM, New York (2007), `http://doi.acm.org/10.1145/1255047.1255057` (accessed January 15, 2011)
6. Ribeiro, C., Jepp, P., Pereira, J.: Lessons Learnt in Building Serious Games and Virtual Worlds for Competence Development. In: Taisch, M., Cassina, J., Smeds, R. (eds.) 14th Workshop of the Special Interest Group (SIG) on Experimental Interactive Learning in Industrial Management of the IFIP Working Group, Milano, pp. 52–61 (2010), `http://sites.google.com/site/ifip57sigexilim` (accessed January 15, 2011)
7. Hauge, J.B., Riedel, J., Fradinho, M., Westra, W.: Addressing Research Fragmentation in Serious Gaming for Manufacturing. In: Taisch, M., Cassina, J., Smeds, R. (eds.) 14th Workshop of the Special Interest Group (SIG) on Experimental Interactive Learning in Industrial Management of the IFIP Working Group, Milano, pp. 62–70 (2011), `http://sites.google.com/site/ifip57sigexilim/` (accessed January 15, 2011)
8. Qualters, D.M., Isaacs, J.A., Cullinane, T.P., Larid, J., McDonald, A. Corriere, J. D.: A Game Approach to Teach Environmentally Benign Manufacturing in the Supply Chain. Journal for the Scholarship of Teaching and Learning 2(2) (2008)

9. Oliveira, M., Andersen, B., Pereira, J., Seager, W., Ribeiro, C.: The Use of Integrative Framework to Support the Development of Competences. In: International Conference on Serious Games Development and Applications, Lisbon (2011)
10. Duin, H., Oliveira, M., Thoben, K.D.: A Methodology for Developing Serious Gaming Stories for Sustainable Manufacturing. In: Katzy, B., Holzmann, T., Sailer, K., Thoben, K.-D. (eds.), pp. 717–725. Strascheg Center for Entrepreneurship (SCE), Munich (2012)
11. Fradinho, M., Andersen, B., Lefrere, P., Oliveira, A.: The New Path to Competence Development. In: Cunningham, P., Cunningham, M. (eds.) eChallenges e-2009 Conference Proceedings (2009)
12. Barrows, H., Tamblyn, R.: Problem-Based Learning: An Approach to Medical Education. Springer Publishing Company, New York (1990)
13. Gabrielsson, J., Tell, J., Politis, D.: Business simulation exercises in small business management education: using principles and ideas from action learning. Routledge, Taylor & Francis Group (2010)
14. Vidani, A., Chittaro, L.: Using a Task Modeling Formalism in the Design of Serious Games for Emergency Medical Procedures. In: Conference in Games and Virtual Worlds for Serious Applications, VS-Games 2009. IEEE Computer Society, UK (2009), http://www.computer.org/portal/web/csdl/doi/10.1109/VS-GAMES.2009.24
15. Petersen, S., Heikura, T.: Modelling Project Management and Innovation Competences for Technology Enhanced Learning. In: EChallenges 2010, Warsaw, Poland (2010)
16. Cerinsek, G., Petersen, S.A., Heikura, T.: Contextually enriched competence model in the field of sustainable manufacturing for simulation style technology enhanced learning environments. Journal of Intelligent Manufacturing (2011), doi:10.1007/s10845-011-0554-0
17. IPMA. ICB - IPMA Competence Baseline, v 3.0 (2006), http://www.ipma.ch/publication/Pages/ICB-IPMACompetenceBaseline.aspx (retrieved May 2010)
18. SAIC – Scientific Applications International Corporation. Life Cycle Assessment: Principles and Practices. National Risk Management Research Laboratory, Office of Research and Development. U.S. Environmental Protection Agency. Cincinnati, Ohio (2006)
19. Feifel, S., Walk, W., Wursthorn, S.: LCA, how are you doing today? A snapshot from the 5th German LCA workshop. International Journal of Life Cycle Assessment 15, 139–142 (2010)
20. Kloepffer, W.: Life Cycle Sustainability Assessment of Products. International Journal of Life Cycle Assessment 13(2), 89–95 (2008)
21. Cowley, B., Bedek, M., Heikura, T., Ribeiro, C., Petersen, S.A.: The Quatric Process Model to Support Serious Games Development for Contextualized Competence-Based Learning and Assessment. In: Cruz-Cunha, M.M. (ed.) Serious Games as Educational, Business, and Research Tools: Development and Design, pp. 491–519. IGI Global, Hershey (2012)
22. Bedek, M., Petersen, S.A., Heikura, T.: From Behavioral Indicators to Contextualized Competence. In: ICALT 2011, Athens, USA (2011)

Evaluating the Validity of a Non-invasive Assessment Procedure

Paul C. Seitlinger, Michael A. Bedek, Simone Kopeinik, and Dietrich Albert

Knowledge Management Institute, Graz University of Technology, Graz, Austria
{paul.seitlinger,michael.bedek}@tugraz.at

Abstract. Recent developments in serious games allow for in-game adaptations to enhance the learner´s current cognitive, motivational or emotional state. Providing suitable adaptations requires a valid assessment of the psycho-pedagogical constructs the game should adapt to. An explicit assessment, e.g. by questionnaires occurring repeatedly on the screen, would impair the learner´s game flow. Therefore, a non-invasive and implicit assessment procedure is required. In the course of the European research project TARGET, we established an assessment procedure which is based on the interpretation of the learner´s actions in the virtual environment, called *Behavioural Indicators* (BIs). A set of 16 BIs has been formulated to assess the learner´s current emotional, motivational and clearness state. In this present work, we describe how these BIs can be validated and focus on the innovative elements of the methodological procedure, the material, experiential considerations and the statistical analysis to be applied in an empirical study.

Keywords: Evaluation, Validation, Non-invasive Assessment, Motivation, Emotion, Problem Solving.

1   Introduction

Serious games have the potential of providing learners with an appealing and intrinsically motivating learning context. Usually, this potential is either taken for granted or examined through questionnaires or interviews in the course of evaluation studies. However, an *adaptive* game would increase the probability that a serious game fully exploits this potential. Providing appropriate adaptations to the learner´s state while she or he is playing a game scenario requires a valid assessment of the psycho-pedagogical constructs the game should adapt to. An explicit assessment, e.g. by questionnaires occurring repeatedly in short time intervals on the screen, would probably destroy the learner´s potential experience of flow [1]. Thus, a non-invasive and implicit assessment procedure is required. In the course of the European research project TARGET (http://www.reachyourtarget.org/), we aim at in-game adaptations based on the ongoing and non-invasive assessment of the learner's *current psycho-pedagogical state*[2]. The non-invasive assessment procedure is based on the observation and interpretation of a learner´s actions and behavioural patterns in the virtual environment. We refer to these actions as *Behavioural Indicators* (BIs). To this end,

M. Ma et al. (Eds.): SGDA 2012, LNCS 7528, pp. 208–218, 2012.

we have formulated a set of 16 BIs to assess the learner´s psycho-pedagogical state during game-play[3]. The psycho-pedagogical state is represented as a row vector encompassing values for the learner´s current *emotional, motivational* and *clearness* state.

The assessment of the emotional state is built upon the *circumplex model of emotion* [6], consisting of the two continuous dimensions of *activation*(also called arousal) and *valence*. With regards to the construct motivation, the emphasis is on *achievement motivation* as described by [4], which can be divided into two independent dimensions: *approach motivation* and *avoidance motivation*, resulting in a *quadripolar*model of (achievement-) motivation[5]. Approach motivation is the motivation to achieve and aim for competence in a particular knowledge domain (for example because of the learner´s intrinsic interest in the topic). Avoidance motivation is the motivation to avoid incompetence (e.g. the learner would like to avoid bad grades in an exam).Finally, *clearness* refers to the learner´s *appropriate problem representation*, i.e. the awareness of the current problem state and the knowledge about the steps to approach a (sub-)goal state of the game scenario.

The five dimensions (*Activation, Valence, Approach Motivation, Avoidance Motivation* and *Clearness*) are assessed by BIs, which are gathered continuously throughout the game-play. For the ongoing assessment, the overall game-play is divided into consecutive and equally long lasting periods of time, so called *time slices*. As a starting point (based on pilot studies), we set the length of the time slices to 30 seconds. The BIs' "raw values" are cumulated at the end of each time slice. They serve as predictor variables in five multiple regression equations (i.e. one for each dimension). Each regression equation consists of a constant intercept, the 16 predictors, and finally, the 16 predictors' weights.

2   Objectives

So far, the predictors' weights have been established as a result of expert ratings on the BIs' predictive validity for each of the five dimensions. However, we aim to establish the predictors' weights by more objective measures in order to increase the validity of the overall assessment procedure.Thus, the main focus of this paper is to describe the innovative elements of the methodological procedure, the material, experiential considerations and the statistical analysis to be applied in an empirical study.

The general aim is to compare the BI-values with establishedquestionnaires on emotion and motivation as well as with self-constructed items on clearness. In particular, the study design is conceived to address the following research question: How predictive are a learner's activities (measured by BIs) in a computer game for her or his internal state?

3   Design

The study design addresses the relationships between the BIs and the five dimensions (activation, valence, approach, avoidance, clearness). The whole data set D consists of criterion variables (questionnaires on motivation, emotion and clearness) and predictor variables (i.e. the BIs). Our general aim is to identify a behavioral profile or pattern of game activities pointing towards a certain internal psycho-pedagogical state.In a first step we compute bivariate correlations and analyze corresponding scatter-plots in order to examine whether the variables are linearly related to each other, as well as to get a first impression of patterns within the data set. In a second step we apply an exploratory factor analysis to figure out the factor structure of the variables and to obtain a clearer picture of interrelations. With respect to our theoretical framework we expect to get at least two factors.

Before turning to our statistical approach the next sections give a description of the questionnaires on the criterions and on the BIs (predictor variables).

4   Material

For the evaluation of the BIs' validity we adopt approaches suggested by [7] and [8] in order to conduct a non-invasive measurement procedure and to elicit the internal state of the participants. The internal state, relevant for this context, encompasses emotional, motivational and clearness-aspects and will be compared with the BIs (see section 4.4). It is measured by means of standardized questionnaires as well as self-constructed items. Similar to [9] we will apply the *Self-Assessment Manikin* (SAM) [10] to measure both dimensions of the emotional model (activation and valence; see figure 1. For the assessment of the motivational state we will apply the German version of the *Questionnaire on Current Motivation* (QCM) [11]. Since standardized questionnaires on the construct clearness (that are appropriate for the TARGET´s game context) do not exist, we elaborated 4 items asking for the participant's current problem representation.

In the following we briefly describe these questionnaires. We conclude this section with a brief description of the BIs by exemplifying a small subset of them.

4.1   Emotion Elicitation

Based on the proposed approach of [12] to use a mixed and dimensional emotion concept, we structure and represent the participants' emotional states in a two-dimensional space of valence and activation. Additionally, we use subjective ratings since they appear to be more reliable than physiological indicators [13]. Instead of using a purely verbal instrument, such as the Semantic Differential Scale [14], we apply the Self-Assessment Manikins [15].

Hence, we do not rely on emotion words, whose meanings are fuzzy and vary between (and even within) cultures, but place the participant's current emotional state in a coordinate system (see figure 2). The inner state is not labeled by an emotional term, such as happy or sad, but with its current x- and y-coordinate within the space spanned by the activation and valence dimension. In addition to the advantage of abandoning an artificial categorization and naming of emotional states this approach is independent of language. Due to its non-intrusiveness, reliability and wide spectrum of emotion recognition [9] researchers have been frequently using SAM to assess activation and valence.

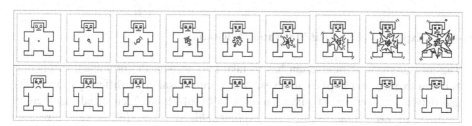

Fig. 1. Activation and Valence scales of the SAM

Figure 1 shows the two SAM-scales that will be applied to measure the experienced activation and valence. Both are 9-point Likert-scales with a verbal anchor on each side. The activation scale (figure 1, first panel) ranges from a relaxed, sleepy figure to an excited, wide-eyed figure, which are verbally anchored by the words "calm" ("ruhig") and "excited" ("aufgeregt"), respectively. Since only Austrian people will participate in this study, we use German terms. The valence scale ranges from a frowning, unhappy to a smiling, happy figure, respectively described by the word "happy" and "unhappy".

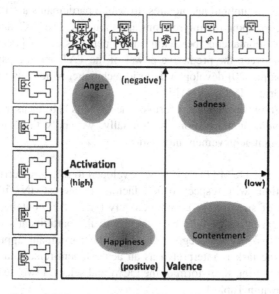

Fig. 2. Activation and Valence scales of SAM constituting a two-dimensional space (figure adapted from [9])

In line with [9] we draw the values of the activation scale (ordinate) against the valence (abscissa). Typically, the four quadrants (I-IV in figure 2) are interpreted in terms of four emotional domains: happiness (or joy), anger, contentment (or pleasure) and sadness. However, rather than assigning labels to the participant's emotional state, we will describe it with an x- and y-coordinate.

4.2   Explicit and Implicit Motivation Elicitation

The measurement of motivation has to take into account the prominent distinction between explicit and implicit motives, which are measured by different instruments and only weakly correlated with each other (e.g.[16]). It has been stated that there is *"growing agreement that implicit and explicit achievement motivation can be seen as distinct constructs"* ([17], p.15). The degree to which the BIs elicit aspects of a participant's explicit or implicit motivational system should influence the correspondence with explicit/implicit instruments. At the moment we can only speculate about the BIs' potential to reveal explicit or implicit state aspects. We therefore have decided to include both an explicit and implicit instrument.

While explicit motives are captured by self-report measures, projective techniques allow for an access to the implicit motives. Self-report measures give access to consciously represented causes or goals of behaviour and support a reliable measurement of a person's goal settings and attitudes [16]. On the other hand, [18] adds for consideration that *"a scientist cannot believe what people say about their motives"* ([18], p.11) and suggests drawing on people's fantasy, e.g. associations to ambiguous pictures. One prominent example of an implicit instrument is the *Thematic Apperception Test* (TAT) that is a set of ambiguous pictures, to which participants are instructed to freely associate their corresponding impressions and thoughts. The TAT has proved to be a good predictor of spontaneous behaviour and a person's career [19].In order to make a compromise between the predictive power of the TAT and the psychometric quality of a questionnaire, [20] developed the grid technique, which has led to the so called Multi-Motive Grid (MMG; e.g. [16]).

In this evaluation study we use a short form of the QCM [11] to measure the participants' explicit achievement motivation. Additionally, we apply the MMG [20] to capture aspects of implicit achievement motivation.

Explicit Instrument. The QCM [11] has been developed to measure current motivation in learning situations with respect to four factors: i) interest (IN), ii) challenge (CH), iii) probability of success (PS), andiv)anxiety (AX). AX contains items that address the negative incentive of failure. PS refers to the participant's certainty to succeed. Items of IN ask for the degree to which the participant appreciates the task.CH measures if the task is interpreted as an achievement-related task. For this study we applied items of the short-form of the QCM and selected two items for each of the four scales, shown in Table 1.

Table 1. Items selected from the QCM

Factor	Items
IN	For tasks like this I do not need a reward, they are lots of fun anyhow
	I would work on this task even in my free time
CH	I am really going to try as hard as I can on this task
	I am eager to see how I will perform in the task
PS	I think I am up to the difficulty of this task
	I probably won't manage to do this task
AX	I feel under pressure to do this task well
	I am afraid I will make a fool out of myself

Implicit Instrument. The Multi-Motive Grid (MMG) confronts a person with a set of pictures (one example is shown in figure 3) to implicitly activate motive dispositions. In contrast to the original TAT, the grid technique assigns a constant set of statements (interpretations) to each picture.The participants' task is to mark those statements that correspond with their own impression. Each statement is associated with one of the "big three" motives: the achievement, power and affiliation motive. The original MMG includes 14 pictures and 12 statements, resulting in a matrix (grid) of 14 × 12 items. The score for a motive's strength is computed by counting the number of times a statement for this motive has been chosen. Additionally, the statements are representative either for approach (hope) or avoidance (fear) tendencies. Consequently, the grid technique yields six scores: a hope and a fear score for each of the three motives.

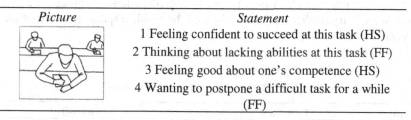

Picture	Statement
	1 Feeling confident to succeed at this task (HS)
	2 Thinking about lacking abilities at this task (FF)
	3 Feeling good about one's competence (HS)
	4 Wanting to postpone a difficult task for a while (FF)

Fig. 3. Example-picture and example-statements of the MMG

Concerning psychometric quality, [16] reported evidence for a sufficient internal consistency (the α-coefficients of the six motives range from .78 to .90) and sufficient retest reliability (retest correlations range between $r=.77$ and $r=.92$). Additionally, [21-23] empirically evidenced the validity of the MMG. In the study of [21] the achievement motive score predicted the performance and flow-experience in a complex reaction task. [22]found significant correlations between the power motive and learning increments in a leadership training program. Finally, [23] evidenced a strong relationship between the scores of the affiliation motive and the number of affiliation related themes in a daily events questionnaire.

In order to keep the work-load of the participants as low as possible we decided to use only three of the 14 pictures. One of them is shown in figure 3 whose label is "taking a test". Additionally, we did not use the whole set of statements but only selected those addressing the hope and fear components of the achievement motive. Figure 3 presents these statements where HS and FF indicate whether the statement represent Hope (of Success) and Fear (of Failure) interpretations, respectively.

Summing up, the items to measure the implicit motivation constitute a 4(statements) x 3(pictures) grid. In contrast to the original MMG, where statements are judged on a dichotomous yes/no scale, we will apply a 9-point Likert-scale ranging from 1 (applies) to 9 (does not apply). We have chosen this format in order to keep the same Likert-scales across the different types of questionnaires. We will average across the participants' reactions to the statements 1 and 3 as well as 2 and 4 to obtain a mean score for hope of success and fear of failure, respectively, with respect to each of the three pictures. In line with [11] we will then transform the hope and fear scores into z-scores to classify the current state as approach- or avoidance-oriented: an approach-oriented state exists if the hope-z-scores are higher than the fear-z-scores.

4.3   Clearness Elicitation

To elicit the current clearness-state we will use five self-constructed items, which are based on the psychological research on problem solving (e.g. [24]). This research suggests clearly defining a problem space in order to reach a particular target. A clear target definition requires a problem solver to reflect on her or his initial state, the intended end state as well as on a proper path of steps leading through the problem space. We will try to elicit such reflections on the problem space by means of the five items presented in Table 2.

Table 2. Five items to measure Clearness

Item	German	English
1	Ich bin mir über das Ziel meiner aktuellen Aufgabe im Klaren.	I know the goal of my current task.
2	Für die Erreichung meines Ziels verfolge ich einen konkreten Plan.	To reach my target I follow a concrete plan.
3	Ich weiß, welche nächsten Schritte mich dem Ziel näher bringen.	I know, which steps will bring me closer to the goal.
4	Es fällt mir schwer, den Dialogen sinnvolle Hinweise zu entnehmen.	I find it difficult to take meaningful hints from the dialogues.
5	Ich habe das Gefühl, planlos durch das Spielszenarium zu navigieren	I have the feeling to navigate through the game scenario without a plan.

4.4   The Predictor Variables: Behavioral Indicators

The whole set of BIs for the non-invasive and on-going assessment of the five dimensions is described and operationalized in [3]. Thus, we focus in this subsection on a smaller subsetconsisting of five BIs to exemplify the underlying principles of the operationalizations. As result of expert ratings, each of these BIs has been evaluated as highly predictive for at least one dimension of the psycho-pedagogical state.

For the dimension activation, a promising BI is *Click Rate*. This BI is operationalized as the amount of key clicks (including mouse and keyboard) per time slice (e.g. within 30 seconds). Valence can be likely measured with a high validity by a BI called *Frequency of emotions*. TARGET´s serious game component offers the opportunity to the learner to apply emotional facial expressions, gestures and body movements of his or her avatar. These emotional expressions can be regarded as indication for positive (e.g. Happiness) or negative valence (e.g. Shame).

We identified three different types of activities the learner may show in the game´s virtual environment: i) *Within-patch processing*, ii) *Between-patch processing*, and iii) *Inactivity*. Each one of these activities constitutes a BI, they are exclusive to each other and they are measured in seconds. Since the length of a time slice is constant it is equal to the sum of the three BIs´ raw values.

Between- and Within-patch processing have been derived from the *theory of information foraging* [25].The theory of informationforaging describes the strategies that people employ to seek for and gather valuable pieces of information. Between-patch processing refers to the time spent on seeking for information sources, so called *patches*. In the context of TARGET, e.g. the non-playable game characters (NPCs) are considered as patches. Thus, the amount of time the learner spends on scanning and exploring the virtual environment constitutes the BI Between-patch processing. This BI is regarded as highly predictive for the dimension avoidance motivation. The time the learner spends on communicating with the NPCs constitutes the BI Within-patch processing and regarded as valid predictor for approach motivation. Finally, the amount of seconds the learner neither explores the environment nor communicates with the NPCs is counted for the BI Inactivity. Inactivity has been evaluated as a highly (negative) predictor for clearness: The lower the BI Inactivity, the higher the learner´s current state of clearness and vice versa.

5   Procedure

For the on-going assessment procedure we are interested in the participant´s *current state*, i.e. in situation-dependent fluctuations of an individual's internal state, which is measured both by means of the BIs and the external criteria (see Design in section 3). Since the external criteria also have to be presented during the game-play, we have implemented a Java-application for selecting and providing the items to the participants, the so-called *evaluation tool*. It intermittently opens a frame in the center of the computer-screen and presents a single item at a moment in time (a statement, question or picture) together with a 9-point rating scale to make a decision on that item. Overall, there are two items to measure the emotional state, 12 items to measure motivation and 5 items to measure clearness (see section 4). All items assigned to a particular construct are presented consecutively in one block. The time intervals between different constructs varied around a mean of a normally distributed random variable (with M=3 minutes and SD=30 seconds). This variation in the item presentation should avoid implicit expectations of the participants who would become accustomed to a regular presentation rate ().

Each construct is represented by one pair of measurement times. For instance, the pair (E_{1i}, E_{2i}) represents the emotional states of a participant i at the first and second measurement time, respectively. The implemented procedure makes sure that a particular construct (e.g. emotion E) is measured a second time, only if the other two constructs (e.g. motivation and clearness) have been measured at least one time. As a consequence, the data vector $\mathbf{D}i$, representing the complete results for participant i, can be split into two row vectors: $\mathbf{D} := [\vec{x}_{1i}, \vec{x}_{2i}]$, with $\vec{x}_{1i} := [C_{1i}, E_{1i}, M_{1i}]$ and $\vec{x}_{2i} := [C_{2i}, E_{2i}, M_{2i}]$. As already described, the measurement of the three constructs for $\vec{x}_{2i}$ begins, only if all data for $\vec{x}_{1i}$ have been gathered.

The first construct of $\vec{x}_{1i}$ to be measured is selected randomly and thus, each construct has a probability of 1/3 to be selected at time 1. The selection procedure is a random sampling without replacement. Therefore, each construct of $\vec{x}_{1i}$ has a probability of 2/3 to be selected at the second or third time $\{[1-(1/3)]*(1/2)\}$. The sequence of the measurement for $\vec{x}_{2i}$ is independent from the one of $\vec{x}_{1i}$.

6   Statistical Analysis

In a first step we will carry out bivariate correlations and a factor analysis on the whole data set, i.e. $\mathbf{D}$ and all BI- raw values.That way we willexamine if the dimensional structure of the constructs based on theoretical considerations and the models described above is supported by the empirical results. In a next step, we will correlate the BIs raw values with the dimensions covered by the factor analyses. Nonsignificant correlation coefficients can be interpreted as BIs being not that valid for that particular dimension. These invalid BIs will be excluded from the multiple regressions. Standardized Beta-Coefficients will support the identification of valid indicators as well as their weights. A linear model would be the simplest case; however, we will evaluate whether statistical requirements, such as linearity of the variables' relationship, are met by the data-pattern. Additionally, we will investigate if other functions, e.g. modelling non-linear relation-ships, provide a better data-fit. Finally, we will vary the length of the time-slices (and thus, the raw-values for the BIs) to find the most suitable length of the time-slices leading to the highest model fit.

As an alternative to this correlational approach, we suggest the following statistical procedure to test the BIs' validity by testing a difference hypothesis (e.g. through analysis of variance).As described in the procedure, each construct$i$ is measured two times, accompanied by the computation of the 16 BIs. The BI-values at a given point in time can be represented by a vector $\vec{x}_{ij} := [BI_{ij1}, ..., BI_{ij16}]$, where the index i represents the construct measured at the corresponding point in time; the index j takes the value 1 or 2, if the construct is measured the first or second time. For instance the vector $\vec{x}_{E2}$ encompasses the 16 BI-raw values that are computed when the construct emotion E is measured the second time.

Experts on cognitive science and media psychology will define optimal vectors for each of the three constructs, denoted by $\vec{x}_{oi}$. To validate the BIs by testing a difference hypothesis, we will compute the similarity between $\vec{x}_{oi}$ and the two observed vectors $\vec{x}_{i1}$ as well as $\vec{x}_{i2}$ (by means of the cosine similarity measure). If the BIs are valid, the similarity between the ideal and the observed vectors should be reflected by the measurement of the external criterions. For instance, if $\vec{x}_{i1}$ is more similar to $\vec{x}_{oi}$ than $\vec{x}_{i2}$, the questionnaires on construct i should also reveal higher scores at time 1 than at time 2. Finally, an analysis of variance will be conducted to examine whether this difference in the questionnaire scores (across all participants) is statistically significant.

Acknowledgements. This paper is part of the EC-Project TARGET funded by the 7th Framework Program of the European Commission. The authors are solely responsible for the content of this paper.It does not represent the opinion of the EC, and the EC is not responsible for any use that might be made of data appearing therein.

References

1. Csikszentmihalyi, M.: Flow: The psychology of optimal experience. Harper & Collins, New York (1991)
2. Kopeinik, S., Bedek, M.A., Seitlinger, P.C., Albert, D.: The Artificial Mentor: An assessment based approach to adaptively enhance learning processes in virtual learning environments. In: Proceedings of the 19th International Conference on Computers in Education, pp. 106–110. Asia-Pacific Society for Computers in Education, Chiang Mai (2011)
3. Bedek, M.A., Seitlinger, P., Kopeinik, S., Albert, D.: Multivariate Assessment of Motivation and Emotion in Digital Educational Games. In: Proceedings of the 5th European Conference on Games-Based Learning, pp. 18–25. ACI, Athens (2011)
4. Atkinson, J.W.: Motivational determinants of risk-taking behavior. Psychological Review 64(6), 359–372 (1957)
5. Covington, M.V., Omelich, C.L.: Need achievement revisited: verification of Atkinson's original 2 x 2 model. In: Spielberger, C.D., Sarason, I.G., Kulcsar, Z., Van Heck, G.L. (eds.) Stress and Emotion: Anxiety, Anger and Curiosity, pp. 85–105. Hemisphere, New York (1991)
6. Larsen, R.J., Diener, E.: Promises and problems with the circumplex model of emotion. In: Clark, M.S. (ed.) Review of Personality and Social Psychology: Emotion, pp. 25–29. Sage, Newbury Park (1992)

7. Insko, B.E.: Measuring Presence: Subjective, behavioral and physiological methods. In: Riva, G., Davide, F., Ijsselsteijn, W.A. (eds.) Being There: Concepts, Effects and Measurement of User Presence in Synthetic Environments, pp. 110–118. IOS Press, Amsterdam (2003)
8. Van Reekum, C.M., Johnstone, T., Banse, R., Etter, A., Wehrle, T., Scherer, K.R.: Psychophysiological responses to appraisal dimensions in a computer game. Cognition and Emotion 18(5), 663–688 (2004)
9. Cai, H., Lin, Y.: Modeling of operators' emotion and task performance in a virtual driving environment. International Journal of Human-Computer Studies 69(9), 571–586 (2011)
10. Lang, P.J.: Behavioral treatment and bio-behavioral assessment: computer applications. In: Sidowski, J.B., Johnson, J.H., Williams, T.A. (eds.) Technology in Mental Health Care Delivery System, pp. 119–137. Ablex, Norwood (1980)
11. Rheinberg, F., Vollmeyer, R., Burns, B.D.: FAM: Ein Fragebogen zur Er-fassung aktueller Motivation in Lern- und Leistungssituationen. Diagnostica 2, 57–66 (2001)
12. Peter, C., Herbon, A.: Emotion representation and physiology assignments in digital systems. Interacting with Computers 18, 139–170 (2006)
13. Lane, R.D., Nadel, L.: Cognitive Neuroscience of Emotion. Oxford University Press, New York (2000)
14. Mehrabian, A., Russell, J.A.: An approach to environmental psychology. MIT Press, Cambridge (1974)
15. Bradley, M.M., Lang, P.J.: Measuring emotion: The self-assessment manikin and the semantic differential. Journal of Behavioral Therapy & Experimental Psychiatry 25, 49–59 (1994)
16. Sokolowski, K., Schmalt, H.D., Langens, T.A., Puca, R.M.: Assessing Achievement, Affiliation, and Power Motives All at Once: The Multi-Motive Grid (MMG). Journal of Personality Assessment 74, 126–145 (2000)
17. Ziegler, M., Schmukle, S., Egloff, B., Bühner, M.: Investigating Measures of Achievement Motivation. Journal of Individual Differences 31, 15–21 (2007)
18. McClelland, D.C.: Biological aspects of human motivation. In: Halisch, F., Kulh, J. (eds.) Motivation, Intention, and Volition, pp. 11–19. Springer, Heidelberg (1987)
19. Spangler, W.D.: Validity of questionnaire and TAT measures of need for achievement: Two meta-analyses. Psychological Bulletin 112, 140–154 (1992)
20. Schmalt, H.D.: The measurement of the Achievement Motivation. Hogrefe, Göttingen (1976)
21. Puca, R.M., Schmalt, H.D.: Task enjoyment: A mediator between achievement motives and performance. Motivation and Emotion 23, 15–29 (1999)
22. Sokolowski, K., Kehr, H.: Zum differentiellen Einfluss von Motivation auf Führungstrainings (MbO). Zeitschrift für Differentielle und Diagnostische Psychologie 20, 192–202 (1999)
23. Schmalt, H.D., Langens, T.A.: Projective, semiprojective and self-report measures of human motivation predict private cognitive events: Strivings, memories and daydreams., University of Wuppertal (2001) (unpubl. manuscript)
24. Pretz, J.E., Naples, A.J., Sternberg, R.J.: Recognizing, Defining, and Repre-senting Problems. In: Davidson, J.E., Steinberg, R.J. (eds.) The Psychology of Problem Solving, pp. 3–31. Cambridge University Press, Cambridge (2003)
25. Pirolli, P., Card, S.K.: Information Foraging. Psychological Review 106, 643–675 (1999)

Challenges and Opportunities in Evaluating Learning in Serious Games: A Look at Behavioural Aspects

Sobah A. Petersen[1] and Michael A. Bedek[2]

[1] SINTEF Technology and Society, Trondheim, Norway
`sobah.petersen@sintef.no`
[2] Knowledge Management Institute, Graz University of Technology, Graz, Austria
`michael.bedek@tugraz.at`

Abstract. In this paper, we describe an approach to modelling competences as learning resources in a serious game environment, where competences are described in detail to identify observable behavioural indicators. This enables the evaluation and assessment of learning, where specific behaviours indicate if a player does or does not have a competence. We have used the OKEI Competence Modelling Framework to describe the competences, where the application of a competence in a specific situation or within a context can be modelled. The main focus of this paper is to analyse and discuss the opportunities and challenges that we have experienced during this work. While the approach is resources intensive to describe the competences in sufficient level of detail, it provides a reusable set of Behavioural Indicators that can be used both in designing and evaluating other Technology Enhanced Learning applications. Most importantly, the work provided important input for the design of the game scenarios in describing situations and relevant contextual information as well as input for improving the believability of the avatars in the game.

Keywords: Evaluation, Serious Games, Behaviour, Competence Assessment, Game Design, Character Design.

1   Introduction

Does technology support learning? And how can we determine if learning is indeed facilitated by the technology and not by some other factors? These are questions that researchers in the domain of Technology Enhanced Learning (TEL) are faced with. Evaluation is an important aspect of TEL and the different approaches to technologies and the different types of support for learning require considerations during iterative evaluation cycles. In this paper, we focus on learning via Serious Games, which has recently gained a lot of attention as a means of rapidly acquiring complex skills and competences in domains such as management and innovation [1].

Learning is often described as inducing a change in the behaviour. Learning has been defined by [2] as a change in at least one of the following constructs: knowledge, skills and attitude. Similarly, they also describe a change in behaviour as a

M. Ma et al. (Eds.): SGDA 2012, LNCS 7528, pp. 219–230, 2012.

change in one of these three elements. Serious Games are intended to induce a change in behaviour of the learners. Thus, the approach that we have taken to evaluate learning in Serious Games focuses on the *behaviour of the learner* and the role that behaviour can play not only on the evaluation of learning, but also in the design of the learning environment including the game scenarios and the virtual characters in the game.

The objective of this paper is to present our approach for the evaluation of the competences of a learner engaged with a serious game environment. The aim of the serious game is to support rapid competence development for Project Managers. Therefore, the approach for evaluation presented in this paper focuses on the behavioural clues and aspects as expression of the competences that the serious game provides a learning environment for. The main contribution of this paper is an analysis of the challenges and opportunities that serious games pose in evaluating if learning takes place.

This work is a part of the European project TARGET (Transformative, Adaptive, Responsive and enGaging Environment, http://www.reachyourtarget.org/), which aims to revolutionize competence development for project and innovation managers by providing technological support to reduce their "time to competence". This project uses serious games to provide life-like learning experiences.

The rest of this paper is organised as follows: Section 2 describes evaluation in general and draws attention to the distinction between assessment of learning and evaluation; Section 3 describes our approach to describing the learning content, i.e. the competence descriptions; Section 4 describes how we evaluate competences using observable behaviour and behavioural indicators; Section 5 analyses and discusses the challenges and opportunities in evaluating learning in serious games using our approach and Section 6 concludes the paper.

2   Evaluating Learning

A general approach that is taken in evaluating learning progress supported by TEL applications is to conduct some evaluations before and after the interventions with the technology, as shown inFig. 1. The learners are tested for what they know before they start using the technology. Then, the learners have a period of intervention where they use the technology or the learning environment and finally, are tested again. In addition to the explicit pre- and post-intervention evaluations, the data that is logged automatically or the content that is generated by the learners during the intervention period provides additional data that can be considered for evaluations. This is a common approach in evaluations conducted in computer-assisted learning or other forms of technology-assisted learning such as Mobile and Ubiquitous learning.

The pre-intervention part of the evaluation may include learner profiling such as the technology literacy of the learner and their interests, tests on the subject that the learner is intended to learn as well as interviews, questionnaires and supplementary behavioural observations to investigate the attitude and behavioural aspects of the learner. Similarly, the post-intervention part of the evaluations can include post-tests on the subject that the learner is intended to learn and interviews and questionnaires to establish if there has been a change in the learners' knowledge and skills, their attitudes and behavioural aspects. However, the degree of evaluation of the behavioural aspects is very limited in most technologies. As Kirkpatrick et al. points out, it takes time before we can see a change in behaviour[2]. Most technologies to support learning are detached from the real world working environment and therefore the chances that what has been learned is transferred to the working environment may vary. While we may be able to establish behavioural patterns, we are unable to observe the learners' behaviour and assess their behaviour, in particular, during the intervention period. All learning efforts are intended to induce a change in the behaviour of the learner. However, this is often very hard or impossible to evaluate.

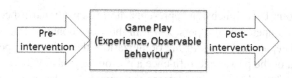

Fig. 1. Evaluating Technology Enhanced Learning

Serious Games offer the unique opportunity to *observe a learner's behaviour during the intervention* period, i.e. while the learner is playing the game. While this is an opportunity to evaluate learning through observing behavioural change, it also poses challenges in the definition and description of competences that the player should learn from the game. In the TARGET serious game environment, we have focused on understanding the behaviour we should be able to observe if a learner does or does not have particular competences that an experienced Project Manager is expected to have. This involved describing the competences that should be learned through the game; i.e. the learning resources supported by the system in a manner that can be related to behaviour that can be observed.

3   Competence Descriptions

We reviewed the literature related to competence modelling and in particular, competence modelling for TEL; an overview is available in [3]. The literature helped to consider competences in a work context, or as Cheetham and Chivers call them, "professional competence"[4]. Thus, parallel efforts in analyzing the competences to identify simpler or atomic elements of each competence or the elements that can be considered as the "ability to do something" and a literature review helped identify how the competences in a work context may be defined [5]. Similarly, from a learning perspective, context is an important aspect. Context has been defined by Luckinas "dynamic and associated with connections between people, things, locations and events in a narrative that driven is by people's intentionality and motivations" ([6], p18). This led to the OKEI Competence Modelling Framework, which identifies different factors of a competence that distinguishes a person's ability to do something, his/her knowledge about something as well as how the ability is exercised by applying the knowledge in a specific context such as within a specific organization [7].

The OKEI Competence Modelling Framework, where OKEI stands for Organization, Knowledge, Environment and Individual, takes into account the Organisational and Environmental factors, plus a person's Knowledge and Individual qualities, all of which may affect the application of the competence. Thus, it goes beyond most modern models used in industry today which aim to assess a person's competence profile rather than their ability to apply the competence. The latter is needed when considering competence modelling from an educational and pedagogic perspective. The OKEI factors are described as follows:

- **Organisation**: This dimension represents the organizational aspects that may influence the competence of a person within the work context. This may include the business strategies and goals of the organization, the role of the person within the organization or the power and influence a person may have within an organization.
- **Knowledge**: This dimension addresses the knowledge that is required to apply or exercise a competence. The knowledge may be academic, theoretical or practical, such as methods or techniques. A person needs a specific knowledge base to be considered as possessing a specific competence.
- **Environment**: This dimension considers the context outside of the organization that may affect the way a competence may be applied. This may include the laws that may affect the work or the norms in the society that should be respected.
- **Individual**: This dimension concerns the individual and personal factors that may affect the way a person is able to apply a competence. For example, if a person is very confident or articulate, the manner that s/he communicates with someone will be influenced by this ability.

Taking this approach to describe competences that can be incorporated in the serious game environment to evaluate if a learner acquires the competences enabled us to describe competences as observable behaviours in a situated context. Table 1provides an example of how the competence "Communication" could be represented using the OKEI Competence Modelling Framework. For someone to communicate appropriately in a given situation, they must know who they are communicating with. For example, the role of the person within the project or the organisation may play a part in determining how the communication should be conducted. This may help in deciding how to address the person or to determine the mode of communication and the information that is communicated, i.e. the context of the information may also be affected by the role of that person. So, the appropriateness of the communication is determined by the context in which the communication takes place, which is de-scribed by the Organisational, Knowledge and Environment factors.

Table 1. Description of the Competence "Communication" using the OKEI Competence Modelling Framework

Organisational Factors	Knowledge Factors	Environmental Factors	Individual Factors
- Roles of people in the organisations, e.g. who will receive what information, and when in the organisation(s) and the project	- Knowledge about the different forms of communication (e.g. oral, text, written, graphic, static or dynamic, formal or informal, requested or volunteered) - Knowledge about the process of communication (plan, prepare, etc.) - Knowledge about the power structure in the organisation (formal and informal)	- Context where the information is communicated	- Verbal communication - Body language and non-verbal communication - Listening skills - Ability to determine appropriate or best time, place and means of communication

Competences are not individual, isolated competences; rather they are related to one another in many ways. Thus, in addition to describing the competences according to the contextual factors, the relationships among the competences, are also considered. In addition to simplifying competences into sub-competences, there are also other relationships across the different competences. For example, several competences such as Negotiation and Trust Building require good communication skills.

4   Behavioural Indicators

The consortium of the TARGET project focused so far on those competences and skills, which are considered important and highly relevant for three knowledge domains, i.e. Project Management, Innovation and Sustainable Global Manufacturing. This intersection consists of quite generic and to some extent fuzzy social skills. In most cases, it is useful to simplify such fuzzy competences into more specific sub-competences. Once a set of specific sub-competences is defined, the process of elaborating a set of observable indicators, or BIs, can be initiated.

As an example, the competence to communicate with different stakeholders can be divided into the sub-competences of verbal and non-verbal communication skills (see Individual Factors in Table 1). One behavioral expression, respectively observable indication for appropriate or inappropriate non-verbal communication is proxemics and the concept of personal space [10-11]. Personal space is the physical distance two or more people keep between each other in different contexts. We adapted this concept directly from research on human behaviour for our own purposes: The "physical distance" a player keeps to his or her interaction partner, i.e. a Non Player Character (NPC) in the virtual environment, constitutes a BI. In TARGET, we applied *contextualized competence assessment*, i.e. the automated scoring of a well defined measurement, respectively its interpretation in terms of high or low performancelevels, by taking a set of contextual factors into account. For example, the appropriateness of the distance to an interaction partner might be dependent on the cultural background of both interaction partners [12].

The assessment of a particular competence builds upon the assessment of a set of BIs as well as the integration of those BIs into a single competence value (e.g. performancelevel). In the most simple case, the integration of several BI values is accomplished by means of linear multiple regressions, with weighted BIs as input variables.

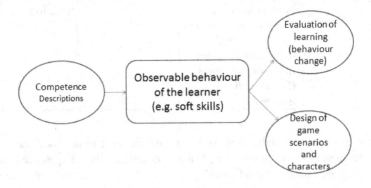

Fig. 2. The role of behaviour

The role of behaviour and BIs are important to the description of the competences and evaluating learning, see Fig.2. As illustrated in the example, it can also be related to the actual game scenarios and the virtual environment

5   Challenges and Opportunities

The behaviour of a learner plays a central role in evaluating if the learner has indeed learnt something and what s/he has learnt. By focusing on the behaviour of a learner, we have identified a number of benefits as well as challenges in designing learning environments and evaluating learning. In this section, we will analyse and discuss the challenges and opportunities in evaluating learning in serious games by assessing competences of a learner, or the game player, using BIs.

5.1   Challenges

In this section, we discuss some of the challenges of describing competences and BIs and evaluating learning in serious games as we have described in this paper.

Resource Exhaustive - The process for a non-invasive assessment procedure described in Section 4, in particular the aim of applying contextualised competence assessment is undoubtedly more resource intensive and time consuming compared to traditional competence assessment in TEL: i) because of the conceptual work, i.e. the definition of BIs to be carried out by domain experts, psychologists or professionals and ii) because of additional software development efforts to extract the game logs and to integrate the parameters into BIs and competence values. In addition to that, some competences or sub-competences might be non-measurable in an on-going procedure simply because of restricted opportunities to act and interact in the virtual environment.

The competence modelling approach that we have followed, i.e. detailing generic competences into more specific ones, identify BIs and operationalizing them by taking contextual factors into account, may also become a time consuming process if a lot of contextual factors are taken into account. This work is optimised by considering the relationships among the competences to identify overlaps among different competences, e.g. Trust Building and Communication, and reusing descriptions of competences and BIs wherever appropriate.

Validation – As pointed out in section 4, the assessment of each competence´s performance level results from the integration of the measurement of a set of BIs. In the most simple case, the integration will be carried out by linear multiple regressions, with weighted BIs as input variables. Even if the BIs have been operationalised by consulting domain experts or based on an extensive literature review and even if the weights (indicating the assumed predictive validity of a particular BI for the specific competence) are resulting from (the same) domain expert ratings, we are not in a position to state for sure that the results of the linear regressions are valid. It is necessary to gather empirical evidence about the competence assessment´s validity. There are different measurements for an assessment approach´s validity but most often it is indicated by the amount of shared variance (= squared Pearson's correlation coefficient) between a predictor and at least one external criteria variable. In general, the validation of automated competence assessments in the context of TEL might allow a wide range of different external criteria, such as standardised questionnaires, self-assessments by the learner, future grades at university courses, etc. Since we are interested on the ongoing assessment of the learner´s current competence performance levels and the fluctuations over time, we are to some extent dependent on an external criterion which also reflects fluctuations and changes over short periods of time. One proposal to deal with this requirement is again based on expert ratings. Domain experts who were not involved in the process of defining the BIs or the BIs' weights for the regressions have to be presented with replays of learner´s gaming sessions. This replay functionality is already implemented in TARGET as indicated by the Graphical User Interface (GUI) of the component assessing the performance, Competence Performance Analyser (CPA) (seeFig. 3). Atvarying time intervals,a particular expert is asked to rate (e.g. on a 7-point Likert scale) the learner´s current competenceperformance level (in this context,"current" means a short time interval before the expert was asked to rate the competence performance level). These ratings should be carried out several times within several game scenarios' replays by a larger amount of experts in order to gather reliable criteria variables. Finally, the BI values at these particular moments in time will be correlated with the experts' ratings for the same time points. The correlation matrices between the BIs and the external criteria serve as starting point to compute standardized Beta-coefficients which determine the BI´s indicators' significance (weight) for the resulting competenceperformance level.

5.2   Opportunities

Describing competences in terms of context as well as to the level of detail where we can identify observable behaviour provides several opportunities, in particular to the design of the game scenarios as well as other aspects. In the rest of this section, we discuss these opportunities.

Competence Development as a Part of Evaluation - Most TEL applications consider evaluation in the broad context, which takes into account several aspects such as usability and the added value of the technology in the bigger context of learning. Since the evaluation of a change in behaviour can often take time or the learning environment is too detached from the real world, the assessment of learning often takes second place in evaluations. In our approach, the competence descriptions which form the basis of the learning resources are directly related to observable behaviours in the virtual learning environment, i.e. the game. With the approach described in this paper, the assessment of learning, observed through the behaviour of the player or the learner brings the focus of evaluations to assessing learning.

Open Student Modelling - TARGET provides a playback functionalityof the previously played game scenarios, called *experiences*, correlated to the performance demonstrated in exercising particular competences. Theuse of this opportunity is enforced at the end of each game session, where the learner engages with the output of the competence performance analysis. The GUI of the CPA as shown inFig. 3, includes a set of graphs on the bottom left of the figure, one for each competence that the scenario was designed to teach, which are listed in the top right window of the figure. The top left window of the screen shows the video recording of the game session. It aims to facilitate the learner´s reflection upon his or herperformance, strengths and weaknesses. The GUI of the CPA is a good example of applying the principles of open student modelling [12] where the learner´s interactions with the GUI and his or her reflection should lead to an enhanced learning process [14].

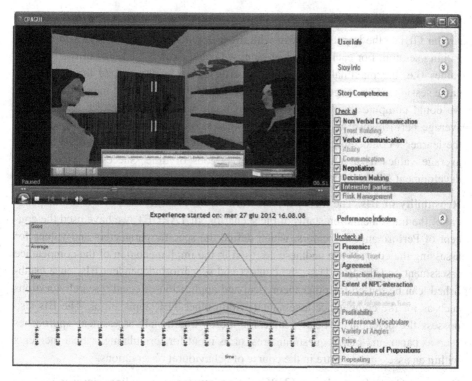

Fig. 3. The Graphical User Interface of the Competence Performance Analyzer

Competence Versus Learning Assessment - The on-going assessment procedure applied in TARGET so far enables the evaluation of the learner´s *current* competence level. The GUI of the CPA provides feedback to the learner of his or her performance levels in very short time intervals throughout the game play, resulting in continuous functions for each competence that is operationalised (seeFig. 3). As mentioned above, this kind of open student modelling aims to facilitate reflection upon the learner´s game experience, and as a consequence, it should support deep and sophisticated learning processes. However, it might be too optimistic to assume that a learner actually develops such generic and complex competences as we are focusing on in TARGET while being engaged with a single game scenario for a short period of time, e.g. about 30 minutes. And it is definitely too optimistic to assume that our assessment of the competence performance levels, respectively the measurements of the single BIs, is sensitive enough to *changes in behaviour*, i.e. the kind of learning or competence development we are aiming for. Thus, the functions shown in the competence graphs in Fig. 3, based on the Performance Indicators listed on the bottom right of the screen,are meaningless for learning assessment if we take only a single gaming session. We have to compare those functions over a longer period of time, gathered from a wider range of different game scenarios to allow for the evaluation of the learner's competence development. One proposal to deal with this is to provide a similar GUI to the learner as above with the difference that the abscissa is in units of gaming session. For each gaming session, we could extract the range of the function values (i.e. the maximal and minimum performance levels reached throughout the game session). This range reflects the variability of the assessment. In addition to that, we could compute the integral of the functions, which would reflect some sort of average performance level for each gaming session. The proposed GUI visualizing the learner's competence development should show both, i.e. the variability and the average values as a function over longer periods of time. Successful competence development would be indicated by increasing average values and decreasing ranges.

Reusability of BIs. The theory-driven work on the identification of BIs is independent of the implementation status of the scenarios. In TARGET, we have used the concept of Performance Indicators, which define the specific parameters and values for assessing the competence andthese are used in the implementation of the competence assessment and the BIs. Thus, the context and scenario independent BIs, once established, can be reused for other theoretical and application-oriented research questions such as for the competence assessment within other TEL applications. The BIs also possess the potential to be re-usable for more "traditional" assessment approaches such as paper-and-pencil questionnaires, or as input for formulating critical incidents within an assessment centre in the course of behavioural observations.

Design of Game Scenarios and NPCs. The competence modelling approach we have followed, i.e. the identification of BIs by taking also contextual factors into account, contributes to the design of the game scenarios in two important ways:

- **Enhancing Narrative Variation.** One of the major aims of the TARGET project is to provide situated contexts by means of complex game scenarios. The higher the variety of different situations the higher the probability that the game scenarios reflect real-life like experiences. The identification of contextual factors supports the narrative design of such situation-rich game scenarios and is necessary for the contextualised competence assessment anyway [15]. For example, the measurement of the BI *proxemics*, respectively its interpretation in terms of appropriateness, could be dependent on the amount of NPC`s involved in the communicative situation. Thus, the game scenario should encompass both kinds of situations: one with a single NPC and one with more than several NPCs.
- **Enhancing Believability.** The rules of appropriate or inappropriate behaviour depending on the context as defined by the contextualized competence assessment approach can be additionally used for modelling the behaviour of the NPCs. For example, based on a particular NPCs "cultural background", the physical distance he or she is preferring to the learner`s avatar or to other NPCs might differ. These variations in the NPC`s behaviour based on their "personal background" enhance the believability of them.

6   Summary and Conclusions

In this paper, we have described our approach to modelling competences as learning resources in a serious game environment, where competences are described in detail to identify observable behavioural indicators. This enables the evaluation and assessment of learning, where specific behaviours indicate if a player does or does not have a competence. We have used the OKEI Competence Modelling Framework to describe the competences, where the application of a competence in a specific situation or within a context can be modelled.

The main focus of this paper has been to analyse and discuss the opportunities and challenges that we have experienced during this work. While the approach is resources intensive to describe the competences in sufficient level of detail, it provides a reusable set of BIs that can be used both in designing and evaluating other TEL applications as well in other situations where behavioural evaluations and assessments are done. And most importantly, the work provided important input for the design of the game scenarios in describing situations and relevant contextual information as well as input for improving the believability of the NPCs. In addition, it supports reflection and retention of learning by revisiting the captured learning experiences.

We have analysed competences in three domains: Project Management, Innovation and Sustainable Global Manufacturing and we have seen that there is considerable overlap among the competences, increasing the reusability of the content. The current implementation of TARGET includes the BIs that we have identified and specific Performance Indicators to measure them. Our current plans include the validation of the BIs based on the results of the user studies.

Acknowledgements. This paper is part of the EU Project TARGET funded by the 7th Framework Program of the European Commission. The authors would like to thank Elisabetta Parodi for providing Fig. 3 and the other members of the TARGET consortium for interesting discussions that have contributed to these ideas.

References

1. Andersen, B., Fradinho, M., Lefrere, P., Niitamo, V.P.: The Coming Revolution in Competence Development: Using Serious Games to Improve Cross-Cultural Skills. In: Ozok, A.A., Zaphiris, P. (eds.) OCSC 2009. LNCS, vol. 5621, pp. 413–422. Springer, Heidelberg (2009)
2. Kirkpatrick, D.L., Kirkpatrick, J.D.: Evaluating Training Programs, The Four Levels. Berrett-Koehler Publishers, San Francisco (2006)
3. TARGET: Deliverable D4.1 - Competence Portfolios (2011), http://www.reachyourtarget.org/index.php?option=com_content&view=article&id=156:d41-competence-portfolios&catid=15:public-deliverables&Itemid=43

4. Cheetham, G., Chivers, G.: Professional Competence: Harmonizing Reflective Practitioner and Competence-based Approaches. In: O'Reilly, D., Cuningham, L., Lester, S. (eds.) The Capable Practitioner: Professional Capability Through Higher Education, pp. 215–226. Kogan Page Limited, London (1999)
5. Engeström, Y.: Learning by Expanding: An Activity-Theoretical Approach to Developmental Research. Orienta-KonsultitOy, Helsinki (1987)
6. Luckin, R.: Re-designing Learning Contexts. Routledge Taylor & Francis Group, London (2010)
7. Petersen, S.A., Heikura, T.: Modelling Project Management and Innovation Competences for Technology Enhanced Learning. In: Proceedings of the eChallenges 2010, Warsaw, Poland, pp. 1–9 (2010)
8. Csikszentmihalyi, M.: Flow: The psychology of optimal experience. Harper & Collins, New York (1990)
9. Bedek, M.A., Petersen, S.A., Heikura, T.: From Behavioral Indicators to Con-textualized Competence Assessment. In: Proceedings of the 11th IEEE International Conference on Advanced Learning Technologies, Athens, United States, pp. 277–281 (2011)
10. Hall, T.: The hidden dimension. Doubleday Anchor, Garden City (1969)
11. Hayduk, L.A.: Personal space: An evaluative and orienting overview. Psychological Bulletin 55, 117–134 (1978)
12. Hall, E.T.: Beyond Culture. Doubleday Anchor, New York (1977)
13. Bull, S.: Supporting learning with open learner models. In: Proceedings of the 4th Hellenic Conference on Information and Communication Technologies in Education, Athens, Greece, pp. 47–61 (2004)
14. Mitrović, A., Martin, B.: Evaluating the Effects of Open Student Models on Learning. In: De Bra, P., Brusilovsky, P., Conejo, R. (eds.) AH 2002. LNCS, vol. 2347, pp. 296–305. Springer, Heidelberg (2002)
15. Cowley, B., Bedek, M.A., Ribeiro, C.S., Heikura, T., Petersen, S.A.: The QUARTIC process model to support serious games development for contextu-alized competence-based learning and assessment. In: Cruz-Cunha, M.M. (ed.) Handbook of Research on Serious Games as Educational, Business, and Research Tools: Development and Design. IGI Global Publishers, Hershey (2012)

AmbiLearn:
Enhancing the Learning Environment
for Primary School Education

Jennifer Hyndman[1], Tom Lunney[1], and Paul Mc Kevitt[2]

[1] School of Computing and Intelligent Systems, University of Ulster, Magee,
Derry/Londonderry BT48 7JL, Northern Ireland
Hyndman-j2@email.ulster.ac.uk, tf.lunney@ulster.ac.uk
[2] School of Creative Arts, University of Ulster, Magee, Derry/Londonderry
BT48 7JL, Northern Ireland
p.mckevitt@ulster.ac.uk

Abstract. Technology is at a stage where it has infiltrated the education system with the potential to enhance teaching and learning. In Northern Ireland a Virtual Learning Environment (VLE) infrastructure is in place. However, statistics and government reports suggest that VLE use amongst the primary school sector is quite limited. In an attempt to redress the limited use of VLEs in the primary school sector this research investigates the potential of serious games and how they may compliment the National Curriculum with the development of AmbiLearn, an enhanced learning environment with a content neutral game-based approach and content creation and reporting modules. This paper presents the design and implementation of AmbiLearn. Preliminary analysis of data from evaluation of AmbiLearn shows promising results and directions for future work are discussed.

Keywords: Virtual Learning Environments (VLEs), Educational Games, Assessment for Learning, AmbiLearn, Content neutral, Game-based approach.

1 Introduction

A Virtual Learning Environment (VLE) is essentially an educational tool which helps monitor students' progress online in terms of assessments and quizzes. In a survey conducted in 2010 within English schools, on behalf of the British Educational Communication and Technology Agency (BECTA), it is reported that 93% of Secondary schools have access to a VLE whilst 67% of Primary schools have access [1]. In Northern Ireland every school and university has access to VLEs. All schools (primary and secondary) funded by the Northern Ireland's Department of Education and Learning (DEL) have access to the *C2K* network [2] which includes a VLE, namely *LearningNI* [3]. Within the Primary school education sector the use of VLEs is quite limited with the Education Inspectorate noting that fewer than 4% of Northern Irish Primary schools accessed *LearningNI* in the month of February, 2010 [4]. One

M. Ma et al. (Eds.): SGDA 2012, LNCS 7528, pp. 231–242, 2012.

explanation for this limited use is that the content presentation style is unsuitable for this level of education. Since 2005 BECTA has referred to VLEs as a 'learning platform' which suggests a greater emphasis on content presentation style [5]. Much of the information available to students through typical VLEs is static downloadable documents. In a higher education setting this provides access to the information online and thus can be downloaded and printed. For a Primary School setting this is unsuitable as most worksheets are usually provided by the teacher as children usually don't have the resources to print during class. From a children's perspective downloading documents lacks interactivity. In 2003, Buckingham and Scanlon [6] suggested that most children's primary experience of home computing is that of playing games which in today's society is understandable due to the fact that the gaming industry (across all platforms and genres) is a large worldwide market reported to be worth $74 billion in 2011 [7]. The fastest growing demographic group for playing games is that of children aged 2-17 [8] with those aged 2-5 as the fastest growing contributors to this category [9]. Using computer games in education is not a new concept but this area has gained much attention due to the increased variety of gaming platforms, rise of virtual worlds and serious games. Considering the role both VLEs and games can play in the Primary School classroom leads to the development of AmbiLearn, an enhanced VLE with a content neutral game-based approach and content creation and reporting modules. The content neutral game-based approach provides a game independent of educational content enabling the game to be reusable for any chosen thematic subject unit. This paper presents related work and the design and implementation of AmbiLearn, suitable for supporting Primary School teachers in assessment for learning and for evaluating their own teaching.

2   Related Work

2.1   Virtual Learning Environments (VLEs)

A Virtual Learning Environment (VLE) is a system which aids the distribution and management of learning materials. The features of a VLE can facilitate different approaches to learning depending on how the VLE is used. The use of such VLEs has had a positive effect in higher education. In this context VLEs are providing opportunities for distance learners and access to course content from any location at any time. Students can catch up on missed lectures/classes, submit assignments and receive feedback at any time [10]. Studies show that assessment tools, for both formative and summative assessments can lead to improved student learning [11][12]. Communication tools have the potential to support collaborative learning and peer learning, as studies show that the use of wikis can help students when developing group documents [13][14]. Similar to VLE usage in higher education, at secondary level VLEs are providing opportunities for distance learning and collaboration [15-17]. The nature of Higher Education allows students the time between lessons to further read up on and study materials presented within VLEs. At lower educational levels the freedom for pupils to study the materials at their own pace is reduced. It is common that a pupil in Primary School will spend at least 5 hours in school each day during which many topics are covered and many different approaches to teaching are used. A pupil in secondary education will spend at least 6 hours in school per day where their time is split between separate lessons with different teachers. In Further and Higher education the time requirement for face to face contact between lecturer and student varies significantly depending on the module/course.

2.2   Serious and Educational Games

Derryberry [18] suggests that serious games are those, "designed with the intention of improving some specific aspect of learning", (p. 3). Similarly, Raybourn [19] states that a serious game is defined as the use of interactive technologies for training and education in private, public, government and military sectors. In education, 'serious games' is one of many terms used to describe the fields of educational games and game-based learning [20]. Studies have shown that the use of video games in the classroom engages and motivates students [21-25]. Gros [25] claims that, "engagement and motivation are interesting benefits of the use of games but they are not enough for educational purposes.", (p. 23) although he continues to point out that environments built on the educational properties of games can be an appropriate way to improve learning. These educational properties can be found throughout the field as pedagogical properties of games, and attributes of serious games/educational games which promote and encourage learning. Charsky [26] outlines such characteristics as competition and goals, rules, choice, challenges and fantasy. Dennis et al. [27] document three key attributes of games as novelty, competition and dynamic interaction.

For educational games to be effective, Fisch [28] suggest that the educational content must be sound, age appropriate, presented clearly and well integrated into the game. Groff et al. [22] conducted a study across Scotland on the impact of console games in the classroom which led to a taxonomy of nineteen educational benefits of console games in schools. One such benefit is that Game-based learning can narrow the gap between home and school. [22]. Mumtaz [29] conducted a study on the use of computers amongst children at home and at school. Results suggest that children make more use of the computer at home playing games than using 'boring' software in school such as word processors. It was concluded that schools should, "learn from what works at home and enable children to work on activities they find valuable, motivational and worthwhile.", (p. 347) [29]. Stone [30] suggests that children today are growing up in an era of fast paced technological change where at home they regard the Kindle as a book and have high expectations of technology. Hence, the classroom must be willing to bridge the gap between home and school in terms of its use of technology [31]. A National survey of 500 Primary (aka Elementary, USA) School teachers from across the USA outlines similar benefits as Groff [22] such as collaboration, increased motivation, engagement, personalised instruction and assess to knowledge [32].

2.3   Assessment Opportunities

Currently, many games within the education system provide educational content specific to one domain or subject such as Mathematics and Literacy. These educational games reinforce core subjects which is appropriate for standardised tests such as InCAS and PIPS [33]. Assessment for learning incorporates formative assessment from a broad range of topics that a child will learn. Overcoming subject specific games, a range of tools are available for an educator to create and determine their own content for activities such as the Black Cat Activity Builder range [34] which enables teachers to input information for science and English worksheets, word search and word games. As standalone software these games do not provide any feedback to the teacher unless he/she is actively observing the child play. Such information is provided within activities in the VLE, e.g. the quiz blocks. Quiz information is logged and a teacher can make judgments based on the scores with their full class data available for that particular activity.

3   AmbiLearn

AmbiLearn follows principles from both *constructivism* [35-37] and *behaviourism* [38- 39] for understanding, remembering (behaviourism) and evaluating and creating (constructivism). Enhancing VLEs with serious games has potential in the Primary School classroom as an assessment tool. AmbiLearn is an enhanced VLE with a content neutral game and content creation and reporting modules. AmbiLearn's game module is content neutral which facilitates the adaption of the game to multiple themes as specified by a plug-in pedagogical model created through the content creation module. In addition, the reporting module provides a graphical representation of game data. Fig. 1 shows a layered view of the architecture of AmbiLearn. The GUI layer provides the visual interface for users accessible through a web browser. The Logic Layer is the VLE scripts which include the VLE libraries, reporting, content creation and game modules. Each of these modules uses common functionality provided by the VLE libraries such as authentication to specify permissions and capabilities. In addition, the game module uses a communication service to access course information from the VLE facilities. The Storage Layer can be implemented via 'plug-in' components. These include VLE database support and all pedagogical model storage which are created through the content creation module. AmbiLearn is implemented with a Moodle VLE as it provides the necessary support (authentication and course libraries) and has the advantage of being Open Source. Additionally, its functionality can be easily extended and customised.

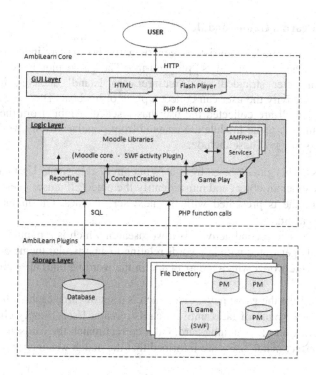

Fig. 1. AmbiLearn Layered Architecture

Typically, a VLE has two main users: teachers/educators and pupils/students. The teachers/educators role in the VLE is to administer pedagogical material whereas a pupil/student's role is to access this pedagogical material. Similarly, as shown in Fig. 2, a teacher/educator accesses the content creation module to define the pedagogical model and administer a game instance to his/her class. The pupil/student plays the game and the teacher can then access game data through the reporting module.

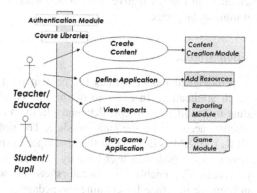

Fig. 2. Component user roles within AmbiLearn

3.1   AmbiLearn's Game Module

AmbiLearn's game module consists of generic activities that are independent of content until a pedagogical model is 'plugged-in'. The game plot is centered around 'Ambi', a character stranded on 'TreasureLearn Island' depicted in Fig.3. By completing an activity the user can collect a piece of his boat. There are six pieces to collect and once all are collected the user has rescued 'Ambi' from the island. The activities within the game module are adapted from popular activity worksheets used within school settings. These include:

- AmbiGuess: This game comes from a `What am I' style game. Users are presented with clues about an object and must identify the object. If a user guesses the object correctly he/she is presented with the next set of clues. On an incorrect guess he/she tries again.
- WordSearch: The second activity is a wordsearch which is a popular activity as it can be easily generated with keywords relating to a particular theme or topic. Users must select the words which are available in the wordlist until all words have been identified.
- FactMatch: Like the game pairs, fact match is a set of cards each with a fact. Users must match the pairs of facts until no cards remain. Users simply click on a card and then click on the matching card. On a correct match the cards are taken away. On an incorrect match users are informed that the match was incorrect and they try again.
- AmbiJig: This is a picture which is split into pieces and scrambled. Users must identify the image and recreate the picture to complete the jigsaw. Users can choose to receive a hint at which point the image will be displayed to aid them in the recreation of the image. If they cannot reproduce the image they can opt to receive help which will result in the pieces being partially arranged making it easier to complete the jigsaw.
- AmbiQuiz: This is a quiz which is multiple choice. Users are provided with the question, and must select the correct answer from a choice of four.

The game was implemented in Flash Creative Suite (CS5) with Actionscript 3 (AS3) as the back end programming language.

3.2   Content Creation Module

AmbiLearn's plug-in pedagogical model defines the content used within the game-based approach for each application. In order to define this pedagogical model the content creation module in AmbiLearn accepts data entry from an educator and builds the content into a structure accessed by the game module. The pedagogical model is implemented as an XML file. XML files enable the developer to specify the structure of the data and the nature of the nodes. A user-friendly interface is designed to input the required data with forms. This enables the educators/teachers who are conducting data entry to have an intuitive interface for creating the pedagogical model. The content creation interface accepts the data entry and creates as output the XML pedagogical model.

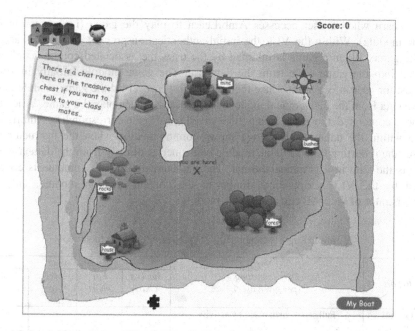

Fig. 3. TreasureLearn Island

3.3   Reporting Module

AmbiLearn's reporting module displays game data in a graphical format. Table 1 shows the scope of the reports provided by the reporting module. As there are five activities defined within AmbiLearn's game module, there are five corresponding reports representing their score (AmbiGuess, AmbiQuiz and FactMatch) and game time (WordSearch and AmbiJig). Also, there is an overall game report. In addition to these reports a personal user report is generated which charts the game data for all AmbiLearn user activity. AmbiLearn's reporting module is implemented with a series of SQL statements that select the appropriate data to display. A Fusion Charts PHP class and compiled SWF charts are implemented to display the data is a graphical format to the user. For each game a chart representing game scores is provided. This is in the form of a stacked chart where the user is defined along the x-axis whilst their overall game score is defined on the y-axis. The overall score represented is displayed as a set of 5 scores stacked, each representing an activity within the game.

AmbiLearn's game, content creation and reporting modules are best viewed in terms of their communication within AmbiLearn. Fig. 4 shows internal communication between AmbiLearn's components. When an instructor chooses the Content Creation capability, the resulting communication within AmbiLearn is as shown in Fig. 4(b). This option is available to those who have administration rights in the VLE, i.e. a teacher or course creator. This module enables them to define an application and create the associated pedagogical model. The pedagogical model is saved within AmbiLearn and becomes a reusable resource. Fig. 4(a) shows communication within

AmbiLearn when a user accesses AmbiLearn to play the game (i.e. accessing the game module). Within the VLE the initial authentication process coordinates access to the game. When a game is initiated by the user, the associated course details are passed into the game code from the database. The game module initially makes a request for user information. Once the information is received the game module reads in the data from the pedagogical model and the user can then play the game. When the game is completed, the game data will be saved back to the corresponding AmbiLearn table within the database. Fig. 4(c) shows communication when the instructor accesses the reporting module. This module calls queries directly from the database and reports the data in a graphical format. The authentication of this module is coordinated by the VLE scripts and similar to the content creation module, only an administrator of the VLE can access this module.

Table 1. Reports Generated by Ambilearn reporting module

Report	Data Reporting (per given user)	Report Format			
		Stacked chart	Bar chart	Average line	Table
Overall game	Full score categorised by activity	✓			
AmbiGuess	Individual activity score in %		✓	✓	
	Number of incorrect guessed objects in %		✓		
	Incorrect objects guessed				✓
WordSearch	Individual activity game time		✓	✓	
FactMatch	Individual activity score in %		✓	✓	
	Number of incorrect facts		✓		
	Incorrect matches guessed				✓
AmbiJig	Individual activity game time		✓	✓	
AmbiQuiz	Individual activity score in %		✓	✓	
	Number of incorrect answers in %		✓		
	Incorrect matches guessed				✓

4   Evaluation of AmbiLearn

To demonstrate and test the educational potential of AmbiLearn evaluation is in progress with Primary School teachers. An evaluation has been conducted for three Primary School classes with their class teacher (Teachers=3, Children=61). The first stage of the evaluation was to create the pedagogical model. The teachers chose their own theme and found it easy to apply the content to the AmbiLearn activities. In this evaluation the themes chosen included *The Water Cycle, Vikings and Rainforests*. The children then played the AmbiLearn game and completed an evaluation booklet on their perceptions of the AmbiLearn game and activities. Results from the children's perceptions of AmbiLearn are promising in terms of enjoyment where 98.36% responded 'yes' when asked: "Did you enjoy playing AmbiLearn?". Exploratory analysis is currently underway to identify any correlations between the children's perceptions of the activities in terms of Fun, Enjoyment, Ability and Difficulty with their class teacher's perceptions of the activities in terms of how useful the activity is in providing relevant formative feedback. The third part of the study involved teachers viewing the reports generated from their class. One teacher suggested that all the graphs provided a true reflection of her class with one single unexpected result for a child on the FactMatch activity. The detailed table reporting incorrect matches for this activity provided evidence that random cards were clicked due to the initial (first clicked) card remaining the same. One teacher commented that he could easily identify many of his class based on the reports without having to obtain their codes since pupil names were not disclosed.

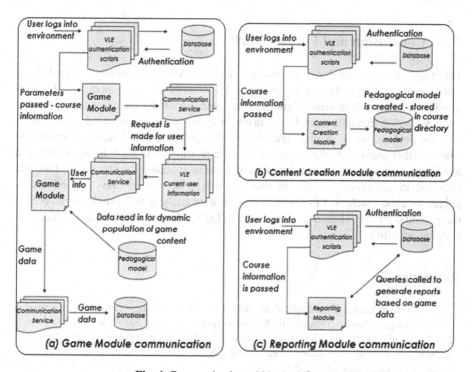

Fig. 4. Communication within AmbiLearn

5   Relation to Other Work

AmbiLearn relates to PlayPhysics [40] for teaching Physics to third-level students and compliments other work [21, 23, 41] but with a focus on game-based assessment. Many games developed in educational settings employ static content. These are mainly commercial Off-The-Shelf (COTS) games and once completed the novelty and attraction begins to fade. AmbiLearn overcomes this limitation as AmbiLearn's game module is designed as a reusable game with a plug-in pedagogical model. Content neutral games are commercially available for the Primary School classroom [34][42], but do not provide opportunities for user logging. A range of games at Content *Generator* [43] overcome such limitations by reporting individual user scores. AmbiLearn extends reporting for full class data in addition to individual instances. Content neutral games [43] offer a range of independent activities and AmbiLearn differs from these as it offers 5 different activities within the one game, including multiple presentation of the educational content. AmbiLearn also differs from other content neutral games due to the 'plug in' pedagogical model. AmbiLearn's game module exists as a single application and the content is linked as an instance of the application. This enables the theme instances to be compared with each other as a tool for evaluation of teaching.

6   Conclusion and Future Work

This paper has presented AmbiLearn, an enhanced VLE with content neutral game and content creation and reporting modules. The content neutral game-based approach provides a game independent of educational content enabling the game to be reusable for any chosen thematic unit. Preliminary analysis of evaluation results has shown that the perceptions of AmbiLearn from both children and teachers are promising whilst further analysis will provide information relating to all modules of AmbiLearn and game components within AmbiLearn's game module. Results show that data provided in the reporting module shows a true reflection of class capabilities as judged by class teachers. Further work on full data analysis will provide evidence on the potential of AmbiLearn as aneffective VLE for Primary School assessment for learning activities.

References

1. British Educational Communications and Technology Agency (BECTA): Harnessing Technology Schools survey (2010), http://dera.ioe.ac.uk/1544/
2. Classroom 2000 (C2K): The Learning Network (2012), http://www.c2kni.org.uk
3. Northern Ireland Curriculum: LearningNI (2012), http://www.nicurriculum.org.uk/pmb/learning_ni.asp
4. Education Inspectorate: A follow up evaluation of the implementation of the revised curriculum in primary, special and post-primary schools (2010), http://etini.gov.uk/index/surveys-evaluations/surveys-evaluations-primary/surveys-evaluations-primary-2010/a-follow-up-evaluation-of-the-implementation-of-the-revised-curriculum-in-primary-special-and-post-primary-schools.pdf
5. Berry, M.: A Virtual Learning Environment in Primary Education (2005), http://www.worldecitizens.net/ftp/Primary%20VLE.pdf
6. Buckingham, D., Scanlon, M.: Interactivity and pedagogy in edutainment software. Information Technology, Education and Society 4(2), 107–126 (2003)
7. JoyStik: Game Industry worth $74 billion in 2011 (2011), http://www.joystiq.com/2011/07/05/report-game-industry-worth-74-billion-in-2011/

8. Downin, J.: Kids gaming market on the rise, UK Gamespot (2011), http://uk.gamespot.com/news/kids-gaming-market-on-the-rise-npd-6339598
9. NPD: The video Game Industry Is Adding 2-17 Year gamers at a rate Higher than that Age Group of Population Growth, https://www.npd.com/wps/portal/npd/us/news/pressreleases
10. Hyndman, J., Lunney, T., Mc Kevitt, P.: AmbiLearn: Multimodal Assisted Learning. International Journal of Ambient Computing and Intelligence (IJACI) 3(1), 53–59 (2011)
11. Peat, M., Franklin, S.: Supporting student learning: the use of computer–based formative assessment modules. British Journal of Educational Technology 33(5), 515–523 (2002)
12. Peat, M., Franklin, S., Devlin, M., Charles, M.: Revisiting associations between student performance outcomes and formative assessment opportunities: is there any impact on student learning? In: Beyond the Comfort Zone: Program and Abstracts for the 21st ASCILITE Conference, Perth, Australia, December 5-8, pp. 760–769 (2011)
13. Kear, K., Woodthorpe, J., Robertson, S., Hutchison, M.: From forums to wikis: Perspectives on tools for collaboration. The Internet and Higher Education 13(4), 218–225 (2011)
14. Thorsen, E.: Student Wiki Pages: e-learning strategy for collaborative student notes. Bournemouth University, Fern Barrow (2011)
15. Foyle Cloud, http://www.foylecloud.com/
16. Hirst, C.: NATE case study: Using a 'Home Learning VLE' (2011), http://www.vital.ac.uk/content/nate-case-study-using-home-learning-vle
17. Homer, S.: Using a VLE. CILT: The National Centre for Languages (2011), http://www.cilt.org.uk/secondary/14-19/ict/general_ict_case_studies/using_a_vle.aspx
18. Derryberry, A.: Serious games: online games for learning. Adobe Whitepaper (2007)
19. Raybourn, E.M.: Applying simulation experience design methods to creating serious game-based adaptive training systems. Interacting with Computers 19(2), 206–214 (2007)
20. Susi, T., Johannesson, M., Backlund, P.: Serious games – An Overview. Skovde: University of Skovde (Technical Report HS-IKI-TR-07-001) (2007)
21. Pastore, R.S., Falvo, D.A.: Video Games in the Classroom: Pre-and in-service teachers' perceptions of games in the K-12 classroom. Instructional Technology and Distance Learning 7(12), 49–61 (2010)
22. Groff, J., Howells, C., Cranmer, S.: The impact of console games in the classroom: Evidence from schools in Scotland. Futurelab, UK (2010)
23. Ritzko, J.M., Robinson, S.: Using games to increase active learning. Journal of College Teaching & Learning (TLC) 3(6), 45–50 (2006)
24. Iacovides, I., Aczel, J., Scanlon, E., Taylor, J., Woods, W.: Motivation, engagement and learning through digital games. International Journal of Virtual and Personal Learning Environments 2(2), 1–16 (2011)
25. Gros, B.: Digital games in education: The design of games-based learning environments. Journal of Research on Technology in Education 40(1), 23–38 (2007)
26. Charsky, D.: From edutainment to serious games: A change in the use of game characteristics. Games and Culture 5(2), 177–198 (2010)
27. Dennis, A.R., Bhagwatwar, A., Minas, R.K.: Play for Performance: Using Computer Word Games to Improve Test-Taking Performance. In: 45th Hawaii International Conference on System Sciences, Maui, HI, USA, pp. 98–107 (2012)
28. Fisch, S.M.: Making educational computer games educational. In: Proceedings of the 2005 Conference on Interaction Design and Children, pp. 56–61 (2005)
29. Mumtaz, S.: Children's enjoyment and perception of computer use in the home and the school. Computers & Education 36(4), 347–362 (2001)

30. Stone, B.: The children of cyberspace: old fogies by their 20s. New York Times (2010)
31. Barron, B., Cayton-Hodges, G., Bofferding, L., Copple, C., Darling-Hammond, L., Levine, M.H.: Take a giant step. In: The Joan Ganz Cooney Center at Sesame Workshop (2011), http://www.joanganzcooneycenter.org/upload_kits/jgcc_takeagiantstep.pdf
32. Millstone, J.: Teacher Attitudes about Digital Games in the Classroom. In: The Joan Ganz Cooney Center at Sesame Workshop (2012), http://connect.nwp.org/sites/default/files/file_file/jgcc_teacher_survey_0.pdf
33. CEM: Assessment and Monitoring Systems (2012), http://www.cemcentre.org/projects/assessment-and-monitoring-systems
34. Black Cat Activity Builder (2012), http://www.semerc.com/semerc/productcategory/curriculum-content/blackcat-literacy-activity-builder.html
35. Piaget, J.: The language and thought of the child. Routledge & Kegan, London (1926)
36. Vygotsky, L.: Thought and Language. MIT Press, Cambridge (1962)
37. Bruner, J.: In search of pedagogy: the selected works of Jerome S, vol. 1. Taylor & Francis
38. Skinner, B.F.: The behavior of organisms. Appleton-Century-Crofts, New York (1938)
39. Watson, J.B.: Psychology as the behaviorist views it. Psychological Review 20, 158–177 (1913)
40. Munoz, K., Mc Kevitt, P., Lunney, T., Noguez, J., Neri, L.: An emotional student model for game-play adaption. In: Ma, M., Antonopoulos, N., Oliviera, M.F. (eds.) Special issue on Serious Games Development and Applications, Entertainment Computing, vol. 2 (2), pp. 133–141 (2011)
41. Habgood, M.P.J., Ainsworth, S.E.: Motivating children to learn effectively: Exploring the value of intrinsic integration in educational games. Journal of the Learning Sciences 20(2), 169–206 (2011)
42. Education Games Network, http://www.educationgamesnetwork.com/learninggames
43. Content Generator, http://www.contentgenerator.net

Developing Serious Games Specifically Adapted to People Suffering from Alzheimer

Bruno Bouchard, Frédérick Imbeault, Abdenour Bouzouane,
and Bob-Antoine J. Menelas

LIARA Laboratory, Université du Quebecà Chicoutimi (UQAC)
555 boul. Universite, Saguenay (QC), Canada, G7H 2B1
{Bruno.Bouchard,Frederick.Imbeault,Abdenour.Bouzouane,
Bob-Antoine-Jerry_Menelas}@uqac.ca

Abstract. To face new challenges caused by society aging, several researchers have initiated the experimentation of serious games as a re-education platform to help slowing down the decline of people suffering from Alzheimer. In the last few years, academic studies have been conducted and some commercial products (*Nintendo's Brain Age, Big Brain Academy*, etc.) have emerged. Nevertheless, these initiatives suffer from multiple important limitations since they do not really suit perceptual and interaction needs of silver-aged gamers, more specifically people suffering from Alzheimer disease. In an effort to address this important issue, we present in this paper a set of specific guidelines for designing and implementing effective serious games targeting silver-aged and Alzheimer's patients. Our guidelines cover the following aspects: (i) choosing right in-game challenges, (ii) designing appropriate interaction mechanisms for cognitively impaired people, (iii) implementing artificial intelligence for providing adequate assistive prompting and dynamic difficulty adjustments, (iv) producing effective visual and auditory assets to maximize cognitive training. Also, as a case study, we present the prototype of our new serious game for Alzheimer's patients.

Keywords: Serious games, Cognitive training, Alzheimer disease, Adaptation and personalization.

1 Introduction

The video games industry actually constitutes the commercial sector having the fastest worldwide growing rate among all entertainment media. As an example, the revenues realized by games development companies were estimated at approximately 60billion in 2011 [1] and the projections suggest that they will reach 75 billion in 2015. This rapid growing is a direct consequence of the new market strategy of the game industry, which is to exploit new interaction methods and gaming platforms, such as the *Nintendo Wii, Microsoft Kinect, Sony EyeToy*, Smart phones, etc., in order to attract a larger community of gamers. This offers new ways of gaming, now enabling non-gamers and the entire family to play together. Recent evolution in these

M. Ma et al. (Eds.): SGDA 2012, LNCS 7528, pp. 243–254, 2012.

technologies paved the way for what is called serious video games. This new type of digital games specializes in other purposes than just entertaining, such as educating [2], leading societal impact on specific subjects [3], enhance individual user's aptitudes [4] and, more recently, train cognitive faculties of silver-aged gamers [5]. Western countries are actually facing one of worst demographic crisis of their history, leading to an increasing number of people suffering from Alzheimer's disease (AD) [6].Because of that, a community of researchers[5], [7], [8], [9] has recently initiated the exploration of a new avenue of solutions for cognitive assistance, based on video games. This consists in exploiting videogames as a software platform allowing the support of new assistive tools, less expensive and more accessible, that could be used, for instance, as a reeducation tool helping to slow the decline of people suffering from Alzheimer[7]. Several academic studies [5], [8], [9] and commercial products, such as *Nintendo's Brain Age*, *Big Brain Academy* or *Vision Focus*, have emerged. However, most of these serious game initiatives provided only memory challenges or a series of random puzzles to play few minutes per day with the aim of "improving brain performances". These initiatives suffer from multiple important limitations since they do not really suit perceptual and interaction needs of people suffering from AD. For example, they do not provide any form of in-game assistance able to recognize cognitive errors and to support the user accordingly and, they do not provide any form of dynamic difficulty adjustment for matching the user's particular skills and cognitive profile [10], [11]. In the same way, proposed interaction methods do not always exploit the naturalness and multimodal capabilities that current technologies can provide. Moreover, their artistic design (colors, borders, perspectives, etc.) are not best suited for a cognitively-impaired person. Development of serious games for AD patients that can be cognitively effective requires specialized training that will focus on all their four cognitive spheres: memory, planning skills, initiative and perseverance [12]. In an effort to address this important issue, we propose, in this paper, a set of specific guidelines for designing effective serious games targeting silver-aged and Alzheimer's patients. Our multidisciplinary contribution takes several forms. Firstly, we will describe thoroughly and synthetically a set of guidelines covering the following aspects: (i) choosing right in-game challenges, (ii) designing appropriate interaction mechanisms for cognitively impaired people, (iii) implementing artificial intelligence for providing adequate assistive prompting and dynamic difficulty adjustments, (iv) producing effective visual and auditory assets to maximize cognitive training. Secondly, as a case study, we will present the prototype of a serious game developed in our laboratory. Finally, the last part of our contribution concerns our ongoing efforts to validate the proposed guidelines and our prototype. Our multidisciplinary team (computer scientists, neuropsychologists, game designers and engineers) has signed formal collaborations agreements with few local organizations (i.e., local Alzheimer Society, regional rehabilitation center, nursing homes for elders) and health facilities to recruit participants. Therefore, in this last section, we will present the developed experimental protocol.

2   Choosing the Right in-Game Challenges for the Patient

Previous researches show that AD patients need specifically adapted challenges [25], and also need help to complete them [16].Consequently, trainings should dynamically adapt themselves to a given profile in order be fully effective. This aspect may also impact positively the player's engagement since it sustains its interest. In this section, we analyze how the in-game features that should be designed in order to fit the patient's profile.

2.1   Guidelines

Keep Trace of the Patient's Cognitive Abilities. One of the important features we were interested in is that the game would be capable of producing an in-game estimation of the patient's cognitive abilities, using the data collected from the different activities. This will allow us to measure the positive impact of the game on the patient's cognitive performance through the training sessions and keep a history of the estimations through time to fully evaluate the game potential. For testing real-life patient's cognitive abilities in smart homes, our lab is using a well-established neuropsychological test called the *Naturalistic Action Test* (NAT) [13]. The test uses adapted activities based on routines actions of everyday life called *Activities of Daily Living* (ADL), in order to assess the patient's errors using predefined score sheets. To answer our need of in-game cognitive evaluation, we decided to develop a game concept based on the activities used in this test, and to integrate the score sheets used for the evaluations in the game, in order to provide a fast estimation of the patient's cognitive abilities during the play sessions.

Determine an Appropriate Number of Steps for the Challenges. Each challenges presented in the game should be completed in a correct number of steps. A high enough number of steps would correctly train the cognitive abilities of the patients. However, too much steps could overload them and lower the benefits of the game. As we decided to use an in-game NAT-based test as explained in the previous subsection, we determined that the game levels should be made of 8 to 12 steps, in order to assure they would be compatible with the NAT.

Keep the Player in his "Flow Zone". Keeping the player in is *flow* zone is important. Flow is a well-known concept in the video games community, representing the feeling of complete and energized focus in an activity, with a high level of enjoyment and fulfillment [28].Maintaining the flow will make the game more fun for elderly gamers, improving their learning experience [14].It is important to remember that it is more difficult for AD patients to learn new paradigms. Hence, the game must be straightforward and easy to learn in order to avoid confusion or frustration of the player. A good way to achieve this is to recreate a well-known environment and choose challenges that reflect the patient's everyday life, as it will prevent the need of understanding complex mechanisms[15]. Also, placing them in a familiar context will smooth the learning curve and assure a less frustrating, and more enjoyable experience.

2.2   Our Choice for the Serious Game Environment

Considering the constraints we defined, and the fact that using ADL would allow the use of a NAT-based test in our game, we decided to base our serious game concept on cooking activities for multiple reasons. First, theses activities respond to the need of recreating a well-known environment for all patients [15]. Secondly, the NAT tests we are using at our lab with real patients are mostly done in a kitchen environment, so the integration in game will be easier since we have plenty of accessible data on the subject. Besides this, the importance of food in everyday life is quite crucial. Thus, not only making the patients prepare meals will train their cognitive faculties, but it will also make them able to repeat such tasks outside the training, i.e., at home [15]. Finally, cooking is a well-established subject in assistive technologies for elders [16], which means information from various researches are easily accessible and will allow us to effectively evaluate the patient through the training process.

3   Designing User Interfaces and Interaction Mechanisms

It is known that physical activities can have benefic effects on brain and cognition [17], [18] as a result, several computer-based rehabilitation systems are based around functional activities. With studies reported in [17] the authors found that exercises effects on cognition were greater for exercice training interventions that exceed 30 min per sessions. Besides many effective results, when implementing these recomendations in traditional therapy approaches, people do often complain about repetive aspects of the exercices and healthcare cost are usually high [19]. In this section we do analyze how interaction aspects of serious games may serve for targetting these aspects.

3.1   Understanding the Success of Wii-like Games

The arrival of the Wii-like games has promoted a strong integration of video games in centers for elderly. All over the world, it is common to see players who are their late eighties or in their early nineties. To understand this true success, it is necessary to analyze whyis the Wii different from others. While interactions with traditional games were essentially based on the couple (keyboard/mouse), with Wii it is rather the natural that prevails. No more need for buttons or arrows in order to move, just do the right gesture and you are done. We refer this as ecological interactions. With such interactions, the learning time is greatly reduced if not absent. Such an aspect is specially important when dealing with elderly. Moreover, because of these realist interactions, the player is more likely to give credit in his task and hence to be engage in it. With more engagement, one can expect more fun and motivations that will let the user perform all the necessary exercises.

Although playing a major role in the Wii success, it is clear that the factors cited above can not, on their own,explainthis console's majorsuccess. Besides, one notes that these factors constitute the core of Virtual Reality (VR) technologies which aimsto create a virtual environment wherethe user would felt being in reality. In fact what differentiates these games from VR applications is primarily their affordability in terms of development, maintenance and usage. This explain why games are particularly adapted to rehabilitation. In contrast to VR applications, games are so accessible, nowadays various games are dedicated to home-based rehabilitation.

3.2 Guidelines

Promote Ecological Interactions. As seen through our analysis, ecological interactions remain a key factor in designing serious games. Effective use of this aspect, should allow at least a significant reduction (maybe elimination) of the learning time. This should lead to greater enthusiasm and can improve engagement of the players in the game. However, it should be noted that interactions must also be thinked in terms of the target group. For example, given that a high proportion of elderly people does suffer from impaired motor skills, interactions based on whole body should a priori be avoided.

Light Interface for Home-Based Exercises. One factor that explains the high cost of traditional methods of rehabillitaion is the costs of travelling to rehabilitation centers. Indeed depending on the health condition of the person, it may necessitate several ressources ranging from familly members to an ambulance. When creating a serious game, design choices should be made in a way to offer home-based rehabillitation training. In order to come up with such effective methods, where ecological interactions can be exploited, portable interfaces that does not required any particular skills for configuration should also be considered.

Take Advantage of the Multimodal Aspect. Thanks to developements of VR technologies, now we have at our disposal a set of tools that let us exploit main sensorimotor channels of human when interacting with a machine. For example, voice can be useful for several tasks (to indicate a command) whereas vibro-tactile feedback has proved to be an effective memory aid for users with impaired memory [20]. In this way, exploitation of such modalities can represent a serious alternative for people facing hearing or sight problems. Therefore we strongly advocate the employement of multisensory interactions both as input and output.

4   Producing Visual and Auditory Assets for Cognitive Training

In order to create a tool adapted to AD patients, it is crucial to consider the effects of aging, as it represents the main risk factor for Alzheimer's disease [21].Indeed most AD patients will suffer from hearing and visual troubles associated with aging, as well as sensory troubles caused by Alzheimer. Visual troubles are well-known [22], but the ability of the patients to react different types of visual and auditory prompting for assistance is important as well. Fortunately, researches in smart homes have proven the efficacy of different assistance prompting methods depending on the patient's cognitive impairments and the level of precision in the assistance we want to provide [11], [23].This section will discuss the importance of creating assets for different types of prompts and the effects on vision to be taken into account when working with colors and textures, luminosity, and contrast.

4.1   Understanding Guidance in Smart Homes

In the field of smart homes, guidance is the action of taking the result of an activity recognition process and the given profile of a patient, in order build an assistance solution consisting of a sequence of pairs (action / effectors), to help the patient in the completion of his task when needed [23]. The assistance is then done on specific actions using prompts to guide the patient in a progressive manner, by providing general to more specific assistance if the patient did not manage to complete the task. However, types of prompting to be used, depending of the patient's cognitive disorders, and the method to use them is also of great importance [11].For instance, it can be more effective to use a sound or a verbal prompt before providing assistance as it get the patient's attention. Furthermore, not every prompt types (auditory, pictorial, video, light, etc.) will be effective with a specific patient, depending on his profile [11]. Since our game makes use of assistance, visual and auditory assets should be created for all the types of prompts to be used.

4.2   Guidelines

Create Simple Scenes and Help the Player. Before anything else, it is important to avoid unnecessary information in the screen, as we know that aging can cause difficulties to find objects in visually complex scenes [24]. Thus, we must pay attention to create relatively simple scenes in our serious game to avoid the players to be discouraged when not finding the correct object. Furthermore, we add different prompts to help them when they experience difficulties, consistently with the recent advances in the field of smart homes [11], [23], [25]. Finally, it is important to pay attention to the speed of the cursor and object's movement to prevent losing the patient during the play sessions.

Use Warm and Bright Colors with Simple Textures. According to Jones et al. [22], bright warm colors such as red, orange and yellow are best seen than others by elderly persons. On the other hand, the vision of blue and purple are reduced, and aging also cause dark and pastels colors to be difficultly distinguished. Moreover, aging cause acuity to be reduced, making nearby images to be blurred and details in textures difficult to discriminate. Thus, simple textures should be used for all objects in the game and colors of important visual information should be brighter to get the player's attention and ensure a good visibility.

Create a Good Luminosity but Avoid Dazzling the Player. When creating a 3D game, colors and textures are not the only thing to consider. To correctly see the scene and the objects, we need to create an environment's luminosity, by choosing what kind of light will be used, their intensity, and how they should be positioned. When working with older people, a good global luminosity is required, but we must avoid dazzling the player from strong light sources, reflections or backlighting. As with bright colors, lightning can be used to get the patient's attention to be directed to an important object or area in the game, as long as it does not disturb his vision. For example, we could generate a gentle spotlight source at the back of the camera to create a cone of light concentrated around a particular object that the player must interact with. If needed, we could also blink this light source to get more of his attention.

Clearly Define Contrasts and Improve Depth Perception. Older persons have difficulties discerning the limits and borders of objects on a surface, and their perception of depth is reduced. Furthermore, AD patients will often lack the capacity of correctly discerning a figure and the background on which it is drawn and will have more trouble to perceive depth when looking at darker objects or areas (e.g. could perceive a rather black object as a hole in the wall). As a result, the serious game need to present objects with well-defined borders to make it easier for the players to distinct them. This task can be done by choosing different colors for the environment and the objects, as well as different colors for objects that will be in juxtaposition. Furthermore, contrasts and shape perception can be improved by exaggerating object's outline thickness using a shader, such as in a well-known technique in video games called toon-shading[26].

Use Different Types of Prompts When Providing Assistance. Each patient presents a specific profile and might not necessarily need assistance in the same contexts or even in the same manner [11]. For example, a patient suffering from auditory disorders can benefit from a visual feedback, in comparison with auditory ones, which will not affect him. Therefore, it is important to dispose multiple visual (arrows, animated circle below objects, video of someone doing the task, etc.) and auditory (sounds, voice assistance, etc.) assets, that the game can exploit in order to provide assistances suitable the player's profile. As stated previously, vibrotactile rendering can also contribute to this point.

5   Implementing Artificial Intelligence for Providing Adequate Assistive Prompting and Dynamic Difficulty Adjustments

Recent researches shows that it is more beneficial for AD patients to be helped through completion of a challenge, rather than see the challenge failed and be presented with a new one [27].Yet, most games on cognitive training such as the popular *Nintendo DS Game*: the *Dr. Kawashima's Brain Training* does not offer either help to the player in the completion of challenges or dynamic adaptation to the player's profile. Therefore, not only these games are not suited to this kind of player, but they does not allow the players to think about their errors and try to correct them, which is an important point in education and re-education [10].Moreover, we noticed that the tools used in previous research [5], [8], [9] do not make use of modern artificial intelligence technologies such as learning, activity recognition (AR) and guidance (prompting) in order to offer a personalized and more effective experience.

To address the problem of *helping* a patient, we are interested in using two methods. The first one is well-known in the field of smart homes and consist of, from a user's profile and type of error [23], providing a feedback using technologic effectors to get the patient attention on a specific object, area or task [11], [25]. Then, we make use of a method called *Dynamic difficulty adjustment (DDA)*, which consists of calculating the level of challenge experienced by the player in order to adjust the difficulty to match the player's abilities. This section will explain how these methods are implemented in our serious game to make it correctly adapted to AD patients.

5.1   Preliminaries on "Dynamic Difficulty Adjustment" (DDA)

Most video games try to suit all types of players by presenting them a static choice of difficulties to choose from (usually from 3 to 5). The major problem of this approach is that we ask the player to choose a level of challenge, without even having a chance to try the game, and without knowing exactly how this choice will impact on his experience [28]. While this can seems acceptable for experienced gamers, it is certainly not the case for more casual gamers or, in our case, for AD patients, which are usually not familiar with digital form of games [5]. DDA addresses this problem by offering an alternative to mismatches between a player's skill and the game challenges, by modulating in-game systems to respond to a particular player's abilities over the course of a game session [29]. In our game, we decided that this should be reflected by providing more or less precision when assisting a patient.

5.2   Guidelines

Use Activity Recognition and Player's Profile to Provide Assistance. Smart homes and other fields interested in rating human routines often uses Markov processes such as POMDP [23] or HMM [30]. One reason for is that these processes are able to manage uncertainty by evaluating signals (movement captors, RFID, etc.) to make an estimation of the action undertaken by the observed person. In the context of a video game, player's actions can often be directly observed and does not require complex mathematical models. However, since a given task can be completed in different manners, the game should implement a model where transitions can be adjusted, such as a simple MDP. This will allow the model to react correctly after been adjusted by the patient's "usual sequence" for a given task. For certain tasks, it can also be necessary to implement policies to add rules on a given sequence (e.g. coffee must be stirred only after adding milk and sugar).

Keep the Player in the Flow with DDA. While assistive prompting can help a patient to complete a given task, one of the main goals of a serious game for AD patients is to train their cognitive abilities. To achieve this, it is important to make sure they experience the right level of challenge so they can be fully concentrated and avoid discouragement [5], [28]. Our DDA algorithm is based on the ELO raking system [31], which ranks players depending on their in-game performance [32].The ELO system makes use of a normal distribution function FN to predict the overcome of a match between two players, depending on their respective relative skill R1 and R2. This prediction is given by FN(R2 - R1), which represents the expectation value of highest ranked player's victory. Since our game is played in solo, the player gets to "compete against the game". Thus, a "skill level" that reflects the difficulty is associated to each level. Then, the result from FN(R2 - R1) gives us a difficulty ratio, which represents the expected level of challenge that will be experienced by the player for the completion of this level. The player's rank will be adjusted through the game as it will increase if he completes tasks easily, and decrease if he repeats errors and need assistance. This smoothes the passage from general to specific assistance and vice-versa.

6   Prototype, Implementation and Upcoming Experiments

With our case study, we want to design an environment that can help users to train their four cognitive spheres while being fun, interactive, safe, and easy to use. In this game, the player is invited to prepare different meals in a virtual kitchen using the provided ingredients and dishes. Each level presents the player with a predefined meal to prepare, in a smooth learning curve. Thus, the player has simple and clear objectives to complete and the game can assist him whenever he experience difficulties.

Our first prototype implementation was made in Torque Game Builder, a 2D game engine, as shown in figure 1. After some preliminary experimentations guided by neuropsychologists, we rapidly realized that a 3D version of the game could better address the need of patients to be in a familiar environment. Based on guidelines described above, we choose Unity 3D,a professional 3D game engine presenting a free license, as development tool.

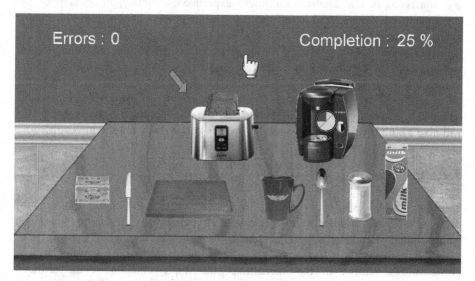

Fig. 1. First prototype in 2D,presenting the player preparing toasts and coffee

The game promotes point-and-click interactions. To challenge planning aspects of the cognitive sphere, a particular attention is paid to the correct order in which the player completes a task. For example, breaking eggs in the frying pan is correct, whereas interacting a cup with the knife results in an error. In the same way, actions in the game levels need to be completed in a logic sequence. For instance, coffee and milk must be added together before any stirring can occur. On the other hand, some actions can take time before requiring the player's attention such as frying eggs. In that case, a timer would appear to indicate the remaining time before completion. All these simple mechanisms have been designed in order to make the game easy to learn and play. The serious game presented in this paper is mainly working and is now in a polish phase concerning mainly the creation of visual and auditory materials. In fact, we are currently working with professional artists for 3D models, textures and user interface development. In the meantime, formal agreements between our lab and ours partners are already established. We are hence in position for preparing our upcoming experimentations and obtain the collaboration of AD patients. Two main partners can be count. The *CSSS Cléphas-Claveau* of *Ville LaBaie*, a regional rehabilitation center which welcomes many AD patients and is in charge of diagnosing all cognitively impaired patients in our region (pop. 150K), and the *Cooperative de solidarité en aide domestique*, a daycare center for Alzheimer patients.

Our experimental protocol will be conducted in three separate phases: experimenting with trial data sets, experimenting with Alzheimer's patients and analysis of the experimental results. The first phase has already begun; it also serves for debugging the proposed game. Once completed, the game will be tested with a group of about 20 AD patients for duration of 3 to 4 weeks. Those tests sessions will be observed and evaluated by a team of multidisciplinary experts, and will be filmed and conserved in our database for future experiments. Finally, the data from the experiments will be analyzed in order to measure the power of our serious video game in cognitive training. This phase will consist of comparing the gathered data from the game to real NAT results obtained for the same patients for testing the validity of our in-game data, and comparing the evaluations made before and after the training period to measure the positive impact of the serious game. Lastly, we want to test whether the results will be sustained after the training or not, by comparing the results obtained at the end of the training period and the ones obtained 3 weeks later. This will give us information on the possibility to train patients in a long-term vision.

7   Conclusion

This paper addressed the exploitation of serious games as a training platform for patients suffering from Alzheimer diseases. To be effective, it appears that such games should meet different criteria. Here we have propose a guideline that structures these requirements under four points. This guideline covers the choice of the in-game challenge, the design of the interactions, the implementation of the artificial intelligence and ends with the production of visual and auditory helps. As a case study, we have presented a game where users are invited to prepare meals. With our upcoming experimentations with patients suffering Alzheimer, this game will serve for the validation of our guideline.

Acknowledgment. We would like to thank our main financial sponsors: the Natural Sciences and Engineering Research Council of Canada (NSERC), the Quebec Research Fund on Nature and Technologies (FQRNT), the Canadian Foundation for Innovation (CFI) and Bell Canada, as well as our collaborators for providing us with Alzheimer patients, allowing the advancement of our experimentations.

References

1. DFC intelligence, Game Market Overview, public report (2011)
2. Miller, D.J., Robertson, D.P.: Using a game console in the primary classroom: effects of "brain training" program on computation and self-esteem. British Journal of Educational Technology 41, 242–255 (2010)
3. Rebolledo-Mendez, G., Avramides, K., Freitas, S., Memarzia, K.: Societal impact of a serious game on raising public awareness: the case of FloodSim. In: Proc. of the ACM SIGGRAPH Symp. on Video Games (Sandbox 2009), pp. 15–22. ACM (2009)
4. Meijer, F., Geudeke, B.L., van den Broek, E.L.: Navigation through virtual environments: visual realism improves spacial cognition. Cyberpsychology& Behavior 12(5), 517–521 (2009)
5. Nacke, L.E., Nacke, A., Lindley, C.A.: Brain training for silver aged gamers: effets of age and game form on effectiveness, self-assessment, and gameplay. Cyberpsychology& Behavior 12(5), 493–499 (2009)
6. United Nations (UN), World Population Ageing 2009, Department of Economic and Social Affairs: Population Division, 129 pages (2009)
7. Imbeault, F., Bouchard, B., Bouzouane, A.: Serious Games in Cognitive Training for Alzheimer's Patients. In: IEEE International Conference on Serious Games and Applications for Health (IEEE-SeGAH), Braga, Portugal, November 16-18, pp. 122–129 (2011)
8. Jiang, C.-F., Chen, D.-K., Li, Y.-S., Kuo, J.-L.: Development of a computer-aided tool for evaluation and training in 3d spatial cognitive function. In: 19th IEEE Symposium on Computer-Based Medical Systems, pp. 241–244 (2006)
9. Hofmann, M., Rösler, A., Schwarz, W., Müller-Spahn, F., Kräuchi, K., Hock, C., Seifritz, E.: Interactive computer-training as a therapeutic tool in Alzheimer's disease". Comprehensive Psychiatry 44(3), 213–219 (2003)
10. Tremblay, J., Bouchard, B., Bouzouane, A.: Adaptive game mechanics for learning purposes: making serious games playable and fun. In: Proc. Int. Conf. on Computer Supported Education: session "Gaming platforms for education and reeducation" (CEDU 2010), vol. 2, pp. 465–470 (April 2010)
11. Lapointe, J., Bouchard, B., Bouchard, J., Potvin, A., Bouzouane, A.: Smart Homes for People with Alzheimer's Disease: Adapting Prompting Strategies to the Patient's Cognitive Profile. In: 5th Int. Conference on PErvasive Technologies Related to Assistive Environments (PETRA), pp. 1–9. ACM (to appear, 2012)
12. Baum, C., Edwards, D.F.: Cognitive performance in senile dementia of the Alzheimer's type: the kitchen task assessment. American Journal of Occupational Therapy 47, 431–443 (1993)
13. Schwartz, M.F., Segal, M., Veramonti, T., Ferraro, M., Buxbaum, L.J.: The Naturalistic Action Test: A standardised assessment for everyday action impairment. Neuropsychological Rehabilitation 12(4), 311–339 (2002)
14. Baid, H., Lambert, N.: Enjoyable learning: the role of humour, games, and fun activities in nursing and midwifery education. Nurse Education Today 30(6), 548–552 (2010)

15. Laprise, H., Bouchard, J., Bouchard, B., Bouzouane, A.: Creating tools and trial data sets for smart home researchers: experimenting activities of daily living with normal subjects to compare with Alzheimer's patients. In: Proc. of the Int. Conf. IADIS e-Health (EH 2010), pp. 143–150 (2010)

16. Bouchard, B., Giroux, S., Bouzouane, A.: A keyhole plan recognition model for Alzheimer's patients: first results. Journal of Applied Artificial Intelligence (AAI) 22(7), 623–658 (2007)

17. Kramer, A.F., Colcombe, S.J., McAuley, E., et al.: Enhancing brain and cognitive function of older adults through fitness training. J. Mol. Neurosci. 20, 213–221 (2003)

18. Hillman, C.H., Erickson, K.I., Kramer, A.F.: Be smart, exercise your heart: exercise effects on brain and cognition. Nat. Rev. Neurosci. 9, 58–65 (2008)

19. Burke, J.W., McNeill, M.D.J., Charles, D.K., Morrow, P.J., Crosbie, J.H., McDonough, S.M.: Optimising engagement for stroke rehabilitation using serious games. The Visual Computer: International Journal of Computer Graphics. SeriousGames and Virtual Worlds, 1085–1099 (2009)

20. Kuznetsov, S., Dey, A.K., Hudson, S.E.: The Effectiveness of Haptic Cues as an Assistive Technology for Human Memory. In: Proceedings of the 7th International Conference on Pervasive Computing, Nara, Japan, May 11-14, pp. 168–175 (2009)

21. Alzheimer's Association. Alzheimer's Disease Facts and Figures. Alzheimer's & Dementia 7(2) (2001)

22. Jones, G.M.M., van der Eerden, W.J.: Designing care environments for persons with Alzheimer's disease: visuoperceptual considerations. Reviews in Clinical Gerontology 18(1), 13–37

23. Mihailidis, A., Boger, J., Canido, M., Hoey, J.: The use of an intelligent prompting system for people with dementia. ACM Interactions 14(4), 34–37 (2007)

24. Ally, B.A., Gold, C.A., Budson, A.E.: "The picture superiority effect in patients with Alzheimer's disease and mild cognitive impairment". Neuropsychologia 47(2), 595–598 (2009)

25. Van Tassel, M., Bouchard, J., Bouchard, B., Bouzouane, A.: Guidelines for Increasing Prompt Efficiency in Smart Homes According to the Resident's Profile and Task Characteristics. In: Abdulrazak, B., Giroux, S., Bouchard, B., Pigot, H., Mokhtari, M. (eds.) ICOST 2011. LNCS, vol. 6719, pp. 112–120. Springer, Heidelberg (2011)

26. DeCarlo, D., Rusinkiewicz, S.: Highlight lines for conveying shape. In: Proc. of the 5th Int. Symp. on Non-photorealistic Animation and Rendering, pp. 63–70 (2007)

27. Pigot, H., Mayers, A., Giroux, S.: The intelligent habitat and everyday life activity support. In: Proc. 5th Int. Conf. on Simulations in Biomedecine, pp. 507–516 (April 2003)

28. Chen, J.: Flow in games (and everything else). Communications of the ACM 50(4), 31–34

29. Hunicke, R.: The case for dynamic difficulty adjustment in games. In: Proc. of the 2005 ACM SIGCHI Int. Conf. on Advances in Computer Entertainment Technology (ACE 2005), pp. 429–433 (June 2005)

30. Wilson, D.H., Philipose, M.: Maximum A Posteriori Path Estimation with Input Trace Perturbation: Algorithms and Application to Credible Rating of Human Routines. In: Proc. of the Ninetheenth International Joint Conference on Artificial Intelligence (IJCAI 2005), Edinburgh, Scotland, UK, pp. 895–901 (2005)

31. Coulom, R.: Le problème des classements. Pour La Science, 20–27 (July 2010)

32. Tremblay, J.: A new approach to dynamicdifficultyadjusment in videogames, Master Thesis (M.Sc.), Université du Québec à Chicoutimi, 108 pages (2011)

Experience in Serious Games:
Between Positive and Serious Experience

Tim Marsh[1] and Brigid Costello[2]

[1] James Cook University, QLD, Australia
tim.marsh@jcu.edu.au
[2] University of New South Wales, Australia
bm.costello@unsw.edu.au

Abstract. This paper discusses the conceptual, practical and ethical considerations towards the development of a framework of experience to inform design and assessment of serious games. Towards this, we review the literature on experience in interaction design, HCI, and games, and identify that the dominant focus for design has been, and still remains, on positive and fun experience. In contrast, anything other than positive experience is often loosely and sometimes inappropriately lumped together under the broad label "negative experience" which can imply bad experience and something to be avoided, while at the same time suggesting it's not useful to design. While work in HCI and the games literature begins to address experience beyond positive, it just scratches the surface. By turning to drama, performance, literature, music, art and film that has shaped experiences and emotion beyond the positive and fun for many years, we describe what experience beyond positive looks like, show how it is not always "uncomfortable" and how it can be classed as entertainment, and argue for the more appropriate term "serious experience". We propose that the focus for design of interaction and serious games should be an appropriate rhythm between positive and serious experience. Finally, we discuss the importance of the take-away message and positive and serious experience in serious games to linger or resonate post-encounter for players in order to encourage reflection and fulfill purpose, and describe associated ethical concerns and make recommendations for designers, evaluators and practitioners in order to safeguard players/users.

Keywords: Positive Experience, Negative Experience, Serious Experience, Framework, Design, Assessment, Linger, Resonate, Reflection.

1   Introduction

The term serious games encapsulates or frames an array of technologies, platforms, applications and environments that can be identified along a continuum from video games through simulation, to interactive art, mixed reality/media and experiential environments [45]. So identifying a framework or categories of user/player experience in serious games needs to be broad enough to be applicable to and encompass the above.

M. Ma et al. (Eds.): SGDA 2012, LNCS 7528, pp. 255–267, 2012.

The serious games community has gone to great lengths to argue that while serious games are for serious purposes (learning, training, education, persuasion, informative, health, well-being, etc), they can also be fun and entertaining [50, 61, 69]. After all, it has been widely argued that positive fun and entertaining characteristics are intended to provide motivation for players to learn [38, 39]. Even further, arguing that fun *and* learning are inextricably linked [20, 46, 47] at least in childhood learning and development.

But what exactly is entertainment in serious games? Is it the same as entertainment in video games? Also, are there any other types of experience in serious games beyond entertainment?

In serious games there may not be a happy or resolved ending at all. Many serious games aim to fulfill their purpose by evoking less fun positive experiences. For example, where the purpose is to provoke thought, provide a message or an experience on a particularly difficult, uncomfortable or unsettling subject or issue. In addition, we argue that experience in serious games may need to resonate or linger with the player after an encounter in order to encourage reflection and so in turn fulfill a serious games' purpose.

While work in the games literature and HCI has long acknowledged experience beyond positive and fun, this largely comes under the broad term of "negative experience" or "negative emotion" [13, 44, 29, 60]. While this work makes great strides in drawing our attention to experience beyond the positive, it only scratches the surface of the possible rich and deep experiences and emotions from interaction, game and serious games play. Furthermore, the term negative experience or emotion suggests the opposite of "positive" which may, intentionally or not, imply bad experience and suggest it is not useful to design. More recently, HCI and CHI has opened shop in a big way on experiences beyond positive and fun as elegantly captured in Benford et al.'s [4] work on "uncomfortable interaction", and how they inform design for overall positive "cultural experience" from techniques in interactive art and drama with rising action followed by denouement.

There are many crossovers with this work and our own in serious games, interactive art and storytelling. However, there are also distinct differences. Most important is that experience beyond positive and fun doesn't have to be "uncomfortable". So while further developing the argument that experience beyond positive and fun is important and can inform design for "cultural experience", including everything under the broad term "uncomfortable" doesn't go far enough and appears to connect more to earlier arguments on "negative experience" or "negative emotion". We argue that as well as "uncomfortable interactions" or "negative experiences" that are beyond positive or fun, there is a further categorization that is neither exclusively positive nor uncomfortable/negative experience, but falls somewhere in-between. For example, interaction or play that is thought-provoking, informing, raises awareness on issues, or where the user/player takes pleasure from negative experience, previously described in interactive art as "pleasurable sense of unease" and "pleasurable thrill of danger" [11], in games as "positive negative experience" [28, 52] and in learning games as "pleasant level of frustration" [27]. This additional categorization of experience is *entertainment without being exclusively fun* and we argue is essential for informing the design repertoire, exposé/portrayal for "cultural experience" beyond "uncomfortable" and "negative" experience.

We propose the new term "serious experience" to frame a broad range of experiences and emotion from interaction/play that encompasses both the thought-provoking and positive/negative categorization and the uncomfortable and negative experience/emotion.

This paper discusses the conceptual, practical and ethical considerations towards the development of a framework of experience to inform design and assessment of serious games. Towards this, we first review the literature on experience in interaction, HCI, and games design, and identify limitations with this work. Next we turn to other media and art forms including drama, performance, literature, music, art, and film to show how these limitations can be addressed. We then propose that design of interaction and serious games should be an appropriate rhythm between positive experience and serious experience, and propose that experience in serious games should linger or resonate post-encounter for players in order to fulfill purpose. Finally, we discuss associated ethical concerns and make recommendations for designers, evaluators and practitioners in order to safeguard players.

2   Background Work: Experience in Play and Interaction

Experience is recognized as a key driver for commerce, retail, leisure and entertainment, etc. [58, 59]. As experience is relatable to everything lived, the appropriate framing and design for emergent experience in specific services, sectors and industries has become a competitive necessity. In interaction design for example, the term *user experience* is widely used to frame experience and emotions associated with product, appliance and interaction design – from both users' and designers' perspectives.

But what exactly is user experience? Much work attempts to shed light on the composition and foundational elements of user experience in interaction design. For over a decade in the design discipline of HCI, we have observed a shift in focus in our design and assessment approaches from being informed exclusively from a usability-centered functional and engineering perspective, towards a user experience-centered design perspective [e.g. 5, 26, 68]. This is demonstrated in proposed theories, levels, threads, frameworks and design research and thinking that emphasizes the pleasure [33], hedonic [24]; ludic [19], emotional [55], enchantment [49] and fun and enjoyment [5] qualities and value in interaction experience. However, while the notion of user experience has been widely adopted in HCI, we have struggled to reach a common understanding and consensus definition [e.g. 25, 36] demonstrating the multifarious and elusive nature of user experience. While there is little doubt that work on user experience has been instrumental in providing a language and in refocusing interaction and product design towards a broader experiential perspective, two major criticisms can be attributed to much of this work. First, it is invariably restricted to positive, fun and aesthetic experience [66, 26]. Second, HCI has largely been concerned with the moment of experience and tends to ignore things that "outlive the moment experience" that people really "value" and "find worthwhile" [10].

Similarly, in computer, video and digital games, *experience* has been the main driver for design since their inception. The term *player experience* is used to frame experience that players get from playing games and specifically, player experience is widely described under the broad term *fun*. According to Salen & Zimmerman [63] "Good games are fun. Fun games are what players want". Fun is "central to the process of making good games" [15]. Strong support for these claims is provided in an Entertainment Software Association[1] survey that reported 87% of the most frequent game players cited fun as the first reason why they play video games [14]. While there have been some attempts that aim to take a closer look at experience in serious games, nonetheless this work focuses on positive experience [e.g. 53].

But what exactly is *fun*? Fun is an abstract and elusive concept that defies easy definition. The Oxford English dictionary [56] describes fun as "light-hearted pleasure or amusement". According to Schell [64], "fun is pleasure with surprises" and Thomas Malone's [38, 39] often cited work on intrinsic motivation - "what makes an activity fun or rewarding for its own sake rather than for the sake of some external reward" - identifies three broad categories: *challenge, fantasy and curiosity*, in an attempt to identify what makes computer games fun. Koster [35] argues that "designing for fun is all about making interactive products like games highly entertaining, engaging, and addictive".

But does it always have to be fun? Or is fun too limiting a term, categorization or label that is not able to describe all potential experiences and emotion from gameplay and may potentially inhibit design and development of games?

2.1   Experience beyond Positive and Fun

For many in the games industry, the shaping of deep and powerful entertainment experiences and emotion, in addition to fun, has been and still is a main driver for design. Consider for example the goal Electronic Arts (EA) set for itself and announced to the world in the well-known advert in The LA Times (1984) and captured in the title "Can a computer game make you cry?" According to Bing Gordon, ex-long term exec of EA, we still haven't reached a point where we can develop games that provide powerful and deep enough experiences and emotion to fulfill this goal. He argues that limitations in models of narrative and characters have something to do with this.

In an interview in Gamasutra [18], Ian Bogost, co-founder of Persuasive Games, similarly argues for the development of more powerful human experiences and emotions beyond fun in games:

> *"For 30 years now we've focused on making games produce fun" "Isn't it about time we started working toward other kinds of emotional responses?" "I know that comparisons to the film industry have grown tired and overused," he says, "but indulge me in this one: When you watch the Academy Awards this year, how many films in the running for awards are about big explosions and other forms of immediate gratification, and how many are about the more complex subtleties of human experience? "Someday, hopefully someday soon, we'll look back at video games and laugh at how unsophisticated we are today".*

The games literature is increasingly identifying that designing exclusively for the experience of fun in games is too limiting. Hunicke, LeBlanc and Zubek [30] argue for a move away from words like *fun* towards a more appropriate vocabulary to describe "the desirable emotional responses evoked in the player, when she interacts with the game system". Similarly, Calleja [9] identifies limitations with the term fun applied to games arguing that "pinning motivation for game-playing on the notion of fun risks missing important dimensions of the game experience". More generally, Seymour Papert proposed the idea of "hard fun" to describe a special kind of fun when words like "pleasure" and "fun" seem inappropriate or inadequate [57].

More recently, work in HCI has begun to look beyond positive experience as typified in Benford et al.'s [4] work that looks to drama to inform design of "uncomfortable interaction" and four primary forms of discomfort: visceral, cultural, control and intimate.

While the HCI community of ACM SIGCHI finally opens-up shop on experience other than positive, fun and aesthetic and the game literature increasingly identifies the importance of moving beyond the fun game experience, much work is still largely tentative, and is only just beginning to scratch the surface. Consider for example the claimed "comprehensive categorization of digital game experience" [60], that identifies two categories, out of nine, associated with "negative experience" (*negative affect:* frustration, disappointment, irritation, anger; *suspense:* challenge, tension, pressure, hope, anxiety, thrill). However, the title appears to identify the authors' point of view that whether or not game experience is positive or negative, "[i]t is always a lot of fun!". For designers to focus on fun means that they might take a shallow or cursory approach to the design of negative affect rather than advocating design and development of deep experiences and emotion beyond fun in games.

Looking to other media, performance, drama, music, art and film that provide powerful and deep experiences and emotion to inform user and player experience provides some leverage to these discussions. In music compositions that create variations in feelings, moods and emotions beyond the positive – it would be quite limiting and tedious if all music was restricted to just positive and fun. In drama, literature, film and storytelling in general, experience beyond positive is necessary to portray suffering, struggle, conflict and adversity, etc. For example, in typical drama and story structure such as the 3 or 5 act play, to set-up a rising action or conflict, that is typically followed by a resolution, but not necessarily a pleasurable one (e.g. Shakespearean tragedies). In film, Grodal [23] has looked to film experience in an attempt to understand video game experience. Building on Zillmann's [70] work on the psychology of suspense in drama and film, Klimmt et al [34] identified suspense in video games. In addition, much work in HCI and games adopted Boorstin's [6] three Vs foundational elements of experience and emotion from film: voyeuristic (new and the wonderful), visceral (thrills, spectacle and suspense) and vicarious (empathy and emotional transfer). In HCI and interaction design, the three Vs also played a prominent role in proposals for shifts "from usability to user experience" [68] and in informing underlying foundational elements for experience and emotion in interaction and product design in influential texts [55, 48]. However, again the emphasis in this work has been on positive and fun experience, as for example captured in the term "enchantment" to inform HCI, but which largely disregards the power of the three Vs to describe experience beyond positive [49].While Norman [55] acknowledges the importance of negative emotion in design as suggested in the sub-title of his book, "Why we Love (or Hate) Everyday Things", he offers only a cursory discussion on the negative.

Interestingly, the three Vs were originally proposed as a potential candidate to inform HCI approaches for design and assessment of experience in games, simulations and virtual environment/reality[2], as well as being an alternative to considering the experience of presence - the dominant experience of the day [40 – 44]. While the three Vs experience continues to be adopted and applied to video games, again this work largely focuses on fun and pleasurable experience. For example, [15] identifies the three Vs as "corresponding" to his framework of fun in "Natural Funativity's Physical, Social, and Mental fun"; [65] adopt the three Vs to help talk about the fun and experience of playing a game; and [62] work directly corresponds to the three Vs to talk about categories of pleasure in games. However, the beauty and power of the three Vs is in its ability to frame a broad range of experience and emotion - both "positive" and "negative" (frightened, disgusted, nauseated, tense, sad, angry, weak, tension, cowardly, serious) as shown in study results from survey and interview approaches experienced by almost all players with our test education and first-person shooter games [41, 44].

Although often using similar technology to games, interactive art has never shied away from creating uncomfortable or unpleasant experiences. Artists might use exaggeration, shock or disorientation to create experiences of alienation. They might also create works that ask their audience to subvert or resist common uses or purposes of a technology [32]. For example, the artwork *Run Motherfucker Run* [54] repurposes a treadmill as a device for navigating an onscreen city, an experience that becomes uncomfortable when the participant realises they cannot stop the treadmill once it has begun. In *Pin Cushion* [67] the audience is invited to distort a representation of a human female face by pricking it with large acupuncture needles. However, they have less control than they think. As a participant touches the needles the artwork reads her or his body's electrical conductivity, resistance and charge. It is this intimate reading that impacts the lifespan and well-being of the character. Working against the usual excitement of interactive technologies, *Perversely Interactive System* [31] uses a biofeedback device to measure tension levels in the participant, with the character in the artwork only responding when tension levels are low. As the artists describe, this was uncomfortable for the participant because it meant that "getting what one desired required controlling or denying that desire". In each case, the audience unease or discomfort is used to provoke interpretative reflection.

In her well-known GDC 2010 talk, Brenda Brathwaite [7] talks about the design process of her "works" within the Mechanic is the Message [8] series of non-digital games that aim to create an experience beyond fun and "capture and express difficult emotions with a games mechanic". These include: The New World (2008) about the Middle Passage and slave trade, Síochán leat aka "The Irish Game" (2009) about the Cromwellian Invasion of Ireland, and Train (2009) a game about the Holocaust and the transportation of people to concentration camps [8]. Participants of these games learn about, and are complicit in, difficult subjects that either emerge during gameplay or are revealed fully after the game (e.g. Train), and the associated difficult experiences and emotions linger after the game has finished.

Our next examples take the idea of negative experience to the extreme by focusing on difficult and dark topics of rape and murder in analogue role-playing "games" in which participants take the role of offender or victim [28, 52]. In debriefing sessions, participants reported feeling extreme negative experiences and that some experiences continued after the game had finished. While it was not the sole reason for developing these games, the authors had fulfilled one purpose, to show that experience beyond the positive or fun can be created in games and there was a weakening of the protective frame of play that allows emotion and experience to "bleed" out from the game and influence the player outside the game [52].

While these examples put into question the idea of play and games - is it still correct to describe taking part as *play* and does the seriousness of the topic make it no longer a *game*? - they show that difficult topics can be designed in an emergent game, that powerful experiences and emotions are felt by participants, and that these experiences and emotions can linger or resonate after gameplay.

Finally, we identify examples in interactive art and games where the user/player takes pleasure from negative experience. Early 20th century conceptions of play included experiences of physical pain and mental suffering. The pleasure that we might take from probing a sore tooth or experiencing the sadness of a tragic artwork being described as a form of playing with emotions that stems from a need to "satisfy our craving for intense impressions" [22]. Recent frameworks from games and interaction design researchers also include experiential categories that go beyond common conceptions of fun. For example, Bartle's [3] model of player types in MUDs includes *killers,* a type of player who derives pleasure from bullying and/or manipulates others.

Costello and Edmond's [11, 12] pleasure framework includes the category of *subversion*, which describes the pleasure that can be had by behaving against the norm, by breaking rules or of seeing others break them. Building on this framework and with a focus on game experience, Arrasvuori et al [2] have added the categories of *cruelty* and *suffering*. Cruelty is the playful experience of acting to cause physical or mental pain in others. Suffering they describe as encompassing the emotions of "boredom, stress, anxiety, anger, frustration, loss and even humiliation". Arrasvuori et al. [2] see these experiences as acting to provide a negativity that, through contrast, makes subsequent positive experiences all the more intense.

While these examples demonstrate that experiences and emotion beyond the positive from interaction and play is an area that continues to be enthusiastically explored in games and interactive art, the negative and potentially extreme experiences from encounters suggests that precautions must be taken to ensure the safety and well-being of players/users. We return to this discussion in a later section.

3   Serious Experience

As the term serious games encapsulates or frames an array of technologies, platforms, applications and environments that can be identified along a continuum from video games through simulation, to interactive art and mixed reality/media, and experiential environments [45], identifying a framework or categories of user/player experience in serious games needs to be broad enough to be applicable to and encompass the above.

As shown in table 1, we argue that experience and emotion from an encounter (interaction or play) with serious games is framed within two main categories: positive and serious; and propose that design should be an appropriate rhythm between these two.

Table 1. Experience and Emotion in Serious Games: Between Positive and Serious Experience

Experience & Emotion in Serious Games		
Positive	**Serious**	
Fun	Thought-Provoking	Negative, Uncomfortable, Unpleasant, Provoking
	Positive-Negative	

As identified above, the dominant focus for design in the HCI and games literature has been on positive and fun experience. In contrast, serious experience encapsulates experience beyond positive and fun, and is composed of two sub-categories. The first category generally identifies experience that is neither exclusively positive nor negative/uncomfortable, but falls somewhere in-between. These are entertaining, likable, or where user/player takes pleasure from negative experience. For example, interaction or play that is thought-provoking, informing, raises awareness on issues, or where the user/player takes pleasure from negative experience, previously described as "pleasurable sense of unease", "pleasurable thrill of danger" [12], "positive negative experience" [28, 52] or "pleasant level of frustration" [27]. This categorization of experience is *entertaining without being exclusively fun*. The second category is "uncomfortable" and "negative experience", as discussed above. These extreme experiences and emotions are disturbing, discomforting and provoking, and in serious games the user/player unease or discomfort is used to provoke interpretative reflection.

We argue that serious experience, both thought-provoking *and* negative, uncomfortable and provoking are essential for informing design of interaction and play of "cultural experience" in serious games beyond positive and fun.

We acknowledge that an encounter with a serious game may be experienced differently at different times by the same user/player or can be experienced differently by different users/players. This depends not on the experience itself but on the perception of the person who experiences it. For example, fun at one time and thought-provoking the next or one person experiences a serious game as negative and unpleasant while another experiences it as thought-provoking. One theory that may help provide some leverage in further investigations is Apter's [1] reversal theory where the exact same type of high (or low) arousal experience could cause one person to experience it as unpleasant and the other as pleasant. Boyle and Connolly (2008) also identify the potential value of reversal theory to help explain the sometimes paradoxical emotions that players experience during gameplay and "the apparently contradictory statements of gameplayers that gameplaying is relaxing but also exciting".

4   Ethics and Code of Practice in Serious Games

As discussed, our concern is not only with the moment-to-moment and in-game experience per se that has dominated work in video games and interaction design, but also on experience that lingers or resonates with users/players after an encounter. This is similar to the idea of bleed in games where a weakening of the protective frame of play allows emotion and experience to bleed out from the game and influence the player outside the game beyond the magic circle [28]. As it is these lingering and resonating experiences that users/players take-away that often provide a measure of success of purpose in serious games, as designers and developers we must be aware of the potential danger and harm that serious games could cause.

While drama, performance, literature and film have portrayed similar extreme and difficult topics, perhaps similar age/rating systems should be introduced. We recommend that developers of games with such extreme topics are aware of the ethics surrounding their development, that guidelines should be drawn-up to inform design and development and, in some cases, they are used only under rigorous procedures and are followed by debriefing sessions (similar to those used in psychology experiments and HCI studies) to safeguard and protect players from harm.

5   Discussion and Conclusion

As discussed, much of the literature on interaction and game experience has tended to focus on positive and fun experience. While emerging work in interaction and video games also identifies "negative" experience as being crucial to provide deeper experience and emotions, discussions are either cursory, don't go far enough, and/or are about the temporary sensations used to set-up a rising action or conflict, and is typically followed by a more pleasurable resolution.

In the serious games community we have gone to great lengths to argue that while serious games are for serious purposes (learning, training, education, persuasion, informative, health, well-being, etc), they can also be fun and entertaining. After all, it has been widely argued, that positive fun and entertaining characteristics are intended to provide motivation for players to learn. Many serious games, however, aim to fulfill their purpose by evoking less positive experiences. In serious games there may not be a happy or resolved ending at all. For example, where the purpose is to provoke thought, provide a message or an experience on a particularly difficult, uncomfortable or unsettling subject or issue.

In order to frame experiences and emotions, we propose *serious experience* (thought-provoking *and* negative / uncomfortable / provoking) as well as *positive experience* (fun) are essential for informing the design repertoire for interaction and play in serious games. We argue that design in serious games should create an appropriate blend or rhythm between positive and serious experience.

Finally, as it is important for serious experience (as well as positive experience) in serious games to linger or resonate post-encounter for players in order to encourage reflection and fulfillment of purpose, we propose that designers, developers, evaluators and practitioners are aware of the ethical concerns and content rating systems are in place in order to safeguard and protect players from harm.

Notes

[1] ESA: Entertainment Software Association, US trade association for video games whose members include Atari, Electronic Arts, Microsoft, Square Enix et al.

[2] INQUISITIVE research project (1998-2002), UK EPSRC funded (GR/L53199), HCI Group, University of York & Rutherford Appleton Laboratories, UK.

References

1. Apter, M.J.: Reversal Theory: Motivation, Emotion and Personality. Routledge, London (1989)
2. Arrasvuori, J., Boberg, M., Korhonen, H.: Understanding Playfulness - An Overview of the Revised Playful Experience (PLEX) Framework. In: Proc. of Design & Emotion 2010 Conference, Design and Emotion Society (2010)
3. Bartle, R.A.: "Virtual Worlds: Why People Play" From Massively Multiplayer Game Development 2 (Game Development). In: Alexander, T. (ed.), Charles River Media, Inc., Rockland (2005)
4. Benford, S., Greenhalgh, C., Giannachi, G., Walker, B., Marshall, J., Rodden, T.: Uncomfortable Interactions. In: ACM SIGCHI 2012 Conference on Human Factors in Computing Systems. ACM Press (2012)
5. Blythe, M.A., Overbeeke, K., Monk, A.F., Wright, P.C.: Funology: From Usability to Enjoyment, pp. 31–42. Kluwer Academic Publishers, Dordrecht (2003)
6. Boorstin, J.: Making Movies Work: Thinking Like a Filmmaker. Silman-James Press, Beverley Hills (1990)
7. Brathwaite, B.: Train: How I Dumped Electricity and Learned to Love Design, GDC (2010), http://www.gdcvault.com/play/1012259/Train-(28or-How-I-Dumped)

8. Brathwaite, B.: The Mechanic is the Message,
   http://mechanicmessage.wordpress.com/
9. Calleja, G.: Game Design Involvement A Conceptual Model. Games and Culture (2), 236–260 (2007)
10. Cockton, G.: Designing worth is worth designing. In: Proceedings of the 4th Nordic Conference on Human-Computer Interaction, NordicCHI 2006, pp. 165–174. ACM Press (2006)
11. Costello, B., Edmonds, E.: A Study in Play, Pleasure and Interaction Design. In: Designing Pleasurable Products and Interfaces, University of Art and Design Helsinki, pp. 76–91. ACM Press (2007)
12. Costello, B., Edmonds, E.: A tool for characterizing the experience of play. In: Proceedings of the Sixth Australasian Conference on Interactive Entertainment, Sydney, Australia, pp. 1–10. ACM Press (2007)
13. Desurvire, H., Caplan, M., Toth, J.: Using Heuristics to Improve the Playability of Games. In: CHI 2004: Proceedings of the SIGCHI Conference on Human Factors in Computing Systems. ACM Press, New York (2004)
14. ESA. Entertainment Software Association, State of the Industry Report 2000-2001. Entertainment Software Association (2001)
15. Falstien, N.: Natural Funativity, Gamasutra (2004),
    http://www.gamasutra.com/features/20041110/falstien_pfv.html
16. Fernandez, A.: Fun Experience with Digital Games: A Model Proposition. In: Leino, O., Wirman, H., Fernandez, A. (eds.) Extending Experiences: Structure, Analysis and Design of Computer Game Player Experience, pp. 181–190. Lapland University Press, Rovaniemi (2008)
17. Forlizzi, J., Battarbee, K.: Understanding experience in interactive systems. In: DIS 2004: Proceedings of the 5th Conference on Designing Interactive Systems, pp. 261–268. ACM Press, New York (2004)
18. Ochalla, B.: From Gamasutra Article: June 29 2007, Who Says Video Games Have to be Fun? The Rise of Serious Games (2007), http://www.gamasutra.com/view/feature/129891/who_says_video_games_have_to_be_.php
19. Gaver, B., Martin, H.: Alternatives: exploring information appliances through conceptual design proposals. In: CHI 2000: Proceedings of the SIGCHI Conference on Human Factors in Computing Systems, pp. 209–216. ACM Press, New York (2000)
20. Gee, J.P.: Learning by design: games as learning machines. Interactive Educational Multimedia 8, 15–23 (2004)
21. Gordon, B.: Can a social game make you cry?, http://justingibbs.com/
22. Groos, K.: The Play of Man. William Heinemann, London (1901)
23. Grodal, T.: Video games and the pleasure of control. In: Zillmann, D., Vorderer, P. (eds.) Media Entertainment: the Psychology of Its Appeal, pp. 197–214. Erlbaum, Mahwah (2000)
24. Hassenzahl, M., Platz, A., Burmester, M., Lehner, K.: Hedonic and Ergonomic Quality Aspects Determine a Software's Appeal. In: Proceedings of CHI 2000: Human Factors in Computing Systems, pp. 201–208. ACM Press, NY (2000)
25. Hassenzahl, M., Tractinsky, N.: User experience a research agenda. Behaviour and Information Technology 25(2), 91–97 (2006)
26. Hassenzahl, M., Diefenbach, S., Göritz, A.: Needs, affect, and interactive products – Facets of user experience. Interacting with Computers 22(5), 353–362 (2010)

27. Henriksen, T.D.: Dimensions in Educational Game-Design: Perspectives on Designing and Implementing Game-Based Learning Processes in the Educational Setting. Paper for Nordic Playground Event (2006)
28. Hopeametsä, H.: 24 Hours in a Bomb Shelter: Player, Character and Immersion in Ground Zero'. In: Montola, M., Stenros, J. (eds.) Playground Worlds, Ropecon (2008)
29. Höysniemi, J.: Games, user interface and performing arts: International survey on the Dance Dance Revolution game. ACM Computers in Entertainment 4, 2 (2006)
30. Hunicke, R., LeBlanc, M., Zubek, R.: MDA: A Formal Approach to Game Design and Game Research. In: Proceedings of the 19th AAAI Conference, Workshop on Challenges in Game AI. AAAI Press (2004)
31. Hughes, L., Laroche, S.: Perversely Interactive System, Interactive Artwork (2004), http://www.interstices.uqam.ca/en/projects/lynn-hughes/item/27-perversely-interactive-system.html
32. Jones, C.: Excerpt from "The Mediated Sensorium". In: Jones, C.A. (ed.) Sensorium: Embodied Experience, Technology, and Contemporary Art, p. 6. MIT Press (2006)
33. Jordan, P.W.: Designing Pleasurable Products: An Introduction to the New Human Factors. Taylor & Francis (2000)
34. Klimmt, C., Rizzo, A., Vorderer, P., Koch, J., Fischer, T.: Experimental evidence for suspense as determinant of video game enjoyment. Cyberpsychology 12, 29–31 (2009)
35. Koster, R.: A Theory of Fun in Game Design. Paraglyph Press (2005)
36. Law, X.E., Roto, C.V., Hassenzahl, M., Vermeeren, A.P., Kort, J.: Understanding, scoping and defining user experience: a survey approach. In: CHI 2009: Proceedings of the 27th International Conference on Human Factors in Computing Systems, pp. 719–728. ACM Press, New York (2009)
37. Lazzaro, N.: Why We Play Games: Four Keys to More Emotion Without Story, XEODesign report, XeoDesign Inc. (2004), http://www.xeodesign.com/xeodesign_whyweplaygames.pdf
38. Malone, T.W.: Toward a theory of intrinsically motivating instruction. Cognitive Science 4, 333–369 (1981)
39. Malone, T.W.: Heuristics for designing enjoyable user interfaces: Lessons from computer games. In: Thomas, J.C., Schneider, M.L. (eds.) Human Factors in Computer Systems. Ablex, Norwood (1984)
40. Marsh, T., Wright, P.: Maintaining the Illusion of Interacting Within a 3D Virtual Space. In: 3rd International Workshop on Presence, Delft, The Netherlands (2000)
41. Marsh, T.: Presence as Experience: Framework to Assess Virtual Corpsing. In: 4th International Workshop on Presence, Temple University, Philadelphia (2001)
42. Marsh, T., Wright, P., Smith, S.: Evaluation for the Design of Experience in Virtual Environments: Modelling Breakdown of Interaction and Illusion. Journal of CyberPsychology and Behaviour, Special Issue on Presence 4(2), 225–238 (2001)
43. Marsh, T.: Presence as experience: film informing ways of staying there. In: Presence, Teleoperators and Virtual Environments, vol. 12(5), pp. 538–549. MIT Press (2003)
44. Marsh, T.: Towards Invisible Style of Computer-Mediated Activity: Transparency and Continuity. Unpublished Ph.D Thesis, Human-Computer Interaction (HCI) Group, University of York, UK (2004)
45. Marsh, T.: Serious Games Continuum: Between games for purpose and experiential environments for purpose. Entertainment Computing 2(2), 61–68 (2001)
46. Marsh, T., Zhiqiang, N.L., Klopfer, E., Chuang, X., Osterweil, S., Haas, J.: Fun and Learning: Blending Design and Development Dimensions in Serious Games Through Narrative and Characters. In: Serious Games and Edutainment Applications, ch. 14, pp. 273–287. Springer (2001a)

47. Marsh, T., Zhiqiang, N.L., Klopfer, E., Chuang, X., Osterweil, S., Haas, J.: Fun and Learning: The Power of Narrative. In: Foundations of Digital Games 2011 (FDG 2011), Bordeaux, France (2011b)
48. McCarthy, J.P., Wright, P.C.: Technology as Experience. MIT Press (2004)
49. McCarthy, J.P., Wright, P.C., Wallace, J., Dearden, A.: The experience of enchantment in human-computer interaction. Personal and Ubiquitous Computing 10(6), 369–378 (2006)
50. Michael, D., Chen, S.: Serious Games: Games that Educate, Train, and Inform. Thomson Course Technology PTR, USA (2006)
51. Monk, A., Frohlich, D.: Computers and Fun. Personal Technology 3(1), 91 (1999)
52. Montola, M.: The positive negative experience in extreme role-playing. In: Proceedings of Experiencing Games: Games, Play, and Players. 1st Nordic Digra, Sweden (2010)
53. Nacke, L.E., Grimshaw, N.M., Lindley, C.: More than a feeling: Measurement of sonic user experience and psychophysiology in a first-person shooter game, vol. 22(5), pp. 336–343 (April 2010)
54. Nijis, M.: Run Motherfucker Run, Interactive Artwork (2001/2004), http://www.marnixdenijs.nl/run-motherfucker-run.html
55. Norman, D.A.: Emotional Design: Why We Love (or Hate) Everyday Things. Basic Books, New York (2004)
56. Oxford English Dictionary. OED Online. Oxford University Press (2009)
57. Papert, S.: Hard Fun. online article, http://www.papert.org/articles/HardFun.html
58. Pine II, B.J., Gilmore, J.H.: Welcome to the Experience Economy. Harvard Business Review, p. 97 (July-August 1998)
59. Pine II., B.J., Gilmore, J.H.: The Experience Economy: Work is Theatre & Every Business a Stage. Harvard Business Press, Boston (1999)
60. Poels, K., de Kort, Y., Ijsselsteijn, W.: It is always a lot of fun!: exploring dimensions of digital game experience using focus group methodology. In: Proceedings of the Future Play Conference. ACM Press (2007)
61. Prensky, M.: Fun, play and games: what makes games engaging, In: Digital Game-Based Learning. McGraw-Hill (2001)
62. Rusch, D.C.: Emotional Design of Computer Games and Fiction Films. In: Computer Games as a Sociocultural Phenomenon: Games Without Frontiers, Wars Without Tears, pp. 22–32. Palgrave Publishers (2008)
63. Salen, S., Zimmerman, E.: Rules of play: Game design fundamentals. MIT Press (2004)
64. Schell, J.: The Art of Game Design: A book of lenses. Morgan Kaufman (2008)
65. Seif El-Nasr, M., Al-Saati, M., Niedenthal, S., Milam, D.: Assassin's creed: a multi-cultural read. Loading 2(3) (2008)
66. Van Vliet, H., Mulder, I.: Experience and Design: Trojan Horse or Holy Grail. In: Proceedings of User Experience, Second COST294 International Workshop Held in Conjunction with NordiCHI 2006, pp. 57–62 (2006)
67. Velonaki, M.: Pin Cushion, Interactive Artwork (2000), http://mvstudio.org/work/pin-cushion/
68. Wright, P.C., McCarthy, J., Marsh, T.: From Usability to User Experience, Computers and Fun 3. Workshop, University of York, UK. Appears in: Interfaces (46), 4–5 (2000)
69. Zyda, M.: From visual simulation to virtual reality to games. IEEE Computer (September 2005)
70. Zillman, D.: The psychology of suspense in dramatic exposition. In: Vorderer, P., Wulff, H.J., Friedrichsen, M. (eds.) Suspense: Conceptualizations, Theoretical Analyses, and Empirical Explorations. Lawrence Erlbaum Associates, Inc., Mahwah (1996)

Author Index